W9-BMY-233

Praise for Death by China

"I myself have escaped the clutches of the Chinese Communist Party and now enjoy a life of freedom in America. It is important for everyone in the nation I love to understand that the aggression of the Chinese government toward human rights does not stop at China's borders. Chinese Communist Party leaders believe they are at war with democracy and freedom, and any governments that support these values. *Death by China* is the perfect book to explain how Beijing's strategists are fighting and projecting that war around the world."

—**Li Fengzhi,** former agent, China's Ministry of State Security

"At a time when there is a perception that China is the next world power, this book puts the spotlight on a different aspect of China, a country that does not seem ready to be a responsible member of the comity of nations. The international community's failure to take this Chinese reality into consideration will not only be detrimental to the rest of the world, but more so to the Chinese, Tibetan, and other people who are confronted with the consequences on a daily basis."

—**Bhuchung K. Tsering,** Vice President,
International Campaign for Tibet

"As a journalist who was born and raised in China and has been reporting on China for many years, I am very impressed with the authors' understanding of the vast scope of China's issues and, most importantly, their clear and discerning insight on China and its relationship with the United States."

—**Simone Gao,** award-winning producer and host
of *Zooming In*, New Tang Dynasty TV

"An important eye-opener for all Americans, *Death by China* is a must-read before your next trip to Walmart—or perhaps the unemployment line."

—**Stuart O. Witt,** General Manager, Mojave Air and Space Port;
test pilot; and USN TOPGUN graduate

"There are 310 million Americans who had better start listening to what Peter Navarro and Greg Autry have written in *Death by China*—about how 1.3 billion Chinese under direction of a totalitarian dictatorship are destroying their livelihoods. This liberty bell of a book should shake American leaders out of their slumber so that they finally—finally—realize that China's economic policies are bankrupting the United States of America. Navarro and Autry describe it as plain as can be and, importantly, how the United States should deal with this threat."

—**Richard McCormack,** Editor and Publisher,
Manufacturing & Technology News

"Like a modern-day Paul Revere, this book offers the most urgent of warnings about how a mercantilist, protectionist, and rapidly militarizing China is systematically destroying the American economy under the false banner of 'free' trade—and in the process, severely weakening our national defenses. It should be required reading for every American citizen—and in the hands of every American Congressman."

—**Ian Fletcher,** Senior Economist,
Coalition for a Prosperous America

"A high-powered rifle shot that hits the Beijing bull's-eye dead-on."

—**Dylan Ratigan**, host of MSNBC's *The Dylan Ratigan Show*

"*Death by China* is further proof that we are sowing the seeds of our own demise. Navarro and Autry detail the way in which Chinese communists steal American technology and jobs, sell back to us products of an inferior quality, and then use the resulting profits to build weapons that put the entire world at risk. This book is shocking and is a must-read for all."

—**Paul Midler**, author of *Poorly Made in China*

"*Death by China* not only accurately describes the enormity of the growing Chinese economic and military threat. The authors rightly and squarely point the finger at all of the corporate turncoats and China apologists in America who are helping to make China's rise anything but peaceful."

—**Alan Tonelson,** Research Fellow, U.S. Business and Industrial Council,
AmericanEconomicAlert.org

"This clarion call carefully researches and intricately details the clear and present dangers an anything but peaceful rising China poses to the world. In doing so, it brings us face-to-face with this inescapable truth: If we do not act now, we will face an almost certain 'Death by China.'"

—**Congressman Dana Rohrabacher,** 46th District (Rep, CA)

"I've been long concerned about China's evolving military challenge to America and our allies, but *Death by China* reveals China's broader strategy of integrated advances on multiple fronts. The authors document how Beijing is using economic weapons of mercantilism and currency manipulation synergistically with espionage, cyberwarfare, space weapons, resource monopolization, and technology theft to gain dominance. In the process, the fundamental economic and geopolitical strengths that underpin America's military superiority are being systematically eroded while China becomes increasingly assertive in regional disputes. Every Western political and military leader should read this book. Now!"

—**Jon Gallinetti,** Major General, USMC, retired

"A chilling compilation of China's gathering storm. The free fall in space I've personally experienced was wonderfully enriching. The free fall I now sense the United States is courting under Chinese domination is to be deeply feared."

—**Brian Binnie,** Commander USN, retired; test pilot; commercial astronaut and winner of the Ansari X Prize

"Be forewarned: Once you start reading, you won't want to stop. *Death by China* lays bare the pivotal, oft overlooked, and sometimes blatantly hidden moves in a massive global chess game. Navarro and Autry have sounded the alarm, calling the free world to act on behalf of its interests and future. Impressively, they call on China as well."

—**Damon DiMarco,** author of *Tower Stories: An Oral History of 9/11* and co-author of *My Two Chinas: The Memoir of a Chinese Counterrevolutionary* with Baiqiao Tang

"At this moment, Chinese officials are poisoning your medicines, polluting your air, and undermining your freedoms. If you're American, Indian, or Japanese, they are planning to wage war on your country. Now looks like a good time to read this book."

—**Gordon Chang,** author of *The Coming Collapse of China*

Praise for Peter Navarro's previous book, The Coming China Wars

"Peter Navarro has captured the breadth of areas where China and the United States have fundamental conflicts of business, economic and strategic interests. He puts this into a global context demonstrating where China's current development course can lead to conflict. His recommendations for nations to coalesce to respond to the challenges posed by China are practical. This book should be in the hands of every businessperson, economist, and policy-maker."

—**Dr. Larry M. Wortzel,** Chairman, US–China Economic
and Security Review Commission

"*The Coming China Wars* is a gripping, fact-filled account of the dark side of China's rise that will be of interest to anyone interested in this complex and fascinating country. Navarro makes no pretense toward searching for the middle ground in the China debate. He issues a call to arms for China and the rest of the world to act now to address the country's mounting problems—pollution, public health, intellectual property piracy, resource scarcity, and more—or risk both serious instability within China and military conflict between China and other major powers."

—**Elizabeth C. Economy,** C.V. Starr Senior Fellow
and Director of Asia Studies, Council on Foreign Relations

"What Al Gore does for climate change, Peter Navarro does for China. This book will hit you right between the eyes. A gargantuan wake-up call."

—**Stuart L. Hart,** S.C. Johnson Chair of Sustainable Global
Enterprise, Cornell University; author of *Capitalism at the Crossroads*

"*The Coming China Wars* has a wealth of fascinating information about the impact of China on the world and the perils it creates. Because of China's great importance, this is a book we should all read."

—**D. Quinn Mills,** Alfred J. Weatherhead Jr.
Professor of Business Administration, Harvard Business School

"This is a well researched and illuminating book, and is a necessary counter to a large body of opinion that posits an inevitable and even peaceful rise of China and chooses to ignore most of the author's message."

—**Richard Fisher,** Vice President, International
Assessment and Strategy Center

DEATH BY CHINA

Confronting the Dragon —
A Global Call to Action

PETER NAVARRO AND GREG AUTRY

Vice President, Publisher: Tim Moore
Associate Publisher and Director of Marketing: Amy Neidlinger
Executive Editor: Jim Boyd
Editorial Assistant: Pamela Boland
Development Editor: Russ Hall
Senior Marketing Manager: Julie Phifer
Assistant Marketing Manager: Megan Colvin
Cover Designer: Chuti Prasertsith
Managing Editor: Kristy Hart
Project Editor: Anne Goebel
Copy Editor: Karen Gill
Proofreader: Debbie Williams
Senior Indexer: Cheryl Lenser
Compositor: Nonie Ratcliff
Manufacturing Buyer: Dan Uhrig

Prentice Hall is an imprint of Pearson.

© 2011 by Pearson Education, Inc.
Publishing as Prentice Hall
Upper Saddle River, New Jersey 07458

Prentice Hall offers excellent discounts on this book when ordered in quantity for bulk purchases or special sales. For more information, please contact U.S. Corporate and Government Sales, 1-800-382-3419, corpsales@pearsontechgroup.com. For sales outside the U.S., please contact International Sales at international@pearson.com.

Company and product names mentioned herein are the trademarks or registered trademarks of their respective owners.

Printed in the United States of America

Second Printing July 2011

ISBN-10 0-13-218023-5
ISBN-13 978-0-13-218023-8

Pearson Education LTD.
Pearson Education Australia PTY, Limited.
Pearson Education Singapore, Pte. Ltd.
Pearson Education Asia, Ltd.
Pearson Education Canada, Ltd.
Pearson Educación de Mexico, S.A. de C.V.
Pearson Education—Japan
Pearson Education Malaysia, Pte. Ltd.

Library of Congress Cataloging-in-Publication Data:

Navarro, Peter.
    Death by China : confronting the dragon—a global call to action / Peter Navarro, Greg Autry.
      p. cm.
    Includes bibliographical references and index.
    ISBN 978-0-13-218023-8 (hardback : alk. paper) 1. China—Commerce. 2. Environmental degradation—China. 3. United States—Foreign economic relations—China. 4. China—Foreign economic relations—United States. I. Autry, Greg, 1963- II. Title.
    HF3836.5.N28 2011
    382.0951'051—dc22
                                            2011003122

To all of our friends in China.
May they one day live in freedom—
and until that day, remain safe.

"It is the job of thinking people not to be on the side of the executioners."

—*Albert Camus*

Contents

Foreword

In the late 1980s, China was abuzz with excitement and possibility as new ideas, personal freedoms, and economic opportunities were flowing in from the West like a river to wash away the dirt of Mao's Cultural Revolution.

During these hopeful times, I was among a group of young student leaders who led calls for political reform to match the new thinking and bring China into the modern world with dignity. We organized rallies and made speeches at schools and squares all across the country, and we fervently believed the top leadership of the Chinese Communist Party would listen. Instead, our movement was crushed by a wave of tanks and the tragic events of June 4th, 1989 in Tiananmen Square that so many of you watched with horror on television.

So much was lost that day—and it was not just the lives of so many brave Chinese that we cried over. Also lost was a once-in-a-generation opportunity to live freely in a democratic China with the very brightest of futures.

Not long after the Tiananmen Square Massacre, I was arrested and jailed, and, along with thousands of other demonstrators, subjected to many months of torture and depravation. During these dark times spent in very dark places, many of my friends died; and to this day, some Tiananmen survivors are still being held in jails or forced labor camps.

Sadly, a whole new generation of Chinese youth knows nothing about what happened at Tiananmen. While we in the West can freely access the videos and images on the Internet associated with the massacre, all of this content has been ritually "cleansed" from the Chinese web by a vast army of censors.

I have now spent half my life fighting against such censorship and for freedom and democracy in China. More than ever, I fervently believe that this is what every thinking person outside of China must clearly understand:

More than two decades after Tiananmen, the totalitarian tiger has still not changed its stripes. In fact, unlike more stable countries, China's spending on police and social control is now rising even faster than China's skyrocketing defense budget!

It is with no small irony or anger that I note it is many of the very same Communist Party officials who supervised the beating, jailing, and killing of my fellow students in the wake of Tiananmen who are today orchestrating the relentless persecution of religious followers like the Falun Gong and the harsh repression of peaceful minorities like the Tibetans and the Uighurs. It is also the very same Chinese Communist Party that has been so quick to crack down on all political opposition movements like the Charter 08 manifesto and the rising Jasmine Revolution Movement; and the only change is that this new century's ruling clique is ever more cunning, more clandestine, and technologically more sophisticated.

Today, as I live comfortably, safely, and free in New York City, I can understand why it is so hard for those in the West to see the Chinese Communist Party clearly for the dangerous enemy that is—to both the people of China and the rest of the world. After all, the leaders in Beijing look very personable on TV, and they now quite strategically refrain from the threatening anti-West rants of Mao.

But facts are facts and the truth is the truth. And as the pages of this incredibly powerful book unfold, you will be confronted with fact after incontrovertible fact that the rulers in Beijing continue to brutally suppress the voices of China's own people even as they systematically flood the world with dangerous products, use a potent arsenal of mercantilist and protectionist weapons to destroy the economies of America and the West, and rapidly arm themselves with the best weapons systems their elaborate spy network can steal from the Pentagon.

I can also understand why these sobering facts and harsh truths may be at odds with your own personal experience. As a tourist to China, you may have taken an enjoyable cruise down the Yangtze, been mesmerized by the Terracotta Soldiers, walked in exhilaration along the Great Wall, or been utterly fascinated by the Forbidden City. Or you may even be an American business executive in Shanghai or Shenzhen making money hand over fist and being hosted to fabulous meals with no reason to see anything but blue skies and a yellow brick road ahead. Unfortunately, most Americans never see the other face of China and how the Chinese people have paid for all this "progress" with a dramatically damaged ecosystem, corruption, social injustice, human rights abuse, poisonous foods, and most seriously, the moral degradation of their souls.

Although I miss China, America has become my beloved second home; and the support of my beautiful wife shows me every day why America is the strongest country in the world. I also see this strength in so many small things in America, like the bumper sticker that reads, "Freedom Is Not Free."

I personally know how true that statement really is. I also know that the cost of freedom isn't always about fighting a military battle. It also includes the individual, political, and economic sacrifices of peacefully defending human rights and standing up for the principals of liberty and democracy.

Demanding that we live up to these principles as Peter Navarro and Greg Autry do in this deeply moving book can never be the wrong choice; and that is why it is long past time for the citizens of the world to truly stand beside the Chinese people—and not the brutally repressive and antiquated regime that rules them. If there is one abiding truth that stands above all after Tiananmen, it is that only a free and democratic China will benefit the world.

—**Baiqiao Tang**, Tiananmen Square protester and co-author of
My Two Chinas: The Memoir of a Chinese Counterrevolutionary
New York City
March 23, 2011

1

It's Not China Bashing If It's True

Death by China. This is the very real risk we all now face as the world's most populous nation and soon-to-be largest economy is rapidly turning into the planet's most efficient assassin.

On the consumer safety front, unscrupulous Chinese entrepreneurs are flooding world markets with a range of bone-crushing, cancer-causing, flammable, poisonous, and otherwise lethal products, foods, and drugs.

- In the kids' collection, these dangerous products range from lead-lined bracelets, necklaces, and toys to flaming pajamas and toxic toddler overalls.

- At your local drug store or online pharmacy, you can find all manner of "cures" that instead kill—from tainted aspirin, counterfeit Lipitor, and fake Viagra laced with strychnine to kidney-busting heparin and arsenic-laden vitamins.

- If you fancy death by explosion, fire, or electric shock, you can choose from a wide selection of booby-trapped extension cords, fans, lamps, overheating remote controls, exploding cell phones, and self-immolating boom boxes.

- Of course, if you're both hungry *and* suicidal, you can always feast on imported Chinese fish, fruit, meat, or vegetables delectably infused with all manner of banned antibiotics, putrefying bacteria, heavy metals, or illegal pesticides.

Even as thousands *literally* die from this onslaught of Chinese junk and poison, the American economy and its workers are suffering a no-less-painful "death to the American manufacturing base."

On this economic front, China's perverse brand of Communist-style "State Capitalism" has totally shredded the principles of both free markets and free trade. In their stead, China's state-backed "national champions" have deployed a potent mix of mercantilist and protectionist weapons to pick off America's industries job by job and one by one.

China's "weapons of job destruction" include massive illegal export subsidies, the rampant counterfeiting of U.S. intellectual property, pitifully lax environmental protections, and the pervasive use of slave labor. The centerpiece of Chinese mercantilism is, however, a shamelessly manipulated currency that heavily taxes U.S. manufacturers, extravagantly stimulates Chinese exports, and has led to a ticking time bomb U.S.–China trade deficit close to a *billion* dollars a day.

Meanwhile, the "entry fee" for any American company wishing to scale China's "Great Walls of protectionism" and sell into local markets is not just to surrender its technology to Chinese partners. American companies must also move research and development facilities to China, thereby exporting the "mother's milk" of future U.S. job creation to a hostile competitor.

Lost so far in China's mockery of free trade have been millions of U.S. manufacturing jobs even as the American blue-collar worker has become an endangered species. Consider the following:

- Since China joined the World Trade Organization in 2001 and falsely promised to end its mercantilist and protectionist practices, America's apparel, textile, and wood furniture industries have shrunk to half their size—with textile jobs alone beaten down by 70%.

- Other critical industries like chemicals, paper, steel, and tires are under similar siege, while employment in our high-tech computer and electronics manufacturing industries has plummeted by more than 40%.

As we have lost job after job across a wide swath of industries, many Americans continue to mistakenly associate Chinese manufacturing only with cheap, low-end products like sneakers and toys. In truth, however, China is steadily marching up the "value chain" to successfully grab market share in many of America's best-paying remaining industries—from automobiles and aerospace to advanced medical devices.

On the wings of massive government support, Chinese companies are busily cornering the market in so-called "green" industries like electric cars, solar power, and wind energy. Of course, it is precisely these industries that American politicians have been so fond of touting as America's best new sources of job creation.

For example, on the wind energy front, China now leads the world in both wind turbine production and protectionist irony. For even as China's state-subsidized companies flood world markets with their own turbines, foreign manufacturers like the U.S.-based General Electric, Spain's Gamesa, and India's Suzlon are prohibited from bidding on projects in China as part of a "Buy Chinese" policy.

One of the most lethal consequences of China's emergence as the world's undisputed "factory floor" has been its increasingly voracious appetites for the Earth's energy and raw materials. To feed its manufacturing machine, China must consume half of the world's cement, nearly half of its steel, one-third of its copper, and a third of its aluminum. Moreover, by the year 2035, China's oil demand *alone* will exceed that of total oil production today for the entire world.

These are indeed lethal appetites. That's because, to support these appetites, Chinese government officials have climbed into a blood-drenched colonial bed with murderous dictators and rogue regimes around the world. In doing so, Chinese government officials and diplomats are engaging in *the* most scurrilous abuse of United Nations diplomacy the world has ever seen.

As a permanent member of the UN Security Council, China can veto any UN sanctions it chooses to. For almost a decade now, top Chinese diplomats have been using China's UN veto power to broker a wide range of "blood for oil" and "rape for raw materials" deals. Consider these facts:

- In exchange for Sudanese oil, China's veto merchants stopped the UN from intervening in the Darfur genocide—even as a relentlessly brutal Janjaweed militia used Chinese weapons to forcibly rape thousands of women and kill 300,000 innocent Sudanese.
- China's veto merchants also blocked UN sanctions against Iran and its anti-Semitic, sham-election president to gain access to the world's largest natural gas fields. This act has blown open the door to nuclear proliferation in the Middle East. It has also dramatically raised the probability of a nuclear strike on Israel and significantly increased the risk of an atomic weapon falling into the hands of anti-American jihadists.

China's abuses of the peacekeeping mission of the United Nations are hardly isolated incidents. Instead, they are part of a broader "going abroad" strategy that has transformed China from a once isolationist nation into arguably the world's biggest budding colonial empire. This is no small irony for a country originally founded on anti-colonial, Marxist principles and once heavily victimized by the British Empire and its opium wars on China.

Throughout Africa, Asia, and America's backyard of Latin America, China's own twenty-first century brand of colonialism always begins with this Mephistophelean bargain: lavish, low-interest loans to build up the country's infrastructure in exchange for raw materials and access to local markets.

Of course, once a country takes this colonial bait, rather than use local labor, China brings in its huge army of engineers and workers to build new highways and railroads and ports and telecommunications systems. This infrastructure then both literally and digitally paves the way for the extraction and transport of raw materials. So it's back to China's factory floors in cities like Chongqing, Dongguan, and Shenzhen for Cameroon's timber, the Congo's magnesium, Djibouti's gypsum, Gabon's manganese, Malawi's uranium, Mozambique's titanium, Niger's molybdenum, Rwanda's tin, and Zambia's silver. As the final colonial coup de grâce, China then dumps its finished goods back onto local markets—thereby driving out local industries, driving up the unemployment rate, and driving its new colonies deeper into poverty.

Arming Itself to the Teeth

Even as China has boomed at the expense of much of the rest of the world, it has used its rapid economic growth to fund one of the most rapid and comprehensive military buildups the world has ever witnessed. In this way, and in the spirit of Vladimir Lenin's dictum that a capitalist will sell the rope that will be used to hang him, every "Walmart dollar" we Americans now spend on artificially cheap Chinese imports represents both a down payment on our own unemployment as well as additional financing for a rapidly arming China. Here's what just some of that vaunted war machine is shaping up to look like:

- China's newly modernized Navy and Air Force feature everything from virtually undetectable nuclear submarines and the latest Russian-designed fighter jets to ballistic missiles that can precisely target America's aircraft carriers on the high seas.
- China's own "Pentagon" is confidently developing advanced weapons systems—many of which have been stolen from us by Chinese hackers and spies!—to shoot down our satellite and GPS systems and send nuclear warheads deep into the American heartland.

- Unlike a fatigued U.S. army now thinly stretched by the conflicts in Afghanistan and Iraq, the People's Liberation Army—
  the largest in the world—has both the overwhelming force and
  troop readiness to roll over the forces of India, South Korea,
  Taiwan, or Vietnam and still have more than enough foot soldiers to crush the Taliban and keep the peace in Baghdad if it
  cared to.
- The "war hawk" wing of China's military is even readying the
  ability to drop virtually untrackable nuclear bombs from space.
  These cosmic nukes simply arrive on target in a few short minutes and far too quickly and quietly for countermeasures.

Of course, America isn't the only country that should fear the emergence of a new and powerful Asian aggressor. China's increasingly nervous neighbors now face a rapidly increasing risk from a rising Asian
hegemon amidst China's brinkmanship and bullying over everything
from access to shipping lanes to long-simmering territorial disputes.

It's Big Brother Meets Silent Spring

Also in danger are the hundreds of millions of innocent Chinese
citizens, who face extreme "Death by China on China" risks from
China's pollution-rife economic growth model, its rigid, class-based
Communist Party theocracy, and an "Orwell on steroids" totalitarianism.

On the pollution front, an overreliance on an export-driven,
heavy manufacturing economy has turned the atmosphere over
China's industrial heartland into the world's biggest toxic cloud and
shroud. More than 70% of China's major lakes, rivers, and streams
are severely polluted. Even a popular tourist cruise down the Yangtze
River, above the Three Gorges Dam, reveals that this once-pristine
Chinese national treasure where Mao once swam is now virtually
devoid of birds and visible signs of aquatic life.

Meanwhile, "What happens in China doesn't stay in China." As
Chinese factories churn out a flood of products destined for the
shelves of Target and Walmart, China's particularly virulent brand of

air pollution rides more than 6,000 miles along the jet stream to California, dropping toxic waste all along the way. Today, most of the acid rain in Japan and South Korea is "Made in China," while an increasing share of the fine particulate found in the air in West Coast cities like Los Angeles likewise started out in a Chinese factory.

As for the risks posed by China's rigid, class-based society, the bitter, ironic truth here is that the ruling Communist Party oversees not a true "People's Republic" but rather its own secular theocracy. While Marx turns over in his grave and a pickled Mao stares glassy-eyed from his crystal coffin in Tiananmen Square, a relatively small fraction of the Chinese population grows fabulously rich even as one billion Chinese citizens continue to live in a Hobbesian world of grinding poverty without access to adequate health care and where even a minor sickness can become a death sentence.

China's totalitarian politics are equally appalling. To quell dissent, the Communist Party relies on a police and paramilitary force numbering more than one million. Its Orwellian web also features some 50,000 cyber cops. Together, these real and virtual jackboots are unrelenting in their repression and suppression.

- Try to organize your workplace, and you are beaten and then fired.
- Stand up for human rights or women's rights, and you are mercilessly hounded, placed under house arrest, or simply "disappeared."
- Be revealed as a Falun Gong practitioner or "closet Catholic," and get ready to have your "deviant thoughts" washed right out of your brain.

The linchpin of such Chinese repression is a grim archipelago of forced labor camps to which millions of Chinese citizens have been exiled—often without trial. For those imprisoned in China's Laogai gulag, it could be worse; according to Amnesty International, the People's Republic annually executes several times more of its own people than the rest of the world combined.

At least lethal injection is now preferred to the traditional bullet to the brain. It is not compassion, however, driving this capital punishment "reform." It is simply that injections are cheaper to clean up, provide less risk of HIV infection to the executioners, and make it much easier to harvest the victim's organs for sale on the black market.

The Big Sellout, the Bigger Copout

Even as these countless Deaths by China play out both within the People's Republic and on killing floors around the globe, America's business executives, journalists, and politicians have had far too little to say about the single greatest threat facing the United States and the world.

In the executive arena, some of America's biggest companies—from Caterpillar and Cisco to General Motors and Microsoft—have been fully complicit in the Chinese politics of "first divide America and then conquer it." The tragedy here is that when China's mercantilist onslaught against American industry began in the late 1990s—and industries like furniture, textiles, and apparel began falling one by one—the business community and organizations like the U.S. Chamber of Commerce were staunchly united.

Over the past decade, however, as each additional American job and each new American factory has been offshored to China, the narrow profit-maximizing interests of many of America's corporate executives have been realigned with their Chinese partners. Indeed, with their bread now being buttered offshore, so-called "American" organizations like the Business Roundtable and National Association of Manufacturers have been transformed from staunch critics of Chinese mercantilism into open, and often very aggressive, soldiers in the pro-China Lobby.

While many American corporate executives have become lobbying warriors for China, American journalists are mostly missing in action. The downsizing of newspapers and network television news in an age of the Internet has led to the closing or shrinking of many foreign news bureaus. As a result, the American media has had to increasingly rely on the flow of news from the government-owned Chinese press—one of the most effective and relentless propaganda machines the world has ever witnessed.

Meanwhile, the cream of America's financial press—most notably the *Wall Street Journal*—clings zealously to a free market and free trade ideology, seemingly oblivious to the fact that China's "one-way free trade" is simply America's unilateral surrender in an age of Chinese state capitalism. The absurdity here is that instead of seeing trade reform as a legitimate form of self-defense against a relentless Chinese onslaught of "beggar thy neighbor" practices, publications like the *Wall Street Journal* continually rail against the threat of American "protectionism." It's all so much nonsense, but the ideological drum beat goes on.

As for America's politicians, no single group of individuals deserves more blame for standing meekly, passively, and ignorantly by as China has had its way with the U.S. manufacturing base and engaged in its massive military buildup. It's not that the American Congress hasn't been fully warned about the dangers of a rising China. Each year, the Congressionally funded U.S.–China Commission publishes both an annual report and ample testimony about this emerging threat.

For example, the U.S.–China Commission has warned that "Chinese espionage activities in the United States are so extensive that they comprise the single greatest risk to the security of American technologies." In fact, to date, China's far-reaching spy network has stolen critical secrets related to the Aegis guided missile destroyer, B1-B bomber, Delta IV rocket, ICBM-capable guidance systems, Stealth Bomber, and Space Shuttle. Chinese hackers and spies have been equally effective at delivering details on aircraft carrier launch systems, drones, naval reactor designs, submarine propulsion systems, the inner workings of neutron bombs, and even highly specific U.S. Navy warship operations procedures.

Similarly, on the economic threat, the Commission has pleaded with Congress to recognize that small and medium-sized American businesses "face the full brunt of China's unfair trade practices, currency manipulation, and illegal subsidies for Chinese exports." Despite these warnings, Congress continues to ignore the advice of its own independent commission and wake up to the rising economic and military threat from China.

Of course, the White House must share equal blame. Both Presidents George W. Bush and Barack Obama have talked softly and carried very little sticks when it has come to China. President Bush's excuse was a preoccupation with the war in Iraq and homeland security coupled with a blind faith in what has been anything but free trade. On Bush's watch alone, the United States surrendered millions of jobs to China.

For his part, *Candidate* Barack Obama on the 2008 campaign trail repeatedly promised to crack down on unfair Chinese trade practices, particularly in key industrial swing states like Illinois, Michigan, Ohio, and Pennsylvania. However, since taking office, *President* Obama has repeatedly bowed to China on key trade issues, primarily because he wants China to keep financing America's massive budget deficits. While Obama mortgages our future to his Chinese banker, he fails to understand that the best jobs program for America is comprehensive trade reform with China.

The Roadmap Ahead: All Roads Careen Toward Beijing

In this book, we will systematically work our way through each of the major categories of Death by China—from China's appalling product safety record and the destruction of the American economy to the rise of Chinese colonialism, China's rapid military buildup, and its bold and blatant espionage adventures. In doing so, our overriding goal is not just to provide you with an exposé and catalog of China's abuses. This book is also meant as a survival guide and call to action at a critical juncture in American and world history. Unless all of us rise up together to confront the Dragon, the rest of our lives and the lives of our children will be far less prosperous—and far more dangerous—than the Golden Age in which many of us grew up.

Part I

"Buyer Beware" on Steroids

2

Death by Chinese Poison:
Bodies for Bucks and Chicks for Free

What do they call Chinese food in China? Food!
—Jay Leno

While that joke is pretty funny, the phrase "Chinese food" has taken on far more serious implications now that China is supplying America with more and more of its fruits, vegetables, fish, and meat—not to mention vitamins and prescription drugs.

For our refrigerator, China is the largest exporter of seafood to the United States, a key supplier of white meat chicken and the world's third largest tea exporter. Chinese farmers also provide 60% of our apple juice concentrate, 50% of our garlic, and significant amounts of everything from canned pears and preserved mushrooms to honey and royal bee jelly.

For our medicine cabinet, China likewise produces 70% of the world's penicillin, 50% of its aspirin, and 33% of its Tylenol. Chinese drug companies have also captured much of the world market in antibiotics, enzymes, primary amino acids, and vitamins. China has even cornered the world market for vitamin C—with 90% of market share—even as it plays a dominant role in the production of vitamins A, B12, and E, besides many of the raw ingredients that go into multivitamins.

These statistics should disturb all of us for one simple reason: Far too much of what China is flooding our grocery stores and drug emporia with is pure poison. That's why Chinese foods and drugs always rank #1 of those flagged down at the border or recalled by both the U.S. Food and Drug Administration and the European Food Safety Authority.

Just why does China keep sending us food and drugs that can sicken or kill us? Sometimes the poisons that show up in its food and drug supply chain are the accidental result of factors such as shoddy production methods, unsanitary processing, or soil toxicity due to a polluted environment. At other times, ethically challenged and morally degraded Chinese "black hearts"—a term used by their own countrymen—purposely contaminate our food and drug supply simply as a way to boost their profits.

Whether it is by accident or by intention, the first thing you need to know about this particular Death by China is that it's nothing personal. Indeed, Chinese farmers, fishermen, food processors, and pharmaceutical peddlers are just as likely to poison their own people as Americans, Europeans, the Japanese, Koreans, and other food and drug consumers around the world. To get just a small acid taste of the truth of this statement in your mouth, consider this "what's in your wok" fact: Fully 10% of all the restaurants in China rely on so-called "gutter oil" for their cooking oil.

Gutter oil is a fetid stew of used oil and waste collected from the traps and drains of commercial kitchens, and it's chock-full of a potent liver carcinogen known as aflatoxin mold. China's guttersnipes sell it at the back doors of many restaurants for a mere one-fifth of the price of new soy or peanut oil. Besides being carcinogenic, this mashup of moldy oils and every possible type of food debris can be a sudden death sentence for anyone with serious food allergies.

China's Serial Melamine Killers

Disgusting though this gutter oil scam may be, it pales in comparison to China's serial melamine murderers. These murderers have struck down numerous victims on both Chinese soil and around the world, and the often futile attempts to catch them graphically illustrate just how difficult it is for either the Chinese government or American regulators to guarantee safe food and drugs when murder for profit is in play.

As for the murder weapon itself, melamine is actually a quite valuable chemical—when it is not being surreptitiously added to food. Combine it with formaldehyde to produce melamine resin, and you get a durable plastic used in products like Formica and dry erase boards. Toss in some other chemicals, and you can use melamine either as a fire retardant, fertilizer, or "super plasticizer" for making high-resistance concrete. But add melamine to products like chicken feed, pet food, milk, or baby formula, and there is no faster way to destroy a pair of kidneys.

Just why do China's black-hearted entrepreneurs add poisonous melamine to our food products? It's because melamine's high nitrogen content mimics correspondingly high protein levels. Such "Chinese protein adulteration," as it has come to be infamously known, thereby fools food inspectors into grading the food with a higher protein content. Because melamine is substantially cheaper than actual protein, this means big bucks for the perpetrators—no matter how high the body count.

Who Killed Fluffy? What Happened to Fido?

The world first learned of Chinese protein adulteration in 2007 when a wave of melamine-tainted pet food killed tens of thousands of cats and dogs in Europe, the United States, and South Africa. And it wasn't just pets that were affected. According to the United States

Food and Drug Administration and the Department of Agriculture, 3 million Americans consumed chicken or pork raised on feed laced with melamine.

And now hear this: If you lost your otherwise healthy pet to a mysterious illness or kidney failure during that time period, chances are it was a "Death by Chinese Poison."

Predictably, when the crisis first broke, the Chinese government stonewalled and even refused to allow foreign safety inspectors in to evaluate the problem. It was a different story, however, when the next melamine scandal crashed on China's own shores.

It's Nothing Personal, Part Deux

"I've completely lost confidence in milk powder made in China," said Emily Tang, 31, a civil servant from the southern city of Shenzhen, who has a 3-year-old daughter.
—*Bloomberg BusinessWeek*

In 2008, almost 300,000 Chinese babies fell ill and 6 died after 22 Chinese dairies conspired to add melamine to the milk and baby formula supply. According to Zhao Huibin, a dairy farmer in Hebei Province: "Before melamine, the dealers added rice porridge or starch into the milk to artificially boost the protein count, but that method was easily tested as fake, so they switched to melamine."

In this particular case, black heart adulterers didn't even use pure industrial-grade melamine. Instead, they relied on the cheaper—and even more toxic—"scrap melamine." No wonder many of the children who recovered from the acute melamine poisoning have been left with significant kidney damage.

What's particularly chilling about this episode is that it came fully a year after Prime Minister Wen Jiabao had authorized an additional $1.1 billion and sent several hundred thousand inspectors to examine food and drug producers. As *The New York Times* opined on the implications of this abysmal regulatory failure:

> *The dairy scandal raises the core question of whether the ruling Communist Party is capable of creating a transparent, accountable regulatory structure within a one-party system.*

And here's a little laugh-out-loud addendum that answers that question while underscoring a fundamental difference between free and open societies and a ruthlessly totalitarian China. In 2010, former journalist Zhao Lianhai went to prison after a sham trial in which he was denied the ability to present evidence.

Zhao's "crime" was not poisoning people. Rather, he was convicted of "inciting social disorder" for his efforts to publicize the melamine murders after his own son was sickened. And that's one more reason why the People's Republic of China will never be able to guarantee us safer food products. Unlike democratic nations where the right to free speech and freedom of assembly are sacrosanct and help shine a bright light on deviant behavior, China sweeps everything under the rug—and any and all protesting voices into its gulags.

China's Heparin Homicides

Now, lest you think China's melamine scandals might be old news, forget about it. To this day, melamine-contaminated products keep popping up precisely because it is so profitable to use the kidney-buster as an additive.

Lest you also think that China's trick of using contaminated "fillers" like melamine to boost profits is limited to foods, forget about that, too. As China's "heparin homicides" graphically illustrate, unscrupulous Chinese entrepreneurs are also busily poisoning our drug supply.

Heparin is an anticoagulant drug used in everything from heart surgery and blood transfusions to intravenous therapy and kidney dialysis; and it is actually made from the lowly mucous membranes of pig intestines. In fact, that's how China has gotten into the heparin manufacturing act: As the pork capital of the world, the Dragon has a seemingly endless supply of pig guts.

To cut costs and boost profits, Chinese manufacturers surreptitiously add a cheap but deadly heparin-mimicking agent called "overly sulfated chondroitin sulfate." This particular poison triggers severe, and sometimes fatal, allergic reactions—from low blood pressure and shortness of breath to vomiting and diarrhea.

Now here's what's particularly nasty about this bait and switch: The heparin contaminant is so close in chemical structure to actual heparin that it is very difficult to detect. It's also 100 times cheaper— $9 per pound versus $900! Because of such low costs, some contaminated heparin batches have been found to have been cut by up to 50% with the counterfeit chemical!

To put a personal face on this particular Death by Chinese Poison, look no further than Leroy Hubley of Toledo, Ohio. He lost his wife of 48 years to tainted heparin. Just a month later and before the contaminant was identified, Hubley's son, who shared his mother's inherited kidney dysfunction, fell victim to the same Chinese cost-cutting scam.

To date, China's heparin poisoners have killed hundreds of Americans while sickening thousands. Bad heparin has also shown up in 11 other countries, including Japan, India, Germany, and Canada. Moreover, despite efforts by both Chinese and American regulators to contain the problem, bad heparin keeps showing up in our operating rooms and dialysis centers to this day.

———————————

At this point, we must ask ourselves this pointed question: Why are so many Chinese black hearts so willing to poison the world's food and drug supply for profit? The answer of at least one noted Chinese scholar provides a penetrating look into the aforementioned "moral degradation" of the Chinese soul. According to business professor Luo Yadong in the *Management and Organization Review*, such degradation—and the rush for profits at any cost—has occurred because of the breakdown of Confucian principles in the moral and ethical vacuum that is Chinese Communism.

It's precisely such moral degradation, working in tandem with corrupt government officials and lax regulatory enforcement, that has led Chinese food processors to deliberately add a long list of poisonous industrial chemicals to foods either to improve taste or to act as preservatives.

In fact, China's own regulators have found such abominations as hot pot soups "seasoned' with formaldehyde to improve taste and soy sauce spiked with hydrochloric acid and human hair to boost amino acid levels. The Chinese black hearts have even added the highly toxic pesticide dichlorvos to make the humble sausage "deliciously" deadly. Just remember these little tidbits the next time you think about eating anything "Made in China."

Sometimes It's Not Murder—Just Manslaughter

There reaches a point where I think it's clear, if China wants to live in the twenty-first century, then they have to produce to those standards.
—Senator Richard Durbin (D-IL)

While "first-degree murder" is the verdict in cases ranging from melamine to heparin, in many other cases, it's simply "involuntary manslaughter"—the killing of another human being without "malice aforethought." A major problem here is that as China has established itself as the world's manufacturing floor, it has also turned itself into a toxic waste dump and the world's most polluted country. Such wholesale environmental trashing now means that the soil China uses to provide the world with its nourishment is riddled with all manner of carcinogens, heavy metals, illegal pesticides, and other toxins. That the poisons from China's soil are leaching into the diets of America, Europe, Japan, and South Korea should be evident to anyone who bothers to look.

A Chinese "Apple a Day" Keeps American Oncologists Fully Employed

Consider, for example, the sweet and cuddly "juice box" you might pack in your child's lunch. There's a good chance this ostensibly "healthy" alternative to soda pop might be dosing your kid with arsenic, a heavy metal that can cause cancer. Here's why:

Over the past 30 years, Chinese exports of apple juice concentrate have soared from 10,000 gallons a year to almost half a billion; and today China commands half or more of the U.S. market. Sure, the juice is cheaper than what American farmers can produce. But one reason is that Chinese orchards rely heavily on illegal arsenic-based pesticides that are absorbed by the tree and concentrated in the fruit.

Do You Like Your Tea Regular or Unleaded?

As for the expression "all the tea in China," well, even that can't be trusted! Here is how a former deputy commissioner of the U.S. Food and Drug Administration described one Chinese method of drying tea leaves on National Public Radio: The manufacturer lays the "tea leaves out on a huge warehouse floor and drive[s] trucks over them so that the exhaust...more rapidly dr[ies] the leaves out." Because China uses leaded gasoline, there is no more effective way of turning a tasty green tea into a lethal weapon.

There Is No Truth in Chinese Food Labeling

In addition, one of the most deceptive black heart practices is to chronically mislabel "organic" food products. Not surprisingly, Chinese farmers have been eager to jump on America's "organic foods" bandwagon, but this admission from a Chinese grocery store owner says it all:

Maybe 30% of farms that put the organic label on their food produce the real thing. I think in the future the government will improve testing. But now, hygiene officers have so much work to do with essential food safety that they don't worry about organic.

Given this admission, it should come as no surprise that Walmart, Whole Foods, and other retailers have found supposedly "organic" products from China to be heavily dosed with pesticides.

Japan's Green Bean Gag Reflex

It's not just America that China is turning toxic. Consider what happened when one Japanese food distributor imported over 50,000 packages of allegedly "fresh" Chinese green beans from the Yantai Beihai Foodstuff Co. in Shandong Province. After consumers experienced nausea and vomiting followed by mouth numbness, Japanese health department officials found the level of a deadly insecticide present in the beans to be almost 35,000 times the legal limit!

Of course, we could continue to chronicle tale after tale of "death by Chinese poison." For example, there's the fiasco in Europe involving Vitamin A supplies contaminated with a deadly bacterium that almost got into infant formula. There have been multivitamins riddled with lead and honey and shrimp dosed with antibiotics. There's also the infamous and well-publicized cough syrup laced with antifreeze that killed thousands around the globe. But examples such as these are only as good as the broader points they illustrate.

The last broad point we wish to illustrate with an example about fish farming in China is this: Given the scope of the environmental problems with Chinese foods and drugs and the pervasiveness of morally degraded Chinese entrepreneurial behavior, it is virtually impossible for agencies such as the U.S. Food and Drug Administration, the European Food and Safety Authority, and the Food Safety

Commission of Japan to adequately police Chinese imports. In fact, the story of how Chinese fish farms have overwhelmed both foreign competitors and food safety regulators represents a microcosm of all that is wrong with relying on Chinese food—and fish!

It's Not Just China's Humans Who Live in Crowded Conditions

Our waters here are filthy. There are simply too many aqua-culture farms in this area. They're all discharging water here, fouling up other farms.
—Ye Chao, eel and shrimp farmer, Fuqing, China

This unfortunately quite true Chinese "fish story" appropriately begins in the Southeastern United States where, during the 1990s, raising fish like the southern catfish represented one of American aquaculture's great success stories. Then, enter the Dragon.

As we discuss fully in Part II, "Weapons of Job Destruction," Chinese enterprises benefit from an array of unfair trade practices, and China's fish farms are no exception. Indeed, beginning in the early 2000s, under the onslaught of Chinese subsidized exports, many American fish farms across states such as Louisiana, Mississippi, and Alabama quite literally dried up.

Today, China is the world's leading source of farm-raised fish and dominates the markets for catfish, tilapia, shrimp, and eel. However, China's fish farms provide no pastoral image of peace and harmony with nature. Rather, they project a Paradise Lost nightmare of hellish filth.

This fish farm filth begins with the fact that less than half of China has access to sewage treatment facilities. How this human waste—along with a flood of pesticides, fertilizers, coal slurry, antibi-otics, dyes, and other pollutants—finds its way onto your Friday night dinner plate is instructive.

This stomach-turning journey begins at the upper reaches of the Yangtze River and runs over 3,000 river miles to China's Eastern Delta. It is at this Eastern Delta where much of the contaminated fish raised for export to the United States, Europe, Japan, and elsewhere is raised.

Along the Yangtze's route, booming large cities such as Chengdu and Chongqing dump billions of tons of mostly untreated human, animal, and industrial waste directly into the river. This toxic mess is then given some considerable time to ferment and stew as it collects in the reservoir behind the gigantic Three Gorges Dam below Chongqing.

In fact, to take a 3-day "luxury" cruise down the Yangtze River from Chongqing to the Three Gorges Dam—as many American tourists do—is to experience a frightening environmental nightmare. The reservoir waters glow an eerie and sometimes malodorous florescent green under an ever-present cloud of smoke from coal burning plants. Like Sherlock Holmes' "dog that didn't' bark," the almost complete absence of waterfowl, turtles, and amphibians—not to mention the once playful, iconic, and now extinct pink river dolphins—underscores the toxicity of one of China's largest rivers and drinking water supplies.

As to why this is in any way relevant to the Chinese fish you eat in America, remember that it is precisely this Yangtze stew—as well as the equally wretched waters of the Pearl and Yellow Rivers—that fill the export-focused fish farms on China's East Coast. Of course, because Chinese eels, fish, and shrimp are raised in such toxic conditions, the creatures suffer from all manner of infections and parasites. As Chinese scholar Liu Chenglin has noted:

> [T]he conditions that aquacultured seafood is grown under in China are deplorable: Producers tightly cram thousands of finfish and shellfish into their facilities to maximize production. This generates large amounts of waste, contaminates the water,

and spreads disease, which can kill off entire crops of fish if left untreated. Even if a disease does not kill off all the fish in an aquaculture facility, remaining bacteria, such as Vibrio, Listeria, or Salmonella, can sicken people who eat the fish.

To treat these conditions, China's fish farmers routinely pump all manner of banned antibiotics, antifungals, antivirals, and dyes into their polluted waters. These toxic substances, which are inevitably absorbed into the creatures' flesh, range from malachite green, chloramphenicol, and fluoroquinolones to nitrofurans, contraceptive drugs, and gentian violet; and they can do everything from cause cancer and trigger rare diseases like aplastic anemia to degrade the human body's ability to use antibiotics to cure infections.

On top of these outrages, Chinese fish processors routinely treat fish for export with substances such as carbon monoxide gas to give the filets a bright red color. This not only increases the visual appeal of the product but disguises any spoilage. Please remember that little trick the next time you see a nice pink Chinese fish and think it is "fresh frozen."

Of course, in China, "what's good for the American goose is often *not* what's good for the Chinese gander." Indeed, this type of "pink primping" is subject to harsh penalties if used in fish designed for domestic Chinese consumption.

Now here is the broader point of this Chinese fish story—and really the only thing you need to remember: The U.S. Food and Drug Administration is so grossly understaffed that although it regulates 80% of America's food supply, it only inspects less than 1% of food imports. It is precisely for this reason that whenever you eat anything from China you are effectively playing "Chinese Food Roulette." And no amount of assurances from either the Chinese government or American regulators should convince you otherwise!

Selling Fake Coals to Newcastle

Certain Chinese companies are now mass producing and sell-
ing fake rice to unwitting villagers. According to a report in
the Korean-language Weekly Hong Kong, *the manufacturers*
are blending potatoes, sweet potatoes, and plastic industrial
resin to produce the imitation rice.
—*Natural News*

To end this chapter, we would be remiss in not sharing with you
two of the most recent, brazen, and outrageous examples of Chinese
product adulteration. These examples put several exclamation points
on the point that if Chinese entrepreneurs will do these kinds of
things to their own countrymen, why would you expect them to send
us safe food, drugs, or products?

The first example involves a scheme to pawn off fake plastic rice
to poor villagers. In this particular con game, the faux rice manufacturers first mash up a blend of regular potatoes and sweet potatoes
and mold the mash into the shape of rice kernels. Synthetic plastic
resin is then added so the grains hold their shape; the giveaway is that
you can boil the faux rice for hours and it remains crunchy. As noted
by an official from the Chinese Restaurant Association, eating three
bowls of this Frankenstein mashup is the same as swallowing an
entire plastic bag. And you thought that wheat bran was hard on your
intestinal track.

As for example number two, this scheme is rampant throughout
major provinces of China, including Gansu, Henan, Qinghai, Shanxi,
and Sichuan. The con involves adding fake flavors and aromas to ordinary rice to make it smell and taste like the much more expensive
premium and aromatic "Wuchang" rice.

By adding a mere half a kilo of fragrance, an unscrupulous
Chinese rice processor can aromatize up to ten tons of rice. That this
scheme is out of control is captured in one laugh-out-loud statistic

reported by the Chinese media: Each year, farmers grow only 800,000 tons of Wuchang rice, but more than 10 million tons are sold at market.

Nor is there any apparent remorse among the perpetrators of this scam. When confronted, one spokesman for a company caught red-handed simply said, "The adulterated rice products have been selling very well due to the lower prices compared to the real thing." We know sociopaths who have more social conscience.

3

Death by Chinese Junk: Strangling Our Babies in Their Cribs

Amber Donnals was sitting on her porch when she heard an explosion, followed by screams. She turned to see her son, Bryan, 6, running toward her, his clothes on fire, and flames shooting up at the rear of the Donnalses' mobile home. He'd been riding his newly minted, Chinese-made ATV...when suddenly it sped up and raced out of control...The red, 110cc four-wheeler barely missed a propane tank before crashing into the trailer and catching fire.

—St. Louis Post-Dispatch

There's nothing funny about this horrific story; fortunately, young Bryan did survive his severe burns. Still, it's worth reporting to you the quite unintentionally comic remark of Bryan's grandfather after the incident because it reflects the ongoing obliviousness of far too many American consumers to the threat of "Chinese junk." Said Tim Donnals, Sr., who bought the ATV for the poor kid, "I didn't think it was going to blow up, or I would not have bought it." Indeed.

Well, we are here to warn you that from now on, any time you buy products from China, you should expect the worst. That's because Chinese manufacturers have an exceedingly long history of junk that blows up in the night—or day—and an equally long history of junk that burns up and breaks up and batters and bruises. Here's just a small sampling of the myriad disasters that can befall you, your family, your neighbors, your coworkers, or your friends if you remain as oblivious to the dangers as Bryan's granddad:

- You break your collarbone when a faulty fender on your bicycle falls into the tire and throws you over the handlebars.
- Your teenage baseball–playing son catches an errant ground ball right in his "protective cup"—which shatters on impact, leaving painful cuts and bruising.
- A guest at your Super Bowl party suffers severe burns when the TV remote overheats in his hand.
- Your next door neighbor's house burns down because of faulty wiring in a fan.
- Your best friend is "fragged" when the cell phone in his chest pocket explodes and sends bone shrapnel into his heart.

The obvious question that arises from these tales from the Manufacturing Dragon's crypt is why we aren't being protected from the myriad dangers. The answer lies in the abject breakdown of five major lines of defense that are supposed to protect you and your family from such abominations.

Your first line of defense should be the Chinese workers assembling your products. Overworked, underpaid, poorly trained, and often abused assembly line workers in China's "worker's paradise" are in no condition to do the sort of quality assurance that the Japanese, Americans, and Europeans take for granted. In fact, stopping a production line in China to fix a problem could get you fired. In his wonderfully told book, *Poorly Made in China*, Paul Midler has noted that reporting quality defects is likely to get any would-be whistle blower branded an "enemy of the state."

Your second line of defense ought to be the Chinese manufacturers themselves. They should have a strong motive to produce safe products if for no other reason than you will sue them if they don't. Oh, but wait. We forgot to tell you. Even if you can find a guilty Chinese company to pin a problem on—a very difficult task—you likely won't be able to sue in either an American or Chinese court. In the extremely rare event you win a legal judgment, just try collecting the money. Even sending back a defective product for rework is nearly impossible because the Chinese customs rules that prevent "importing defective products" offer a nice excuse to the manufacturer. The point: Liability flows across the Pacific in only one direction.

As for your third line of defense against Chinese junk, this should be the Chinese regulatory system. Good luck with that, too. China's product safety bureaucracy is not only grossly understaffed. It ranks as one of the most corrupt in the world. It's not just that Chinese inspectors can be bought at the rate of a few dimes per dozen. It's also that many of the Chinese manufacturers producing deadly junk are owned by the government—and it will be a blue sky day in Beijing before the government will crack down on itself.

Still a fourth line of defense should be America's own border inspectors and consumer protection agencies. However, what America's product cops sadly share in common with their Chinese counterparts is an understaffing problem. As we saw in Chapter 2, "Death by Chinese Poison," only 1% of the Chinese food entering America is even inspected. As you will soon see, we have a similar problem when it comes to agencies like America's Consumer Product Safety Commission.

This leaves you with your fifth and final line of defense: the American companies stuffing America's retail channels with cheap Chinese imports while they're supposed to be conducting rigorous tests for quality control. What's particularly troubling here is not just the naïveté of so many American corporations so ready to trust the Chinese to police their own factories. It's also the willingness of far too many of these corporations to quickly deny culpability or even cover up problems whenever things go so terribly wrong. Hey, we're talking to you, Walmart, among many others.

So, dear friend, please read this chapter and weep accordingly as we regale you with tale after tale of the myriad Chinese products that can sicken, maim, or kill you. Then, once you finish this chapter, dry your eyes and call, write, or e-mail your Congressional representative. It's well past time for all of us to stand up just like Peter Finch did in the movie *Network* and shout, "We're mad as hell, and we won't buy your 'Chinese junk' anymore."

China's Appalling Record on Product Safety

Import from China. Save money. Lose your life.
—Leslie LeBon

Before we explain why Chinese manufacturers are so prone to producing lethal junk, it's important to debunk one of the favorite myths of China apologists, namely, that Chinese products are as safe as other countries. The indisputable fact of the matter here is that while all countries on occasion produce defective and dangerous products— hey, even a company like Toyota known for its superb quality messes up big sometimes—the Chinese are in a league all by themselves.

To prove this, we could quote you statistic after statistic. However, this quick reprise of China's product safety record in Europe should more than suffice.

Consider that in 2009, China captured fully 58% of the product safety notifications issued by European regulators while only 2% of United States exports to Europe were flagged. And please note: Chinese exports to Europe are only slightly higher than that of United States exports—18% for China versus 13% for the United States. A simple calculation with these ratios shows that Chinese products are flagged for safety violations at a rate 22 times higher than that of the United States.

Now here is the kicker. Despite vigorous attempts by the European Union to improve China's product quality compliance—including a special inspection process for Chinese goods and sending

European inspectors to China to train government officials on product safety standards—China still managed to outdo itself by capturing an astounding 61% of all EU notifications in 2010.

Here's the broader point: You can't trust Chinese regulators to protect you. Indeed, almost half of the time European regulators notify their Chinese counterparts of a product defect or safety violation, the Chinese do *nothing*. Nada. Zero. Zip. The major reason: The responsible Chinese manufacturer typically cannot be tracked down by government officials. (This is either a remarkably convenient circumstance for China, Inc. or a true test of the fly-by-night character of so many of China's "black heart" factories.)

Why Chinese Manufacturers Produce So Much Chinese Junk

Only the Chinese can turn a leather sofa into an acid bath, a baby crib into a lethal weapon, and a cell phone battery into heart-piercing shrapnel.

—Ron Vara

Now that we know that China produces more dangerous products than any other country in the world even after adjusting for its huge global market share, it's useful to drill down a bit deeper to examine just why this is so. As we shall now show you in a series of Chinese "junk-ettes," the problems range from shoddy production methods and sheer stupidity to the more nefarious games of "Chinese Product Adulteration" and a national pastime of the Chinese black hearts we like to call the "Quality Con."

Blame Shoddy Production: Chinese Drywall Leaves Many High and Dry

When Bill Morgan, a retired policeman, moved into his newly built dream home in Williamsburg, Va... his wife and daughter

suffered constant nosebleeds and headaches. A persistent foul odor filled the house. Every piece of metal indoors corroded or turned black. In short order, Mr. Morgan moved out. The headaches and nosebleeds stopped, but the ensuing financial problems pushed him into personal bankruptcy.
—*The New York Times*

The Curious Case of the Corrosive Chinese Drywall provides a classic lesson in the art of shoddy Chinese production methods. The millions of sheets of drywall in question came to be contaminated with corrosive sulfurous compounds when Chinese manufacturers first started using cheaper, high sulfur gypsum. Then, to save even more money, the manufacturers cut the gypsum with power plant fly ash from China's notoriously high-sulfur coal. As a middle-finger salute to this whole shoddy process, the corrosive drywall was then mixed and shipped to the United States without proper oversight or testing.

To be clear here, the sulfur contaminant in the Chinese drywall not only makes the air in homes smell like rotten eggs and attacks the respiratory system. The sulfurous gasses are so powerful they corrode pipes, cause appliances and HVAC units to fail, turn silver jewelry black, and kill family pets.

In fact, contaminated Chinese drywall has been found in as many as 100,000 new American homes in at least a dozen states. Those states hardest hit have been those with a hot and humid climate, which facilitates the release of the sulfurous gasses.

Florida is the epicenter of the crisis—with the only upside being an inadvertent but effective "Keynesian stimulus" to the local economy. Indeed, the business of replacing toxic Chinese drywall has boomed. Said Congressman Robert Wexler (D-FL), "Florida is hypersensitive to hurricanes, and this is like a silent hurricane. Whole neighborhoods are being wiped out...."

And speaking of hurricanes, New Orleans likewise got more than its fair share of this Chinese junk during the post-Katrina rebuilding process. Even the head coach of the New Orleans Saints, Sean Payton, had to move out of his Mandeville, Louisiana home. How's that for a double whammy?

Writ large, China's putatively "low cost" drywall has cost American homeowners as much as $15 billion above its purchase price. That's because the remediation cost per home has run anywhere from $100,000 to $250,000. Of course, the vast majority of the Chinese manufacturers involved have not only refused to pick up the tab; as in our earlier European example, most can't even be identified.

Costs to the taxpayers have likewise been stiff. To investigate the scandal, the Consumer Product Safety Commission incurred the highest compliance costs in the agency's history, while the IRS had to create a special deduction just so affected homeowners could write off the cost of the damages and drywall remediation. That's right, folks: The rest of us are paying for this drywall debacle in our tax bill even if we didn't take the hit. If there ever were a lesson that cheap Chinese goods aren't really cheap, this is it. If there were ever validation of the claim that "you get what you pay for," this is it, too.

Blame Sheer Stupidity: Would You like Eczema with That Sofa?

One night I found him with blood all over his face because he had been scratching himself in his sleep. We had to put gloves on him.

—Rebecca Lloyd-Bennett

While shoddy production methods are the source of at least some of the problems with Chinese junk, sometimes it's just sheer stupidity. How else can you explain the use of one of the most potent allergic sensitizers known to medical science—dimethyl fumarate—in the production of leather goods for sofas and other furniture?

This particular Death by China farce started in the hot and humid warehouses of Guangdong. That's a province on the southern coast of China near Hong Kong and a place that Americans more generally refer to as Canton.

To prevent mold from growing on insufficiently cured leather used for pillows and cushions, a group of Chinese furniture producers began treating their leather goods with dimethyl fumarate. This "DMF" is an extremely powerful chemical that can burn its victims right through their clothing and that even at very low concentrations produces extensive eczema that's difficult to treat.

The further interesting twist in this dumb and dumber tale is the way the manufacturers applied the DMF. They put it in small packets inside the leather cushions under the assumption that the mold-fighter would be released whenever temperatures got too high in their warehouses or along the transportation routes to market. What these Guangdong imbeciles didn't count on is that the DMF would also be released from body heat as people sat on their chairs, sofas, and love seats. And released the DMF was, as thousands of consumers across Finland, France, Poland, Sweden, and the United Kingdom quite literally got burned by their furniture. In the UK alone, close to 2,000 victims "suffered severe skin or eye complaints, breathing difficulties, or other medical complications."

As with so many "Deaths by Chinese Junk," young children would suffer the most. British infant Archie Lloyd-Bennett was burned over much of his body. In a heart-wrenching twist, 3-year-old Scottish lass Angel Thomson was torched so badly that hospital staff felt the child may have been intentionally burned with cigarettes. On these suspicions, the staff contacted Social Services to report a possible case of parental abuse; Angel's mother Ann was terrified for a time that her daughter was going to be taken away from her before the real Chinese culprit was identified.

As for the now-predictable epilogue to this tale: While a judge ordered the British businesses who sold the deadly leather goods to pay $32 million to the victims, the Chinese manufacturers got off scot-free—which is an insult to both our sensibilities and Scotland.

Blame Product Adulteration #1:
It's Impossible to Get the Chinese Lead Out

> *On August 2, Mattel recalled about 1.5 million Chinese-made Fisher-Price toys—including characters such as Dora the Explorer, Big Bird, and Elmo—that contained lead paint. In June, about 1.5 million Thomas & Friends wooden railway toys, imported from China...were recalled because of lead paint. Lead is toxic if ingested by young children.*
> —MSNBC.com

We are already familiar with the role of Chinese product adulteration in creating deadly food and drugs. We saw it in Chapter 2 when black-hearted Chinese entrepreneurs cut their costs by adding ingredients like melamine to pet food and chondroitin sulfate to heparin. Regrettably, Chinese manufacturers play the same game with many other products. Nowhere is this more evident than in the ongoing battle to keep heavy metals like lead and cadmium off America's retail shelves.

Lead hits young children the hardest because their developing brains and bodies are particularly sensitive to even relatively small amounts of the heavy metal. From just small lead doses, young kids can suffer irreversible injuries that later in life result in anything from attention deficit disorder and hyperactivity to criminal behavior, brain swelling, and major organ failure. Because children are so much at risk from the effects of lead, it is all the more despicable that so many of the Chinese products contaminated by lead are aimed at our children—whether it be iconic Sesame Street toys, teen heart throb jewelry, or classic wooden trains.

And by the way, China's black-heart product adulterers love to put lead in paint because, despite causing permanent brain damage, lead paint dries a lot faster and thereby significantly reduces production costs. Lead is also a low-cost and more pliable substitute for more expensive metals like nickel and silver in products like jewelry and trinkets.

As the MSNBC excerpt at the beginning of this section indicates, a poster child for Chinese lead woes has been the Mattel Corporation. Several years ago it was involved in one of the most high-profile product scandals in the modern era—one that resulted in millions of toys being recalled.

One important lesson to draw from the Mattel lead meltdown is that, contrary to the popular spin of some China apologists, it does not appear to matter how many years of experience American companies have in China or how closely they believe they have developed relationships with their Chinese suppliers. Companies like Mattel can still be fooled—and kids around the world can still be put in harm's way.

Blame Product Adulteration #2: What's That Powder on My Tricycle, Daddy?

In talking about lead, we would be remiss if we did not share with you this little story involving Chinese tricycles that were powder-coated with paint containing a high level of lead. This story is particularly interesting because it illustrates how sometimes all of us can be victimized by the "sins of omission" of complicit American corporations.

This particular "Trike Story" begins following the Chinese product quality scares of 2007 when a vendor to a major urban school district decided to test its Chinese-manufactured products for lead. These tests did, in fact, reveal the toxic tricycles.

At that point, according to a purchasing manager for the company at the time, the company put a "stop ship" order on all of the products to prevent them from going out to additional customers. The company then sent out its remaining inventory to a local vendor to have the powder coating stripped from each bike and the tricycles refinished. That was exemplary corporate behavior.

What was not exemplary was this "sin of omission": According to the purchasing manager, the company failed to inform the school district of the tricycles that had *already* been shipped. To her knowledge, none of these bikes was ever recalled.

In fact, a recall would have been devastatingly expensive to the vendor and damaging to the long-term customer relationship. What this story, like so many others, illustrates is that when a reputable U.S. firm goes into business with a Chinese manufacturer to save money, it will often find itself catapulted into a compromising position. At least based on this story, you shouldn't count on American companies to always "do the right thing."

Blame Product Adulteration #3:
If They Don't Want Lead, Let Them Eat Cadmium

Walmart said Wednesday it is pulling an entire line of Miley Cyrus-brand necklaces and bracelets from its shelves after tests performed for The Associated Press found the jewelry contained high levels of the toxic metal cadmium.. ... Walmart had learned of cadmium in the Miley Cyrus jewelry, as well as in an unrelated line of bracelet charms, back in February...but had continued selling the items.

—Associated Press

Having been busted on numerous occasions for the unauthorized use of lead, China's black hearts have figured out a way to adulterate their products with other equally deadly but less detectable heavy metals such as antimony, barium, and worst of all, cadmium.

In fact, cadmium is a veritable cornucopia of catastrophe. A known carcinogen, it can trigger severe respiratory responses like toxic pneumonitis and pulmonary endema. Cadmium can also suck the mineral densities out of bones, thereby causing severe back and joint pain while increasing the risk of fractures; and it can cause kidney dysfunction that can lead to coma.

Of course, the extreme toxicity of cadmium hasn't stopped China's product adulterers from substituting it for the more easily detectable lead. Furthermore, China is the world's largest producer of the metal. Regrettably, in this new variation of an old shell game, some major American corporations have been willing accomplices.

For example, in 2010, the Associated Press conducted its own undercover operation by running a series of independent tests on Chinese products. These tests found the presence of cadmium in an entire line of Miley Cyrus jewelry that Walmart had trumpeted as a teen exclusive. Inexplicably—and despicably—Walmart did not stop selling the jewelry for months on the grounds that it would be "too difficult to test products already on its shelves." In this same year, Walmart was busted for selling cadmium-laced children's pendants produced to match characters from the Disney film, *The Princess and the Frog*.

In a similar incident, Warner Brothers Studio Store in Burbank, California was caught with its heavy metal pants down when its *Wizard of Oz* Tin Man drinking glasses were found covered in lead at levels up to 1,000 times higher than the federal limits. High lead levels were also found in Batman and Superman glasses—while the decorative enamel in many of the glasses also had relatively high levels of cadmium.

When asked why they were willing to put American kids in harm's way, studio executives for this American icon chose to protect themselves with this incredulous response, "It is generally understood that the primary consumer for these products is an adult, usually a collector." Oh really....

Blame the "Quality Con": While Our Corporations Lay Sleeping

A major customer complained that our bottles were being made too thin. The [Chinese] factory had quietly adjusted the molds so that less plastic went into making each bottle. As a result, when the bottle was given the slightest squeeze, it collapsed...After investigation, [we] discovered that the bottle had gone through more than one change. The factory had been making downward adjustments over a several-month period. The first bottles that came off the line were sturdy, but then they came out as merely acceptable. When none of us noticed the first changes, the factory decided to go for it again...Putting less plastic in the bottles generated savings, but these were not shared with the importer. The only thing passed on to the importer was the increase in product risk.

—Paul Midler, *Poorly Made in China*

It's time for all of us now to become more familiar with one of the favorite games China's product adulterers love to play with naïve and trusting foreigners. This game we call the Quality Con goes hand in glove with a complementary game we have dubbed the "Shanghai Sting." Here's how the games begin.

An American executive, hot to outsource his company's production to cut costs, travels to China to find a cheap Chinese manufacturer. Upon finding a possible candidate, the American exec shows plans or blueprints to the Chinese manufacturer detailing exactly what is needed. At this point, one of three things can happen.

In the best-case scenario, the Chinese manufacturer enters into a long-term agreement with the American company, produces high-quality products at a low cost, and the two live prosperously ever after.

The second, far more likely possibility is the Shanghai Sting. Here, the Chinese manufacturer declines the offer to produce the product—but keeps the American company's design. Within a few months, that same Chinese manufacturer is producing the American company's product for sale as a competitor—using the American company's stolen design.

The third possibility is the Quality Con described by Paul Midler in the earlier excerpt from his revealing book *Poorly Made in China*. The Quality Con starts when the Chinese manufacturer quickly produces a high-quality beta test version of the requested product *exactly* to specs. On the basis of that high-quality sample, the American company contracts with its new Chinese supplier for a given amount of the product on a weekly or monthly basis.

At first, the American company will be extremely pleased with the deal. Costs are cut significantly—often by as much as 50%. In this honeymoon period of the Quality Con, the American company makes money hand over fist; and it is at this happy apex in the relationship that the Quality Con begins in earnest. For, over time, the Chinese manufacturer slowly, and sometimes infinitesimally, begins to substitute inferior raw materials or components as a means of boosting margins. Shave a little here, shave a little there. But never shave too much all at once so that the quality adjustment is noticed.

Of course, the more naïve the American company's management team, the more that team will trust its Chinese counterpart to continue producing quality products and dispense with intensive testing. In this way, the American company not only offshores its production but its risk management.

Hangzhou Zhongce Rubber Cuts Corners and Kills Americans

> *Hangzhou Zhongce has refused to tell Foreign Tire Sales' officials how long it omitted the gum strip from its manufacturing process. ...Foreign Tire Sales said it believed that it purchased about 450,000 of the tires in question from the Chinese company. Hangzhou Zhongce sold the tires to at least six other importers or distributors in the United States.*
> *—The New York Times*

A classic example of China's Quality Con is offered up by the Hangzhou Zhongce Rubber company. This case is particularly interesting because it once again illustrates the ethical dilemmas that American companies can find themselves in the midst of because of the machinations of Chinese manufacturers.

The American company that got conned was Foreign Tire Sales of Union, New Jersey. In fact, Foreign Tire Sales had been importing tires for several years when Hangzhou began to use only half of a key gum strip that ensured the integrity of the tires. When this change went unnoticed, Hangzhou then escalated the con by leaving the entire gum strip out. This was done, of course, to shave a few pennies off the production cost.

The cost of this Quality Con has been numerous tire failures, the crash of an ambulance in New Mexico, and a fatal collision in Pennsylvania that killed two and severely injured another. Incredibly, the management team of Foreign Tire Sales "waited more than 2 years to pass on their suspicions about problems with the tires."

Meanwhile, throughout this whole con game, Hangzhou executives stonewalled their American counterparts about the missing gum strip, but Foreign Tire Sales went on selling its tires anyway despite its suspicions. In the ensuing recall of close to half a million tires, Foreign Tire Sales almost went bankrupt while Hangzhou ducked all responsibility.

Why You Can't Trust American Regulators

In its Hidden Hazards series, the Tribune *has documented how the understaffed and sluggish Consumer Product Safety Commission fails to protect children from dangers in toys and other products. The paper's examination of Simplicity's popular cribs underscores that, even in the aftermath of a child's death, the agency can fall short in its watchdog role, leaving children vulnerable to a documented hazard. Interviews and records show that the federal investigator assigned to [Baby] Liam's death failed to inspect the crib in his initial inquiry and didn't track down the model or manufacturer. "We get so many cases," the investigator, Michael Ng, said in an interview this month. "Once I do a report, I send it in and that's it. I go to the next case. We could spend more time, but we are under the gun. We have to move on."*

—Chicago Tribune

One of the longest-running Chinese junk sagas in American history—the battle to keep our babies safe in their cribs and strollers—aptly underscores the point that you will not be adequately protected from Chinese junk by the American product safety and regulatory system. In fact, Chinese-made cribs and strollers have been cutting, suffocating, trapping, and strangling American children for more than five years.

The first recorded victim of Chinese cribicide was the baby Liam Johns in 2005. Said his grief-stricken mother on *CBS News*: "The side of the crib had come off forming a 'v,' which caused him to get stuck feet first and he got stuck in his neck at the crib. I gave him CPR and waited for the ambulance to arrive, and they took him to the hospital where he was pronounced dead."

In fact, baby Liam would die in vain. Neither the company that sold the imported Chinese crib—the Pennsylvania-based Simplicity—nor the Consumer Product Safety Commission warned parents about the deadly crib danger in a timely manner. As the *Chicago Tribune* reported, "Despite 55 complaints, seven infants left trapped, and three deaths, it took years for the Consumer Product Safety Commission to warn parents about 1 million flawed cribs."

Why You Can't Trust American Corporations

The problem with China is that they have routinely shoddy manufacturing. There is always a chance that something they make is going to hurt or kill kids. In fact, the Maclaren Strollers did the same thing to young children. It amputated their fingers...I have to wonder why our United States' companies are continuing to send work to China, effectively continuing to endanger our children. They must understand the danger, but in the name of profit they are willing to put young children and babies at risk.

—Gary Davis, retired CEO

If China keeps sending us so many dangerous and toxic products, why don't American distributors like Foreign Tire Sales, Simplicity, and Walmart take more precautions before selling them to an unwitting and trusting public? That's a very good question, particularly because many of the American corporations that have been implicated in various product recall scandals—from Burger King and Coca-Cola to Mattel, Walmart, and Warner Bros.—have very valuable brand names to protect.

As we have seen by how companies ranging from a tiny foreign tire seller to the behemoth Walmart have handled their Chinese product quality crises, the answer to this question is unsettling. It reveals that the knee-jerk reaction of far too many American corporations is to simply cover their collective derrieres—rather than own up to their own failures and redouble their efforts to police the Chinese junk they purvey. Because this is true—and because all five lines of defense against Death by Chinese junk have broken down—we now need to take matters into our own hands. We will show you exactly how to do that in the final chapter of this book. But in the meantime, we must come to understand that we cannot change our buying and consumer behavior until we fully embrace this fundamental principle:

> Seemingly "cheap" Chinese products are really a lot more expensive than China-free alternatives after you factor in the risks of injury or death and then add to that buying calculus all the various legal, regulatory, and taxpayer costs that Chinese product failures entail.

So the first thing we all need to do as we shop is to carefully scrutinize all labels. If it's "Made in China," put it back down unless you absolutely, positively need it and can't find a reasonable substitute. And if you positively absolutely have to have that product, do take appropriate precautions.

Part II

Weapons of Job Destruction

4

Death to America's Manufacturing Base: Why We Don't Play (or Work) in Peoria Anymore

China has become a major financial and trade power. But it doesn't act like other big economies. Instead, it follows a mercantilist policy, keeping its trade surplus artificially high. And in today's depressed world, that policy is, to put it bluntly, predatory.

—Paul Krugman, Nobel Laureate Economist

Over the past decade, riding tall astride the Trojan Horse of free trade, a "predatory" China has stolen millions of American manufacturing jobs right from under our noses. If we had held on to those jobs, America's unemployment rate would be well below 5% instead of near double digits, the U.S. government budget would be in balance, and our once-fair country would be facing a far brighter future than any we can currently envision. The obvious question is this: Why have we as a nation stood so passively by in the face of one of the greatest heists in global economic history: China's theft of the American manufacturing base?

"Oh, but wait!," you say, "China is taking America's jobs fair and square using a cheap and well-disciplined labor force." That, of course, is the spin of the China apologists who refuse to acknowledge even the existence of unfair trade practices.

In fact, when you carefully research the *real* sources of Chinese competitive advantage, it becomes crystal clear that more than half of China's edge comes from a complex array of eight unfair trade practices, each of which is expressly forbidden under the normal rules of free trade. These exceedingly potent "Eight Weapons of Job Destruction" include:

1. An elaborate web of illegal export subsidies
2. A cleverly manipulated and grossly undervalued currency
3. The blatant counterfeiting, piracy, and outright theft of America's intellectual property treasures
4. An incredibly short-sighted willingness by the Chinese Communist Party to trade massive environmental damage for a few more pennies of production cost advantage
5. Ultra-lax worker health and safety standards so far below international norms that they make brown lung, butchered limbs, and a dizzying array of cancers not just occupational hazards but virtual certainties
6. Unlawful tariffs, quotas, and other export restrictions on key raw materials from A to Z—antimony to zinc—as a strategic ploy to gain greater control over the world's metallurgy and heavy industry
7. Predatory pricing and "dumping" practices designed to push foreign rivals out of key resource markets and then gouge consumers with monopoly pricing
8. China's vaunted "Great Walls of Protectionism"—to keep all foreign competitors from setting up shop on Chinese soil

Make no mistake about it. These are real economic weapons with considerable firepower. The simultaneous firing of these weapons at America's manufacturing base has already led to the shutdown of thousands of American factories and turned millions of American workers into collateral damage—all under the false flag of so-called "free trade."

Why There Is Nothing "Free" about Free Trade with China

If you want to find out what free trade isn't, try reading any one of the economic textbooks our kids are reading in college these days. Your eyes will roll, your head will spin, and your stomach will turn because these texts are so divorced from the reality of the global trading arena. It's as if Gandhi had replaced Clausewitz and Sun Tzu in military strategy courses.

Indeed, despite abundant evidence to the contrary, these textbooks, continue to tout the virtues of free trade and the so-called "gains from trade" that we all should benefit from. But here's what these unwitting propaganda tracts fail to acknowledge: While free trade is great in theory, it rarely exists in the real world. Such conditions are no more found on Earth than the airless, frictionless realm assumed by high-school physics texts.

In the case of *China* v. *the United States*, this seductive free trade theory is very much like a marriage: It doesn't work if one country cheats on the other. Instead, when China systematically engages in the eight unfair trade practices described in this chapter, the "positive sum" game in which both countries are supposed to win quickly devolves into a "zero sum" game with one big prosperous winner and one big recessionary loser. In precisely this way, "free trade" between the Dragon and Uncle Sam has simply become a code word for "Death to the American Manufacturing Base!"

If *They* Build It, American Jobs *Won't* Come!

Just why should we care about the loss of America's manufacturing base? Haven't we been told by pundits like *The World Is Flat* Thomas Friedman that America's prosperous future lies in the rapid expansion of service sector jobs? And haven't talking heads like *Newsweek*'s Fareed Zakaria and even the *Atlantic*'s James Fallows insisted over and over again that the migration of manufacturing jobs from America and Europe to low-wage countries like China and India is as inevitable as the tide rising and sun setting?

Yes, of course we have been force-fed this pabulum. But journalists like Fallows, Friedman, and Zakaria are, and excuse the pun here, flat-out wrong. What these misfiring pundits and others of their ilk have failed to grasp is one of the most fundamental principles of economics:

> American workers can compete with their low-wage counterparts anywhere in the world as long as they are more productive—and the free trade playing field is level!

This has always been the American worker's competitive edge: using superior machines, technologies, and innovative processes to boost productivity. Through the highest rates of productivity in the world, America's blue-collar manufacturing workers have always been able to earn a decent wage and thereby finance their own versions of the American dream.

Instead, America's blue collar dream of a white picket fence and kids in college has turned into a nightmarish phantasm because, no matter how much the American manufacturing workers of today produce, they can't possibly defend themselves against China's "Eight Weapons of Job Destruction." In fact, while manufacturing once accounted for fully 25% of the American gross domestic product, today that share has shrunk to a mere 10%.

Not coincidentally, as China has systematically hollowed out the American manufacturing base, its economy has grown at the astonishing rate of 10% annually. In contrast, over the past decade, the U.S. economy has expanded at a rate of only 2.4%. Note that this paltry 2.4% growth rate during the 2000s is fully 25% below America's historical growth rate of 3.2% between 1946 and 1999.

"Wait, wait," you say, "a mere 0.8% drop in America's annual GDP growth rate over the past decade can't have made that much of a difference." But here's the rub. That 0.8% difference equates to a failure to create almost 1 million jobs a year and, cumulatively, over 10 million jobs over the last decade. Not coincidentally, that's almost the exact number of jobs we need to get the American economy back to full employment and producing at its full potential output.

If *We* Build It, American Jobs *Will* Come!

Now here's the bigger manufacturing base picture: It's not just these raw job loss numbers over the past decade of over 10 million jobs that make manufacturing so important to the American economy. A strong and vibrant manufacturing base is also critical to long-term prosperity for at least four reasons.

For starters, manufacturing jobs create a lot more jobs downstream than service sector jobs. In fact, for every dollar of final manufacturing output, America creates almost a dollar and a half in related services such as construction, finance, retail, and transportation.

Manufacturing jobs also pay more on average—a lot more—particularly for female and minority workers. This higher blue-collar purchasing power provides a critical stimulus for the rest of the economy. It's not for nothing that when factories close, the retail centers, doctor's offices, hotels, and restaurants that grew up around them die with them. When factories leave, city and state tax revenues fall as well, and government jobs and services must be cut.

Most importantly, a strong manufacturing base is critical to spurring the technological innovation that America needs to power its economy over the longer term. The sobering fact here is that U.S.-based manufacturers account for fully two-thirds of all private research and development in America. When these manufacturers leave for China, they take their research and development expenditures with them—and America's ability to innovate!

A fourth and final reason America must staunchly defend its manufacturing base has to do with the critical relationship between large, finished goods manufacturers like Boeing, Caterpillar, and General Motors and the rest of America's manufacturing supply chain. Keeping the factories of these heavy industries in America is important because a whole host of other companies large and small depend on their business.

For example, big companies like AC Delco headquartered in Kokomo, Indiana and Cummins Engines headquartered in Columbus, Indiana supply products like auto parts and diesel engines to firms like GM and Ford. Thousands of medium-sized and smaller companies in hundreds of cities across America likewise contribute generic components like high-pressure hoses and electrical cables, as well as build customized inputs like injection-molded plastic and precision-milled parts.

Now here's the problem: When a firm like DuPont or Medtronic offshores its production to China, it usually takes all the supply chain business with it. This is not just for logistical reasons. It's also because of protectionism: China forces the Western firms that offshore to China to use Chinese domestic content and thereby to help develop Chinese domestic suppliers on Chinese soil. In fact, interviewing a Shanghai manager at a major American supplier of aircraft assemblies, we learned this firsthand: The firm routinely brings in U.S. engineers to educate underperforming Chinese suppliers on how to improve the quality of precision subcomponents. Through this process, the firm is able to replace U.S. partners it has worked with for years.

So from now on, whenever you see a big company like 3M, Cisco, or Ford offshoring another plant to China, please understand that the loss of jobs is not confined to the company in question. Rather, in this twenty-first century version of "trickle down economics," initial job losses ripple through the rest of North America's manufacturing base, then through all of our service sectors, and finally, once-vibrant manufacturing hubs like Warren, Ohio, and Windsor, Ontario, become new ghost towns.

For all these reasons, it should be crystal clear why manufacturing jobs are so critical to long-term prosperity not just in America but in Europe and Japan and the rest of the world. It should be equally clear why China's hammer blow to America's manufacturing bases has made it so difficult for the United States to create enough jobs to significantly cut its unemployment rate. For even though a desperate White House has thrown a massive stimulus at America's flagging economy, our unemployment lines continue to stretch for miles. Just why do you think this is so, Mr. President?

Well, here's one reason: Trying to jumpstart our economy with a massive stimulus in the absence of a vibrant manufacturing base has been like trying to start a car without spark plugs or gain traction on slick tires. It just can't be done. Sadder yet, a great portion of that stimulus money leaks right out of our economy and stimulates Guangzhou and Shanghai rather than Gary and Pittsburgh. Indeed, the false Keynesian vision of a virtuous cycle of spending just won't play in Peoria when so much of what we buy isn't made here and our biggest trading deficit partner never reciprocates.

How Does China Cheat? Let Us Count the Ways

Let's turn now to a more detailed analysis of China's Eight Weapons of Job Destruction. And let's start with China's elaborate web of illegal export subsidies.

#1: The Export Subsidies' Dagger to the Heart

On the face of it, the term *export subsidies* seems pretty innocuous. But to understand just how such subsidies represent a real dagger to the heart of any American business, imagine for the moment you are a Chinese entrepreneur ready to start up a company that will do battle with a competing manufacturer in Ohio, Pennsylvania, Michigan, or Tennessee.

To jumpstart your enterprise, the Chinese government will provide you with free land, subsidized energy, and almost unlimited access to low- or no-interest loans. And, by the way, if you get into trouble, you won't have to pay the loans back, as the government owns and controls all the banks, and the Communist Party appoints all the bank's executives.

Now, once you are ready to export your product to America, you will get a nice and juicy direct subsidy for every item you sell—on the order of 10 to 20 cents for every dollar shipped. In addition, when the profits start rolling in, you'll be eligible for some hefty income and property tax breaks.

On top of all this, your Chinese enterprise need never worry that an American competitor will attack you in your own backyard. If foreigners want to sell into your market, they will be forced to set up shop on Chinese soil and become your *minority* partner.

Now that you see what American businesses are up against with China's export subsidies alone, do you have a better understanding of why a refrigerator manufacturer in Madison, Wisconsin, a washing machine maker in Clyde, Ohio, or a blender maker in Orem, Utah, has such a hard time competing with the Dragon? And now does it make more sense why a vacuum cleaner manufacturer in Palm City, Florida, a hand tool crafter in New Britain, Connecticut, or a baby crib maker in Barrington, New Jersey, must struggle so hard to stay afloat on the global seas of Chinese mercantilism?

In fact, the continued existence of China's elaborate web of illegal export subsidies represents one of the biggest broken promises in world economic history. That's because when China joined the World Trade Organization in 2001, it promised to promptly eliminate all illegal subsidies—along with all other forms of unfair trade practices.

Well, Communist China, Democratic America is still waiting for you to keep that free trade promise. And, as we wait, your massive illegal export subsidies continue to hammer hardest at some of North America's most important pillar industries: steel, petrochemicals, paper, textiles, semiconductors, plywood, and machinery. The list is as long as the unemployment lines in Stockton, California; Las Vegas, Nevada; Monroe, Michigan; and Rockford, Illinois.

#2: The New "Great Game": Chinese Currency Manipulation

China has intervened on a gigantic scale to keep its exchange rate down...This surely is currency manipulation. It is also protectionist, being equivalent to a uniform tariff and export subsidy.

—Martin Wolf, *Financial Times*

Chinese currency manipulation is so important to the understanding of the damage being done to America's manufacturing base that we are going to devote the whole next chapter to it. For now, however, suffice it to say that by virtually all creditable estimates, the Chinese yuan (aka the renminbi) is grossly undervalued—in the range of 40%.

In practical terms, this means that for every $1 of product that China sells into the United States market, Chinese exporters only have to charge the equivalent of 60 cents. That's a huge subsidy!

At the same time, for every $1 of product that an American business tries to sell to China, it has to charge the equivalent of considerably more than a buck. On top of that indirect tariff, an American manufacturer exporting to China gets slapped with an additional and very direct 30% tariff.

Knowing how China's currency manipulation acts as both a subsidy and tariff, is it a little more clear now why it is so difficult for a cutting tool manufacturer in South Easton, Massachusetts or a fastener producer in Corry, Pennsylvania, to compete with their Chinese counterparts in Shenzen, Guangzhou, and Chengdu?

#3: They Think It's Not Stealing If They Don't Get Caught

Now what about the effects of China's rampant counterfeiting, piracy, and intellectual property theft on America's manufacturing base? Well, here's the felonious deal.

Every time China steals another technology, design, or process from the good old U.S. of A., it drains a little bit more blood from our manufacturing veins. That's because when an American company wants to discover a new cancer-fighting drug, build a new fuel-efficient automobile, or develop higher efficiency solar panels, that process of discovery is going to cost both money and time—lots of money and time. If a Chinese pirate or counterfeiter can simply steal the fruits of such innovation—without regard or respect for property rights—that translates into a real cost advantage.

To understand the scale and scope of the cost advantage piracy provides to Chinese manufacturers consider that drug companies like Merck and Pfizer spend up to 20% of their sales on research and development, while tech companies like Intel and Microsoft devote 15% and car companies like General Motors and Ford devote 5%. So when a Chinese competitor simply counterfeits a Pfizer drug like Viagra, reverse-engineers a semiconductor design from Intel, unlawfully replicates an operating system from Mr. Softie, or breaks into a computer to steal a hybrid car design from General Motors, guess what? Yep, that Chinese pirate can charge substantially less for his competing product because this intellectual property thief doesn't have to recoup any research and development expenditures.

And please know this: The Chinese pirate never suffers remorse—whether it's a tiny Shanghai street vendor hawking an unreleased *Harry Potter* DVD for 80 cents or a top executive from the giant Chery Automotive Company that has stolen both the name and car designs from the American Chevy brand. That lack of remorse exists because over a billion mainland Chinese citizens have been raised in an ethics vacuum where property rights are meant to be trampled—and the state owns everything. It's an ethics skew that runs straight back to Chairman Mao and straight through the lunacy of the Cultural Revolution. This amoral skew has created an attitude of, "Do whatever you can get away with to better your own situation." While such disdain for property rights is well understood among China's Asian neighbors, far too many Westerners remain clueless about the cultural and political roots of Communist China's amorality.

#4: Trashing China's Environment for a Few Pieces of Silver

Let's turn now to arguably the most shortsighted of China's Weapons of Job Destruction. This is the Chinese government "shoot yourself in the head" willingness to trade off the wholesale destruction of the environment for a few more pennies of production cost advantage.

Despite having some strong environmental laws on the books and despite constantly spewing green rhetoric for Western consumption, the reality is that the Communist Party has no more respect for such fluff than it does for its own constitution, which supposedly guarantees freedom of speech and worship. As an executive at one of China's biggest factories put it to one of us bluntly, "If you can show performance, you can be promoted very quickly—but nobody cares about the environment."

To see how this environmental trashing works in China's favor, suppose an American chemical company in Cincinnati, Ohio, must install sophisticated pollution control equipment to prevent the dumping of chemical waste into the Ohio River. In sharp contrast, a Chinese competitor in Chongqing can simply use the Yangtze River as a toilet for whatever witch's brew it wants to dump. So guess which company is going to grab a bigger share of the international chemical market?

Or suppose an American paper producer in Waterford, New York, has to install expensive, low-emissions boilers in its steam plants while its Chinese competitor does not. This, too, adds up to more Chinese paper produced and fewer American jobs—and a whole lot more Chinese citizens choking on their own atmosphere.

In fact, China's "more pollution, lower prices" competitive edge cuts the deepest with precisely those manufacturing industries in the United States that face the highest environmental compliance costs. Consider that companies like Dow Chemical and U.S. Steel spend about ten times as much on environmental protection as do Chinese competitors such as Sinopec Oil and Bao Steel.

That China has trashed its environment to boost its export trade is evident in this stark fact: In the space of the three short decades it has taken China to emerge as the world's factory floor, China has also earned the dubious distinctions of both "most polluted country on the planet" and "biggest contributor to climate change." And it's not just American workers taking the hit. Chinese citizens are paying an exceedingly high price in the form of soaring rates of cancer, heart attacks, strokes, emphysema, and skin disease.

The plight of China's "non-human inhabitants" is a good barometer of the scope of the problem as well. Any observant visitor to China will note that both the countryside and cities are almost completely devoid of birds. It's a silent spring, summer, fall, and winter in China's toxic landscape.

#5: Maiming and Killing Chinese Laborers for No Fun but Lots of Profits

Just as the trashing of its rivers and streams and thrashing of its air basins helps China gain a competitive edge, so, too, does the butchering, battering, and brown-lunging of its workforce. On

China's deadly factory floor, silicosis and respiratory failure, severed fingers and sawed-off limbs, organs racked by cancer, and skin etched by acid are not just occupational hazards; for millions of workers, they are virtual certainties. This passage from *The New York Times* aptly captures the surreal, *Slaughterhouse Five* nature of the problem:

> *Yongkang...just south of Shanghai, is the hardware capital of China. Its 7,000 metal-working factories...make hinges, hub-caps, pots and pans, power drills, security doors, tool boxes, thermoses, electric razors, headphones, plugs, fans, and just about anything else with metallic innards. Yongkang, which means "eternal health" in Chinese, is also the dismemberment capital of China. At least once a day someone...is rushed to one of the dozen clinics that specialize in treating hand, arm, and finger injuries.*

The primary culprits in this carnage are China's ultra-lax health and safety regulations; and those Chinese workers at highest risk toil in industries ranging from building materials, chemicals, and machinery to metallurgy, plastics, and textiles. In China's coal mines alone, thousands die every year compared to less than 50 fatalities annually in the United States.

From the standpoint of international competitiveness, all this workplace carnage adds up to the most grisly of the competitive advantages that China holds in its arsenal of weapons—and the phrase *blood, sweat, and tears* has never had a more literal meaning than in the sweatshops and "blood shops" of China.

#6: The Neutron Bomb of Export Restrictions

Now what about this sixth Weapon of Job Destruction called "export restrictions"? To understand why the World Trade Organization bans them outright—and why they represent a neutron bomb dropped on America's heavy industries—one need only look at some of the specific raw materials China restricts the export of using both stringent quotas and tariffs as high as 70%.

At the top of the restricted list are such basic industrial building blocks as bauxite, coke, fluorspar, magnesium, manganese, silicone carbide, and zinc. Bauxite is the ore from which aluminum is extracted. Coke is a key fuel and reducing agent in the iron ore smelting process. Fluorspar is critical to both steel and aluminum production. Magnesium is the third most commonly used structural metal behind only iron and aluminum, while manganese is used by steelmakers to prevent rust and corrosion. As for silicon carbide, it's used to make ceramic materials for products ranging from bulletproof vests to brake disks. And zinc? This versatile staple has applications in everything from galvanizing steel and die-casting brass and bronze to adding pigment to paint and providing a catalyst in the manufacture of rubber.

In other words, virtually all the raw materials that China holds large reserves of and that it now restricts the export of are materials vital to both heavy industry and the world's metallurgy. Of course, in a global market, Chinese restrictions of basic materials ratchet up costs. So, for an American steelmaker in Gary, Indiana, a Canadian aluminum smelter in Lac Saint-Jean, Quebec, a Japanese die-caster in Hiroshima, or a German glass maker in Düsseldorf, the inevitable result is an increase in world prices for their raw inputs and a reduction in their competitive positions relative to China.

As a further turn of the production cost screw, while American and other Western companies have to endure these higher costs, their Chinese competitors get preferential access *and* regulated domestic prices. Together, these two effects add up to yet one more Dragonian cost and price advantage over foreign competition.

It is well worth repeating here that the World Trade Organization expressly forbids any such export restrictions, precisely because they convey such an unfair trade advantage. But China doesn't care. Neither the United States nor Europe has done anything substantive to enforce these particular rules. So a protectionist China keeps these illegal restrictions in place as a means of gaining greater control of— indeed, a tighter chokehold over—virtually all metallurgy and heavy industry in the world.

#7: Predatory Pricing, Dumping, and the Dragon's Rare Earth Cartel

As bad as China's export restriction situation is, it is only half of the story. The other half has to do with China's export restrictions on a wide range of so-called "rare earths." Rare earths, with far-out names like cerium, erbium, scandium, and terbium, represent the high-tech manufacturing version of the mouse that roared. Because of their critical magnetic and phosphorescent properties and their ability to transmit, produce, and store energy, small quantities of rare earths provide a big punch in a range of high-tech products.

For example, the voice coil in your iPod's hard drive, that battery in your neighbor's hybrid car, and the solar panels you might be considering for your home all require one or more of the rare earths. So, too, are the rare earths needed for the automobile catalytic converters that keep our air clean, portable x-ray machines that allow doctors to quickly diagnose problems, lasers used in scientific and industrial applications, and magnets that run the modern navigational systems upon which both commercial and military aircraft depend.

Given the importance of the rare earths in all of our lives, it is chilling to learn that China has effectively cornered the market in many of them. What's astonishing about China's market power is that it holds only about a third of the world's proven reserves of the rare earths, yet it currently accounts for over 90% of world production.

Just how did China manage to create what is effectively its own "Rare Earth Cartel?" That's where China's tactics of predatory pricing and dumping come into play; and it's a lesson straight out of the "Cartel Handbook."

This lesson started more than a decade ago. That's when some key Communist Party officials recognized China's rich endowment of rare earths and began pouring massive government subsidies into their production. Their avowed aim was to turn the People's Republic into the "OPEC of Rare Earths."

To develop its Rare Earth Cartel, China's state-owned mining companies purposefully built up a huge overcapacity and then, with equal purpose, dumped huge quantities onto world markets. The practical effect of this dumping was to drive down world prices well below actual production costs and thereby drive foreign competitors out of the market.

In fact, one of the biggest victims of Chinese dumping was an American company based in Denver, Colorado, called Molycorp. At one time, Molycorp was the king of rare earths, and its Mountain Pass mine in California was the largest in the world. But under China's predatory onslaught, Molycorp was forced to shut down its mines in 2002.

Over the last several years, with its rare earth cartel now well established, China has moved from the Phase I dumping part of its predatory scheme to Phase II: that of price gouging. In this phase, having successfully shut down many foreign mines with its dumping, China has begun to dramatically raise the prices of its rare earths.

Consider, for example, cerium oxide, a critical component in fuel cells and catalytic converters. In 2007, the world spot price was just about $3 a kilogram. Today, after China's export restrictions, the price of cerium oxide has jumped to over $23 a kilogram—a more than seven-fold increase in just 3 years.

And how about samarium oxide, a rare earth important for the manufacture of high-performance magnets and used in the radiation treatment of lung cancer? Its price has increased by close to 1,000%.

Of course, these whopping price hikes have begun to draw foreign competitors gingerly back into the market (even Molycorp has reopened its mine). However, all of China's competitors face one very huge risk: At any time, China's state-run rare earth companies can turn the spigot back up, flood the market once again, drive down prices, and, in a déjà vu all over again moment, put companies like Molycorp right back out of business. Not surprisingly, the ever-present risk of renewed Chinese dumping of rare earths has had the quite intentional effect of suppressing rare earth production outside of China—just as the Chinese government has intended.

As a final dimension of its ultimate rare earth strategy, China is even changing its predatory game from that of mere economic domination to some very real, brass-knuckled, political blackmail. For example, in a well-publicized 2010 event, Japan backed down and released a criminally reckless Chinese boat captain who had been rightfully detained for ramming a Japanese Coast Guard cutter in waters surrounding the Senkaku Islands—territory controlled by Japan but claimed by China. Of course, one very big reason why Japan bowed to Chinese pressure is because China completely cut off the export of rare earths critical to production in the Japanese auto and electronics industries.

#8: Goodness Gracious, Great Walls of Protectionism

As a final Weapon of Job Destruction, China's "Great Walls of Protectionism" loom large. These imposing edifices are built with many kinds of bricks: outright tariffs, thinly disguised quotas, inflated customs duties, "Buy China" domestic content laws, all manner of technical barriers to trade, and corrupt practices like rigged bidding.

In practical terms, these walls mean this: While a Chinese manufacturer of computers in Shenzhen, garments in Dong Yang, or aircraft components in Shanghai can freely sell into the North American market, its counterparts and competitors in San Jose, Mexico City, and Dorval, Quebec cannot do the same. Is it any wonder that our manufacturing base is on life support?

The Sum of All Our China Fears

When you sum up China's Eight Weapons of Job Destruction, the total is millions of American, Canadian, European, Mexican, and Asian jobs lost and the entire Western manufacturing base brought to its knees. When you connect the dots that link each of China's Eight Weapons of Job Destruction to the unemployment lines in America, economic malaise in Japan, debt crisis in Europe, and civil disorder in Mexico, you also see this much bigger picture: a mercantilist and protectionist Chinese industrial policy strategy aimed at nothing short of the total domination of world manufacturing, the total penetration of global markets, and the economic subjection of the Western World.

As the CEO of Nucor Steel, Dan DiMicco has eloquently described the situation: "We've been in a trade war with China for more than a decade. But they are the only ones firing the shots!" Even the normally kowtowing GE Chief Jeffery Immelt remarked in a rare moment of clarity, "I really worry about China; I am not sure that in the end they want any of us to win or any of us to be successful."

Clearly, it's long past time that America and its free market and fair trading allies fired back. It's also well past time for China's Communist Party leaders to know this: The World Trade Organization was founded for a reason: to promote *real* free trade and advance the growth of *all* countries around the world. By using its Eight Weapons of Job Destruction, China systematically subverts the entire free-trade framework—even as it invades American market after American market under WTO cover. This is one of the great obscenities in global economic history; and Chinese mercantilism and protectionism must be stopped. If not now, when? If not by America, then by what nation? As Winston Churchill once said, "The Americans can always be counted upon to do the right thing, after they have exhausted all other possibilities." We've reached that point.

5

Death by Currency Manipulation: Crouching Tiger, Nuking Dragon

American workers can compete dollar for dollar against Chinese workers. They just can't compete dollars against manipulated yuans.

—Eric Lotke, Campaign for America's Future

If money is the root of all evil, then China's manipulation of its currency, the yuan, is the tap root of everything wrong with the U.S.–China trade relationship. For more than a decade, chronic U.S. trade deficits with China have dramatically slowed America's economic growth rate and spiked our unemployment rate. Yet it would be impossible for China to keep sucking the lifeblood out of the American economy without its fangs of currency manipulation.

China manipulates its currency by artificially "pegging" the Chinese yuan to the U.S. dollar at a grossly undervalued fixed exchange rate. To understand why this debilitates the American economy, it is critical to understand that any nation's economy is driven by only four factors: consumption, business investment, government spending, and "net exports."

This last growth driver—net exports—is the most important for our discussion of Chinese currency manipulation because it measures the difference between how much we export to the world minus how much we import. And here is a critical observation that underscores the essential role that net exports play in our economy:

> When America runs a chronic trade deficit with China, this shaves critical points off our economic growth rate. This slower growth rate, in turn, thereby reduces the number of jobs America creates.

Of course, as the American economy suffers from slow growth and high unemployment, China enjoys just the opposite effect. The Dragon booms while America goes bust.

Another Day Older, Deeper in Debt, and Slower in Growth

So just how big is our trade deficit with China? Just how many jobs has our "Chinese import dependence" cost us? And why is currency manipulation a principal reason the United States is unable to significantly reduce its trade deficit? Only by knowing the answers to these questions can we escape from China's currency manipulation trap. Let's start then with the size of the U.S. trade deficit.

In terms of *absolute* size, America imports almost $1 billion a day more than it exports from China every business day of the year. That's not a typo; it's *billion* not *million*.

In terms of *relative* size, the U.S.–China trade deficit is equally astonishing. China accounts for almost half of our annual trade deficit in goods and fully 75% when petroleum imports are removed from the calculation. Here is one logical policy inference from these statistics:

> If America wants to reduce its overall trade deficit to increase its growth rate and create more jobs, the best place to start is with currency reform with China!

As for the actual impact our Chinese import dependence has had on America's growth and unemployment rates, this, too, is mind-boggling. Over the past decade, our trade deficit with China has typically shaved off close to half a point of GDP growth a year. While that might not seem like a large sum, it translates into a cumulative impact of millions of jobs that the American economy failed to create. If we had those jobs right now *plus* the millions more manufacturing jobs that China's unfair trade practices have destroyed outright, we wouldn't be seeing unemployment lines wrapping around government buildings, fields of padlocked houses under foreclosure, and America's empty factories pushing up weeds. Instead, we'd be on the sunny side of Easy Street.

As a side note, these stunning statistics always remind us of the story about Willie Sutton, the famous bank robber. When they asked Sutton why he robbed banks, he famously replied, "Because that's where the money is." Just as banks are where the money is, China's currency manipulation is where our best hope of reducing our trade deficit—and reclaiming robust economic growth—lies.

Hard Times for America from China's Hard Dollar Peg

So, just how does China manipulate its currency? It does so by effectively "hard pegging" its yuan to the dollar at a grossly undervalued fixed exchange rate: around six yuan to the dollar. This ultracheap yuan, in turn, provides a lucrative subsidy for Chinese exporters while levying a hefty tax on U.S. exports to China. The result of this currency manipulation, working in league with the other Chinese unfair trade practices we have discussed, has been the chronic U.S. trade deficits we have just weighed and measured.

Now here's the key currency manipulation point: America's trade imbalance with China could never persist in a world of free trade where China allowed its currency to float freely alongside other float-ing currencies around the world like the euro, Japanese yen, Swiss Franc, Brazilian real, Indian rupee, and U.S. dollar.

In a world of free trade characterized by completely floating exchange rates, the U.S.–China trade imbalance could never persist because as the U.S. trade deficit rose, the dollar would fall relative to the yuan. As the dollar fell, U.S. exports to China would rise, Chinese imports would fall, and trade would come back into balance. How-ever, by pegging the yuan to the dollar, a mercantilist China subverts this free trade adjustment process—even as it undermines a global free trade framework based on the promise of mutual gain.

The Nuking Dragon Declares a New Kind of War

The Chinese government has begun a concerted campaign of economic threats against the United States, hinting that it may liquidate its vast holding of U.S. treasuries if Washington imposes trade sanctions.... Described as China's "nuclear option" in the state media, such action could trigger a dollar crash.... It would also cause a spike in U.S. bond yields, ham-mering the U.S. housing market and perhaps tipping the economy into recession.
—The London Telegraph

It's bad enough that Chinese currency manipulation has left the American economy stuck in first gear while destroying millions of jobs. It is worse that this particular "Death by Chinese Currency Manipula-tion" also threatens the "Death of American Political Sovereignty." At the heart of this matter is what the war hawks running China's central bank have threatened us with. These hawks call it the "financial nuclear option," and it involves using China's vast foreign reserves to destabilize America's banks, stock market, and bond market.

To understand just how credible China's threat of "dropping the big one" on America's financial system is, it helps to illustrate more precisely how China manipulates its currency. This process begins when you or I walk into a store like Walmart and buy a Chinese product, after which our dollars are shipped overseas. At this point, to maintain the U.S. dollar's fixed peg to the yuan, China must promptly recycle our "Walmart dollars" back into the United States by buying financial assets such as U.S. government bonds, U.S. real estate, or U.S. companies; otherwise, upward pressures would build on the yuan.

Now here's perhaps the most interesting little twist on this currency manipulation tale: Before the Chinese government can recycle any of our Walmart dollars, it must gain control of those dollars from the Chinese exporters that accumulated them. This requires a convoluted process known as *sterilization*.

To sterilize our Walmart dollars, the Chinese government forces its exporters to buy Chinese government bonds denominated in U.S. dollars. In return for surrendering their greenbacks, exporters then receive about 4% interest on the sterilization bonds. The Chinese government then turns around and reinvests the captured sterilized greenbacks back into U.S. government bonds that pay less than 2% interest. China thereby loses 2% or more in interest on every dollar it sterilizes—and the losses run into the billions!

Just why is the Chinese central bank willing to shoulder such huge losses? It is because the Communist Party is far more interested in creating jobs to maintain political stability and its totalitarian grip on the country than it is in actually making money. That's one of the big differences between true American capitalism and China's perverted "beggar thy neighbor" brand of state capitalism. And never mind that in this zero-sum currency manipulation process, many of the jobs that China gains are exactly the ones lost by the American economy.

In fact, this process of Chinese currency manipulation has led to an accumulation of over $2 trillion in U.S. foreign reserves now held by the People's Bank of China, aka, American's mortgage banker. To put this astonishing sum in perspective, it's more than the gross national product of India or Canada, and it's nearly equal to that of the United Kingdom. It is also bigger than the GDP of South Korea, Mexico, and Ireland *combined*!

What this astonishing sum means is this: China could take its foreign reserves and buy a controlling interest in all the big American companies listed on the Dow Jones Industrial Average, including giants like Microsoft, Exxon, and Walmart—and still have enough cash left over to buy up majority stakes in Apple, Intel, and Ford.

It is precisely China's massive accumulation of dollar-denominated foreign reserves that now allows the Chinese Communist Party to credibly threaten to nuke our financial system. As He Fan of the Chinese Academy of Social Sciences has said in threatening the financial nuclear option, if China were to begin dumping dollars, this would "lead to a mass depreciation of the dollar." And as the excerpt leading off this chapter has aptly described, such a "dollar crash" would "cause a spike in U.S. bond yields, hammering the U.S. housing market and perhaps tip the economy into recession."

In fact, there is clear evidence that a kowtowing Uncle Sam has already begun to surrender at least some of America's political sovereignty to China because of the credibility of China's financial nuclear option. Indeed, any time now that the White House, the Congress, or the U.S. Trade Representative threatens to crack down on unfair trade practices, China fires a missile across our bow by threatening to dump—and in some cases actually dumping—U.S. dollar reserves. Indeed, the existence of this financial nuclear threat goes a long way toward explaining the perennially timid behavior toward China of various U.S. Secretaries of the Treasury over the last decade—from Bush's Hank Paulson to Obama's Timothy Geithner.

And please understand this: Over time, it would be extremely naïve for any American to think that China's "greenback blackmail" will be limited to merely trade issues. At some point, Chinese officials are likely to use this weapon on any one of a number of geopolitical issues: from White House visits by the Dalai Lama and arms sales to India to the ever-present conflict on the Korean peninsula, and the ever-touchy U.S. backing of Taiwan.

China, Can You Spare Us a Gazillion Dimes?

Chinese currency manipulation has not only led to a loss of American political sovereignty. It has also greatly facilitated America's self-inflicted "Death by Fiscal Profligacy." Remember: In the process of currency manipulation, the Chinese government must maintain the peg between the yuan and the dollar principally by buying U.S. government bonds. In this way, our Chinese mortgage banker helps American politicians finance our massive budget deficits.

That China helps us finance programs like America's serial fiscal stimuli and the Federal Reserve's easy money printing press is no small irony. After all, it is largely because of America's blood-sucking trade deficits with China that America's politicians feel they need to keep priming the economic pump with deficit spending—even as we keep getting deeper and deeper into debt to a totalitarian regime benefiting greatly from our demise.

In fact, this whole sad process in which China has become America's mortgage banker has been part of a Devil's bargain President Barack Obama has engaged in ever since he took office and broke his promise to get tough on Chinese mercantilism. Here, we need to clearly remember that on the 2008 campaign trail, in key industrial swing states like Illinois, Michigan, Ohio, and Pennsylvania,

Candidate Obama repeatedly promised to crack down on unfair Chinese trade practices.

Since taking office, however, *President* Obama's Treasury Department, led by the aforementioned Timothy Geithner, has repeatedly refused to brand China a currency manipulator. However, it is precisely such a move that would allow the United States to impose appropriate countervailing duties to eliminate one of China's most important mercantilist edges. But instead of fulfilling his campaign promise, President Obama has chosen this dangerous devil's bargain: "You keep buying our bonds, China, and we won't take any meaningful actions on trade reform." In this way, the President has wrongly put politics and his administration's short-term financing needs ahead of America's prospects for long-term economic recovery. This is dead wrong, because no matter how many trillions of Walmart dollars we borrow back from China to throw at the American economy, these stimulus bucks won't make any difference—until we achieve constructive currency reform with China.

America Trapped in the Global Economic Elevator

> *We're fed up. China's mercantilist policies are hurting the rest of the world, not just America. It helped create the global recession that we're in. The Chinese want to be treated as a developing country, but they're a global giant, the leading exporter in the world.*
> —Senator Lindsey Graham (R-SC)

As a final observation from 30,000 feet, China's currency manipulation is not just debilitating the American economy. It is threatening to tear asunder the entire global economic fabric and free trade framework. The problem is this: Whenever the U.S. dollar declines against other currencies such as the euro, real, won, and yen—as it now does frequently—the Chinese yuan falls with it. This fall in the yuan against these other currencies in turn provides a mercantilist

China with an even sharper edge against competitors around the world—from Europe and Brazil to Japan and South Korea. The results have included the flagging export demand that drove Europe into economic stagnation and the prolonging of Japan's now decade-long persistent slow growth. Meanwhile, inflation runs rampant in countries like Australia and Brazil due to speculative hot money flows and commodity price appreciation that can be traced directly back to the undervalued yuan.

Throughout all of this—and despite repeated calls from institutions like the International Monetary Fund and World Bank for China to strengthen its currency—China has taken the hardest possible line against reform. This hard line begins right at the top of China's leadership; as the proverb says, "A fish rots from the head down."

Consider, for example, this incredulous response from Prime Minister Wen Jiabao to pressure from other members of the G-20 to revalue. Said Wen: "First of all, I do not think the [yuan] is undervalued." Right, Mr. Wen, and the air is clean in Beijing, Tibetans love being part of China, the people speak freely in Shanghai, and your lunar space probe has shown that the moon is made of Swiss cheese.

In fact, with these kinds of absurd responses to international pressure from top Communist Party leaders, it's hard to tell whether China's currency manipulation denial is more akin to a Shakespearean tragedy or a Molière farce. After all, of all the countries that stand to benefit from China strengthening its currency, China would benefit the most!

For starters, a stronger yuan would fight rapidly rising inflation in China by lowering the cost of oil, raw materials, and the myriad other inputs China needs to run its factories. As an important inflation-fighting bonus, a stronger yuan would also promptly halt the speculative inflows of "hot money" now inflating both a Chinese stock market and real estate bubble.

Most importantly, a stronger yuan would put significantly more purchasing power in the hands of a woefully underdeveloped Chinese consumer. In this way, Chinese currency reform would make China far less dependent on selling exports to the rest of the world— a vulnerability that represents the true Achilles' heel of China's growth model.

Unfortunately, China's leaders refuse to accept the compelling logic of this message. Instead, these brittle ideologues defend their intransigent position by claiming that strengthening the yuan would destroy China's economy by sharply reducing its exports. But this is just another way of saying that the only way China can keep growing is by beggaring the rest of the world. One must also consider the obvious possibility that beggaring the rest of the world and, in particular, emasculating America's economy and manufacturing base is, in fact, one of China's long-term strategic and military goals.

6

Death by American Corporate Turncoat: When Greenbacks Trump the Red, White, and Blue

General Electric plans to sink more than $2 billion into China through 2012. The conglomerate has shifted more production from the U.S. to China, adding more than 1,000 new jobs...Last month it shut a lightbulb factory in Virginia and will relocate those 200 jobs to China.
—London's *Daily Mail*

There is no honor among thieves—and no patriotism among American corporations. That's the clear message companies like General Electric, Caterpillar, and Evergreen Solar are sending to the American people these days as they shut down aging factories in the United States and open up gleaming, new state-of-the-art facilities in Dragonland. By running off to China, these corporate turncoat lemmings are not only helping drive their countries right off a cliff; they are signing future death warrants for their own firms. It was not always so.

At the turn of this century, when China first joined the World Trade Organization and began its mercantilist assault on the American manufacturing base, U.S. corporate executives stood shoulder to shoulder with American workers to strongly protest China's unfair trade practices. The dire warning of this business-labor coalition fell on deaf ears, however, in a rigidly ideological Bush White House that couldn't tell the critical difference between free trade benefiting all and unfair trade benefiting mostly China.

Now, a decade later, America's business-labor coalition is as dead as a democracy protester in Tiananmen Square. In the new political calculus, as each additional American job and each new American factory has been offshored to China, so-called "American" organizations like the Business Roundtable, National Association of Manufacturers, and U.S. Chamber of Commerce have been transformed from staunch critics into meek apologists for a mercantilist and protectionist China having its way with the American economy and its workers.

The ultimate irony of America's corporate betrayal is this: In the process of helping China decimate the U.S. manufacturing base, many of America's corporate turncoats are destroying the future of their own companies. They are doing so by turning over to China not just their current technologies but also their ability to invent new ones. To understand why this is so—and why so many American corporate executives have been so willing to let the worship of greenbacks trump the red, white, and blue—it is first useful to understand the "three waves of offshoring" that have characterized the exodus of millions of American jobs to China.

The First Offshoring Wave:
The Chinese Plantation Rises

The first wave of offshoring was a slow-moving affair that began shortly after the Communist Party opened China's "Worker's Paradise" to the West in 1978. This opening featured so-called "market reforms" that effectively stripped Chinese laborers of their health care and pension benefits along with any rights to decent wages and safe working conditions—while ironically not actually freeing the Chinese economy from domination by state-owned enterprises and communist central planners. Not coincidentally, over the next several decades, Western companies like Mattel, Reebok, and Schwinn began producing more and more of their low-end, labor-intensive products—toys, sneakers, bikes—with cheap Chinese labor.

It was during this first offshoring wave that the model of indentured servitude so prevalent in the China of today was perfected. On industrial plantations, young men and women—and no shortage of children—fresh from the farm sign onerous binding contracts that most are too uneducated to comprehend. They work shoulder to shoulder on hot, dirty, and crowded factory floors, typically for 12 to 16 hours a day. They sleep and eat in cramped dormitory-style quarters, often with bars on the windows or fences around the company's perimeter. If they try to escape, they are beaten. If they try to organize the workplace, they are first beaten and then fired.

It is precisely these modern-day slaves who, at 40 cents an hour, still make the toys that please our children, mold the running shoes that propel us on our jogs, and stitch the shirts that find their way onto our backs. As stark testimony to the ultimate chains that bind these workers to a "Dickensian World with Chinese Characteristics," many are relatively happier in their new plight because, as bad as the Dragon's industrial plantations are, Chinese peasant farm life is worse.

The Second Wave:
If You Can't Beat Them, Join Them

The second wave of American offshoring began shortly after China joined the World Trade Organization in 2001 and began its full frontal assault on the American manufacturing base using "weapons of job destruction" like illegal export subsidies and currency manipulation. Under intense siege from Chinese factories, more and more American corporate executives came to this realization: By taking advantage of China's elaborate web of illegal export subsidies, they could produce more cheaply on Chinese than U.S. soil, and if they did not, their competitors surely would. This realization inspired America's corporate catchphrase, "If you can't beat China, join it." Soon thereafter, America's second wave of offshoring turned into a tsunami.

It is important to emphasize that during this second wave, the primary goal of American executives was not to sell to the hypothetical 1.3 billion ravenous consumers in the Chinese market. Rather, it was to produce for export to the rest of the world—including *back* to America! To be crystal clear here, the advantage that American executives believed they could gain from offshoring during this second wave was not just from cheap labor; there was plenty of that in other countries like Bangladesh, Cambodia, and Vietnam. Rather, the real lure was China's unfair trade practices, lax environmental and safety regimes, and artificially subsidized export trade. If the American government was not going to crack down on China's unfair trade practices—and the Bush administration provided precious little help during this siege—it would be better at least for the shareholders and executives (if not for the workers) of these corporations to shift their production to China.

The Third Wave: The Grand Illusion of 1.3 Billion Consumers

The third and far most dangerous wave of American offshoring is now in progress. It is fueled partly by cheap labor as in the first wave and partly by the mercantilist advantages of producing in China as in the second wave. But the far more important propellant for this third wave is the grand illusion among American corporate executives that their next big market opportunity lies in selling to the 1.3 billion consumers residing in the world's most populous country. This wave of offshoring is ultimately the most dangerous because it is driven by the illusion that most Chinese consumers have adequate purchasing power to propel the market—when in fact, many are dirt-poor. This dangerous offshoring wave also requires any American corporation wishing to sell into the Chinese market to accede to three protectionist conditions as set forth in China's policy of "Indigenous Innovation."

The first protectionist condition requires minority ownership; American companies must form a joint venture with a Chinese partner and hold no more than 49% of the enterprise. Most obviously, this condition means loss of direct control of the enterprise by the American company. More subtly, this condition gives the Chinese majority partner—most often a state-owned enterprise—the power to access any and all information about the venture, including trade secrets.

The second protectionist condition constitutes one of the egregious Chinese violations of free trade rules; it mandates *forced technology transfer*. To wit, American companies must surrender their intellectual property to their Chinese partners as a condition of market entry. The practical effect of this condition is to facilitate the dissemination of various technologies not just to the Chinese partner directly involved but also to the Chinese government and other potential Chinese competitors. By surrendering to this condition, Western companies, in effect, create their own Chinese competitors virtually overnight.

The third condition goes mercantilist hand in protectionist glove with the second condition of forced technology transfer. It is the equally *forced export of Western research and development facilities to China*—likewise a gross violation of World Trade Organization rules. This is the unkindest cut of all because it is equivalent to selling America's seed corn; as any economist will tell you, it is only through research and development that the technological innovation necessary for new job creation can take place. If that R&D and innovation take place on Chinese rather than American soil, guess which nation is going to reap the lion's share of new job creation?

It should be obvious at this point why any American company that surrenders to China's three protectionist conditions of indigenous innovation virtually ensures its self-destruction. For once an American company surrenders its autonomy, its current technologies, and its ability to develop future technologies, it is only a matter of time before Chinese companies "digest" these technologies and use them to outcompete the American company—not just on Chinese soil but in the global marketplace. In this way, American companies learn the hard way that the lure of 1.3 billion Chinese customers is more siren song illusion than dollars and cents reality. In this way, "Death by Corporate Turncoat" also turns into corporate suicide.

A Tale of Two Countries and Four Companies

To put a more personal face on this, let's contrast the activities of four major corporations in China and their CEOs: Westinghouse, the most naïve; General Electric, the most schizoid; Caterpillar, a poster child for the lure of Chinese mercantilism; and Evergreen Solar, the once "Great Green Hope" of the Obama administration and now an exclamation point to the failure of America's politicians to defend our business community from Chinese aggression.

Westinghouse's Wishful Fission Thinking

> Westinghouse Electric has handed over more than 75,000 documents to its Chinese customers as the initial part of the technology transfer deal it hopes will secure its place in the fastest-growing nuclear market.... Jack Allen, president of Westinghouse for Asia [said] the company had "no guarantees" of its role in China once the four AP 1000 [nuclear] reactors were completed.
> —Financial Times

Just as Frodo could not resist the seductive lure of the lethal Ring, Westinghouse apparently cannot resist the Chinese nuclear power plant market. Oh, we get that: The Chinese nuke market *is* the largest and fastest-growing in the world, with 23 reactors under construction and plans to build over 100 more. But while grabbing a significant share of that growing market would certainly be a huge prize for Westinghouse, the worst possible way to compete for that prize is to do what its CEO Jack Allen has done: turn over to China everything it needs to build future reactors without Westinghouse's help.

The situation is not without comic irony. On its website, Westinghouse Nuclear boasts that "nearly 50% of the nuclear power plants in operation worldwide...are based on Westinghouse technology." Well, guess what, you corporate Candide? Now that you have surrendered those 75,000 documents to China, it's likely that 50% or more of the nukes in China will also be based on Westinghouse technology; it will just be pirated Westinghouse technology.

Westinghouse's naïveté is all the more surprising because, while it is a U.S. corporation, it is effectively controlled by Toshiba of Japan. And many a Japanese corporation has already been burned by China's forced technology transfer conditions and the previously noted astonishing ability of Chinese manufacturers to rapidly digest foreign technologies and use them to turn themselves into fierce competitors. Just consider how a coterie of Japanese and European executives shot themselves in the head with their own bullet train technology transfers, as wryly noted by *The Wall Street Journal*:

> *When the Japanese and European companies that pioneered high-speed rail agreed to build trains for China, they thought they'd be getting access to a booming new market, billions of dollars worth of contracts and the cachet of creating the most ambitious rapid rail system in history. What they didn't count on was having to compete with Chinese firms who adapted their technology and turned it against them just a few years later.*

The Big Cat Kowtows to the Red Dragon

Now check out these two recent news stories. Their juxtaposition sums up Caterpillar's global strategy: Shut it down in America and build it up in China.

> Caterpillar on Tuesday announced plans to lay off more than 2,400 employees at five plants in Illinois, Indiana, and Georgia as the heavy equipment maker continues to cut costs amid the global economic downturn.... In response to the worsening conditions, Caterpillar in January announced job cuts that will ultimately eliminate 20,000 positions.
>
> —Huffington Post

> During the past three decades, Caterpillar has grown from a single sales office in Beijing to our cross-country footprint of today—which includes eleven manufacturing facilities, three research and development centers, nine offices, and two logistics and parts centers.
>
> —Jiming Zhu, Vice President, Caterpillar

Driving the Big Cat's strategy are the powerful rip currents of Chinese unfair trade practices that inevitably pull American companies like Caterpillar offshore. To see these rip currents in all of their inglorious suck, consider the company's decision to produce mini excavators for sale into the Chinese market in Wujiang, China, rather than in Peoria, Illinois. Caterpillar opted for Chinese soil—and workers!—because if it were to produce its mini-excavators domestically and try to export them to China, it would face a stiff, protectionist 30% tariff upon entry into the market.

But that's not all. The Big Cat would face an equally stiff, mercantilist tax in the form of a Chinese currency grossly undervalued by as much as 40%. These two beggar thy neighbor tariffs and taxes alone make U.S. production for export to China a nonstarter for many American companies.

What hurts the most about this particular offshoring decision is that Caterpillar is not just an icon in American industry. It has been a key source of jobs and income throughout the American Midwest for over a century. That manufacturing quite *literally* doesn't play in Peoria anymore is truly an American tragedy.

Now here is a final laugh-out-loud tidbit: Even as Caterpillar was getting ready to create new jobs in China to build its mini excavators and send thousands of Americans to the unemployment line, it had both hands out grasping for benefits from the Obama administration's fiscal stimulus program. Yep. That turns our stomach, too.

Evergreen Solar Offshores Our Energy Future for a Few Pieces of Silver

If you can't beat China and can't get the U.S. government to understand what you're up against, then you may as well join them. That is what Evergreen Solar has decided to do, shifting production of solar fabrication and assembly from its factory in Devens, Massachusetts, to Wuhan, China.
—*Manufacturing & Technology News*

Evergreen Solar produces some of the highest efficiency solar panels in the world. If we are to believe President Barack Obama, it is precisely companies like Evergreen Solar that are supposed to be one of America's best sources of new job creation. For shouldn't America's so-called "green industries" experience some of the fastest job growth in an age of dwindling oil supplies and global warming?

If we are to believe Evergreen's CEO Rick Feldt, however, his company did everything possible to convince the Obama administration to help Evergreen keep its production facilities in Massachusetts. Feldt's actions even included going to Washington to beg key administration officials like Energy Secretary Steven Chu and Commerce Secretary Gary Locke to fight back against the massive illegal subsidies that the Chinese government was throwing at its own solar power industry. But Evergreen's political entreaties fell on deaf ears.

So it was that when the Chinese government offered Evergreen low-interest loans on 65% of the cost of building its new plant in China instead of Massachusetts, Evergreen's CEO believed he had no other choice other than to accept China's 30 pieces of silver and send his company's production offshore. Said an exasperated Feldt, "The United States keeps talking about keeping jobs. You go to the President's State of the Union Address and he said, 'I want to keep jobs in the United States.' It's easy if you say it, but you've got to do something to do that." That's exactly right, Mr. Feldt, but America will surely miss your new factories being offshored to China.

In fact, America, and particularly Massachusetts, will miss your American factory as well—and the 800 workers it employed. That's because shortly after promising to maintain a factory presence in Massachusetts, Evergreen announced it was closing its plant in the Bay State altogether. And yes, that's the same state-of-the-art plant built in 2007 that Massachusetts taxpayers shelled out $52 million to support. And here's the final insult: Evergreen will also force U.S. tax-payers to pay for the closure as it takes a $340 million write-down on the closed plant. You just can't make this kind of stuff up.

General Electric: Would You Like a Spoon with That Forked Tongue?

A pattern is developing. One [foreign] company cedes its intel-lectual property to a Chinese State Owned Enterprise (SOE), and then all of them are squeezed to the margins of China's domestic market and face a new competitor. None of this is accidental or a case of over-eager SOEs crossing the line. China wants to transform from being the factory of the world to an advanced economy and is using its market power to take a short-cut by "digesting" others' intellectual property.

—John Gapper, *Financial Times*

In shining bright spotlight on America's Corporate Turncoats, it is useful to cycle back to the company that opened this chapter: General Electric. At least on the surface, GE's dance with the Dragon doesn't look like a bad gamble. GE now has over 15,000 (mostly Chinese) workers in more than 50 locations in China, and each year, it is deriving an increasing amount of revenue from its China operations. Still, GE continues to experience revenue shortfalls relative to the pots of gold that its expansion in China is supposed to provide.

The bigger issue with GE, however, is the schizophrenic behavior of the CEO Jeffrey Immelt. On the one hand, Immelt has lashed out at Chinese protectionism and gone so far as to opine, "I really worry about China. I am not sure that in the end they want any of us to win, or any of us to be successful."

On the other hand, Immelt, doing his best impression of Vichy France President Marshal Pétain, has surrendered a staggeringly large array of new technologies to China in exchange for what Immelt apparently considers is the high honor and privilege of doing business in the People's Republic. For example, in one of the most disturbing of Immelt's giveaways, GE transferred its entire global avionics business just so it could participate in the development of a Chinese passenger jet. GE has also handed over important pieces of technology in industries as diverse as rail locomotives, wind energy, and antipollution equipment.

That's incredibly shortsighted because, as the earlier words from John Gapper of the *Financial Times* reinforce, once Chinese companies digest GE's existing technologies and newer technologies are developed in GE's research and development facilities sited on Chinese soil, GE will be "marginalized" in the Chinese market—and face even fiercer Chinese competition in international markets.

The Political Calculus of Divide and Conquer

On behalf of the undersigned organizations and their members, we write to express our strong opposition to H. R. 2378, the Currency Reform for Fair Trade Act.
—Letter to Congress by 36 American companies and groups

It's not just manufacturers like Caterpillar, General Electric, and Westinghouse that have turned their backs and coats on America. As the above excerpt from a letter to Congress illustrates, many other American companies and industries that stand to benefit in the short term from the parasitic relationship that China has with the United States have switched sides in the China debate. In fact, every time the subject of trade reform with China comes up now, these companies come right out of the woodwork.

Just consider powerful agricultural groups like the American Soybean Association, American Meat Institute, Corn Refiners Association, and USA Poultry & Egg Export Council. They regularly oppose constructive trade reform with China because they fear retaliatory tariffs. While such fear may be justified, it doesn't excuse lobbying actions that materially harm the broader interests of the United States and its workers as America tries to come to grips with one of the worst economic dilemmas this country has ever faced.

A critical second part of America's "divide and conquer" pro-China coalition includes retail groups like the American Apparel & Footwear Association, the National Retail Federation, and the Sporting Goods Manufacturers Association. These groups fear a rise in prices and a collateral hit to their bottom line if China were to take steps such as fairly valuing its currency and eliminating its illegal export subsidies. What these groups fail to understand—and what many American citizens have yet failed to grasp—is this: The flood of artificially cheap Chinese goods putting America out of business has merely been a down payment on this country's present and future unemployment. Furthermore, more unemployed Americans just means less purchasing power for consumers and less business for these American retailers over the longer run.

And here is one lobbying group that is particularly troubling: the American Chamber of Commerce in Shanghai. This group was last seen lobbying against key provisions in a proposed Chinese law that would have expanded protections for Chinese workers—and thereby given American workers a better chance to compete.

What all of these American business groups and corporate executives now doing business with China must come to grasp is this variation on John Donne's famous poem: No American business is an island entire of itself; every business is a piece of this country, a part of the broader economy. If a job be washed away by Chinese mercantilism, America is the less... And therefore never send to know for whom the bell tolls; it tolls for thee.

7

Death by Colonial Dragon: Locking Down Resources and Locking Up Markets Round the World

To defeat your enemy, first offer him help so that he slackens his vigilance; to take, one must first give.
—Sun Tzu

In the greatest movement of people the world has ever seen, China is secretly working to turn the entire [African] continent into a new colony. Reminiscent of the West's imperial push in the 18th and 19th centuries—but on a much more dramatic, determined scale—China's rulers believe Africa can become a "satellite" state, solving its own problems of overpopulation and shortage of natural resources at a stroke.
—Daily Mail Online

While America's factories gather ever more dust, while U.S. diplomats and military leaders continue to focus myopically on the Middle East, and while Washington's politicians dreamlessly sleep, China is on the march. Its million-man army is moving relentlessly across Africa and Latin America locking down strategic natural resources, locking up emerging markets, and locking out the United States, Europe, Japan, and other economies of the world from the building blocks of future prosperity. It's all just one more nail in the coffin of the U.S. and global manufacturing bases; and it's long past time that the world started paying attention to the rising colonial empire in our midst.

China's Colonial Dragon is the misbegotten son of its voracious Manufacturing Dragon—a factory floor that already consumes half of the world's cement, nearly half of the world's steel, a third of its copper, a fourth of its aluminum, and vast quantities of everything from antimony, chromium, and cobalt to lithium, timber, and zinc. It is all of these resources and more, which come from all around the world, that contribute to every nation's economic growth and quality of life—and that collectively are the raw material sources of all manufacturing jobs and the community of service workers they support.

It is the bauxite and iron ore from countries like Guinea and Tanzania that are transformed into the aluminum and steel we need to manufacture airplanes in Seattle, Washington and build ships in Bath, Maine. It is the copper from Chile that wires our home, the cobalt from the Congo that helps run the machine shops of Michigan, and the niobium from Brazil that goes into everything from rocket engines for our national defense to nuclear reactors for lighting our homes.

And it is the lithium from Bolivia and Namibia that will fuel the batteries that will run our hybrid cars, the manganese from Gabon that helps mold the billions of recyclable cans we need for our soft drinks, and the titanium from places like Mozambique and Madagascar and Paraguay that helps produce anything that requires a high-strength to weight ratio—from twenty-first century marvels like Boeing's new ultra-fuel efficient 787 Dreamliner to Johnson & Johnson's artificial hips and knees.

It is all of these natural resources from all of these different nations that China now wants all to itself for its own manufacturing base and job creation machine. And if we stand idly by on the global stage and allow this to happen, we might as well dig our own economic grave using a gold-plated shovel made in Shanghai. But happening it is, and we all need to clearly understand Beijing's "bait and switch" colonial game if we are to confront this rising empire on issues critical to both economic survival and national defense.

The Colonial Dragon's Bait and Switch

The people of this bewitching, beautiful continent, where humankind first emerged from the Great Rift Valley, desperately need progress. The Chinese are not here for that. They are here for plunder.
—Daily Mail Online

China's strategy of bait and switch always begins the same way: Its president or premier or trade minister arrives in the capital of some far-off country like Djibouti or Niger or Somalia that most Americans can't even point to on a map. He comes waving a huge checkbook offering the promise of lavish, low-interest loans to build up the country's civilian or military infrastructure—whether it be useful roads, ports, and highways; a wasteful and opulent palace for the ruling dictator; or AK-47s to keep a restive population under a repressive boot.

In exchange for China's largess, all the budding colony has to do is two things. First, it must surrender control of its natural resources in exchange for the loan—thereby allowing China to lock down the colony's resources for its own use. Second, it must open its markets to all the finished products that China's factory floor will make with the raw materials the colony surrenders—thereby allowing China to lock up yet another emerging market.

In fact, China's brass-knuckled approach to resource acquisition is radically different from that of much of the rest of the world, which relies on global markets to distribute energy and raw materials through the price system. Such a market-based approach to natural resource distribution is the essence of a global economy based on a community of interests. But rather than rely on cooperative capitalism, Beijing's colonial capitalists put an exclamation point on the "colonial" part of the equation.

In fact, the Dragon's bargain now being struck across Africa and Latin America—and much of Central Asia—is the very definition of colonialism: Seize control of the natural resources that represent the true wealth of a colony. Export these resources back to China rather than allow the colony to use the resources for its own economic development. Then re-export the raw materials back to the colony in the form of finished, manufactured goods. This thereby creates jobs in the homeland, boosts the profits of the homeland's corporations, and of course lengthens the unemployment lines in the colony. What's left in the colonies are mostly dangerous, low-paying jobs in extractive industries, while all the high-value manufacturing work moves to Guangzhou or Chengdu or Shanghai. It's all good for China, but all bad for the colonized mark.

China's Checkbook Diplomacy

When we look at the reality on the ground, we find that there is something akin to a Chinese invasion of the African continent.
—Libyan Foreign Minister Musa Kusa

In fact, China's colonial bait and switch is playing out all over the globe. The Chinese mortgage on Angolan oil is already well over $10 billion and counting. The Democratic Republic of the Congo has encumbered billions of dollars of its copper in exchange for infrastructure. Ghana is bartering away its cocoa beans, Nigeria is trading natural gas for power plants, and the Sudan is literally up to its military arms in oil-backed Chinese debt. And none of these countries ever gets the better end of the deal.

Meanwhile, in Peru, China now owns an entire mountain of copper; and in buying Peru's Mount Toromacho, Beijing's colonialists have taken a page right out of the W.C. Fields playbook and his famous motto, "Never give a sucker an even break." In fact, a hard-bargaining China picked up this copper treasure for a mere $3 billion in payouts and pay-offs and now stands to make a 2,000% profit on its investment. Mean-while, hunger, illiteracy, and poverty—and horrific mining accidents and environmental dumping—remain daily facts of Peruvian mountain life.

As bad as this Peruvian deal is, it is easily topped by Beijing's fleec-ing of the murderous dictator Robert Mugabe of Zimbabwe. This dod-dering old tyrant, who rules one of the most resource-rich and job-poor nations in the world, mortgaged off fully $40 billion of Zimbabwe's pre-cious platinum reserves for a mere $5 billion. He then used a good chunk of the funds on a new palace along with helicopter gunships, fighter jets, and assault rifles to keep a Chinese-made jackboot on the neck of the Zimbabwe people. Only the Chinese can make Zimbabwe's Apartheid of old look good by comparison.

"So what?" you say. Aren't the Chinese just as entitled to these resources as America or Europe or Japan? And why should U.S. citi-zens care if the Chinese rip off some corrupt African dictator or some poverty-stricken Latin American backwater? If the leaders of these Third World hell holes are too stupid or greedy to resist China's checkbook diplomacy, so be it. For what possible difference can it make to the employees of a company manufacturing machined graphite components in Bensenville, Illinois, cathedral stained glass in Kokomo, Indiana, or hardwood furniture in Asheboro, North Carolina? And how could any of China's colonial gambits affect in any way the job prospects of a young man graduating from Cal-Berkeley with a degree in chemistry or a young woman leaving Georgia Tech with a degree in engineering? Well, here's at least one answer.

By establishing its colonial relationships across Africa, Asia, and America's back yard of Latin America, China is keeping more and more of the world's natural resources out of the global marketplace and all to itself. This colonial lockdown strategy thereby gives Chinese manufacturers exclusive access to essential resources at the lowest possible cost—and China thereby gains yet another competitive advantage over America and the rest of the world.

In fact, to see clearly what China is doing is to understand that its resource acquisition lockdown strategy is nothing more than a thinly disguised *de facto* embargo on natural resource access imposed upon the rest of the world. For if Chinese manufacturers can lock down the bauxite from Brazil, Equatorial Guinea, and Malawi; the copper from the Congo, Kazakhstan, and Namibia; the iron ore from Liberia and Somalia; the manganese from Burkina Faso, Cambodia, and Gabon; the nickel from Cuba and Tanzania; and the zinc from Algeria, Kenya, Nigeria, and Zambia, well, that's just that much less for the factories of Cincinnati and Memphis and Pittsburgh—and Munich and Yokohama and Seoul.

China's *de facto* colonial embargo also offers up a billion more tons of natural resource reasons why the automobiles of the future are going to be manufactured in Lanzhou and Wuhu rather than Detroit and Huntsville; why tomorrow's airplanes will be built in Binzhou and Shenyang rather than Seattle and Wichita; why the next generations of computer chips will be fabricated in Dalian and Tianjin rather than in Silicon Valley; and why twenty-first century steel will be forged more and more in Tangshan and Wuhan rather than in Birmingham, Alabama and Granite City, Illinois.

This is not the way the free market or international cooperative relationships are supposed to work. Not by a long shot. And we should all be outraged at this prospect. But in the political salons of Berlin, Tokyo, and Washington, the attitude seems a lot more like Rhett Butler in *Gone with the Wind*: "Frankly my dear, I don't give a damn."

The Overpopulated Dragon Overruns the Dark Continent

Whatever they say, it is a fact that the Chinese come to Africa not just with engineers and scientists. They are coming with farmers. It is neo-colonialism. There are no ethics, no values.

—Egyptian Parliament Member Mustafa al-Gindi

Even as China booms and other manufacturing nations of the world stand to go bust, China's budding new African colonies—from Angola to Zimbabwe—remain mired in hunger, poverty, and often bloody civil wars. This is despite the fact these colonies sit atop some of the most valuable treasures of the earth.

This ongoing poverty and civil strife is a direct result of the "switch" portion of China's "bait and switch" checkbook diplomacy. Here's how this switch works: At the outset of the colonial relationship, a "baiting" China promises that all of that borrowed Chinese money to build the colony's infrastructure will flow down to the local population in the form of thousands of jobs and robustly rising wages. The switch, however, is when China quite literally exports its own "million-man army" to build the infrastructure.

For rather than hire local architects, engineers, construction workers, and trucking companies, a "switching" China uses as much of its own labor force as it can get away with according to the terms of whatever deals it signs. Here's what this sad and sorry colonial situation looks like on the ground in the Sudan to the authors of the book, *China Safari*:

> *So there are Chinese to drill the oil and pump it into the Chinese pipeline guarded by a Chinese strongman on his way to a port built by the Chinese, where it is loaded onto Chinese tankers headed for China. Chinese laborers to build the roads and bridges and the gigantic dam that has displaced tens of thousands of small [land]holders; Chinese to grow Chinese food so other Chinese need eat only Chinese vegetables with their imported Chinese staples; Chinese to arm a government committing crimes against humanity; and Chinese to protect that government and stick up for it in the UN Security Council.*

And here's the biggest dirty little secret about China's colonial ambitions. While locking down natural resources and locking up new markets are the primary strategic goals, Beijing's central planners also want to systematically export millions of Chinese citizens to the "satellite states" of Africa and Latin America to reduce pressures on a grossly overpopulated homeland. In *China Safari*, one Chinese scientist framed this population dumping strategy in this way:

> *We have 600 rivers in China, 400 of which have been killed by pollution.... We will have to send at least 300 million people to Africa before we begin to see the end of our problems.*

And here's just one small case in point that illustrates the emigration screws China is putting to the Dark Continent: When Namibia defaulted on billions of dollars in Chinese loans, Beijing's loan sharks collected by negotiating the acceptance of thousands of Chinese families to Namibia. In fact, this secret deal only surfaced through WikiLeaks; and perhaps needless to say, when the news hit, it outraged the Namibia people.

You'd probably be outraged, too, if these forced migration shoes were on American feet. Just think about it: If a few billion dollars of debt gets China the right to settle thousands of Chinese immigrants in Namibia, how many hundreds of thousands of Chinese immigrants do you think Beijing might want the American government to accept to get rid of our $2 trillion debt to China? But hey, there's plenty of room in Montana and Wyoming.

As to the startling scope of the strategic—and incredibly racist—Chinafication of Black Africa, here's how award-winning journalist Andrew Malone has described the grim progression:

> *With little fanfare, a staggering 750,000 Chinese have settled in Africa over the past decade. More are on the way. The strategy has been carefully devised by officials in Beijing, where one expert has estimated that China will eventually need to send 300 million people to Africa to solve the problems of over-population and pollution.*
>
> *The plans appear on track. Across Africa, the red flag of China is flying. Lucrative deals are being struck to buy its commodities—oil, platinum, gold, and minerals. New embassies and air routes are opening up. The continent's new Chinese elite can be seen everywhere, shopping at their own*

expensive boutiques, driving Mercedes and BMW limousines, sending their children to exclusive private schools....

All over this great continent, the Chinese presence is swelling into a flood...Exclusive, gated compounds, serving only Chinese food, and where no blacks are allowed, are being built all over the continent. "African cloths" sold in markets on the continent are now almost always imported, bearing the legend: "Made in China."

From Malone's scathing narrative, you can glean that it's not just construction crews that China is exporting to Africa, Asia, and Latin America. China also brings its own farmers, merchants, and even hookers!

To put China's land grab in its proper perspective, suppose the America government swept into Iowa and Nebraska, seized millions of acres of prime cropland, turned it over to China, told local farmers to take a hike, and racially segregated the neighborhoods and eating establishments. Just how enraged do you think Americans would be?

Well, that is exactly what is happening right now in Africa where there are *already* over a million Chinese farmers. That's right, over a million Chinese farmers. These Chinese émigrés are tilling African soil to produce food for export back to China exclusively for Chinese tables—even as hunger and poverty remain rife around them.

Here's just a small bitter taste of the Sino-African land grab trade: According to *The Economist*, China has snagged over 7 million acres of prime Congolese palm oil turf to grow biofuels. In Zambia, Chinese farms already "produce a quarter of the eggs sold in the capital, Lusaka." In Zimbabwe, according to the *Weekly Standard*, the Mugabe regime went so far as to offer "formerly white-owned farms for free to Chinese state-owned firms." Meanwhile, the Trojan Horse of the ironically named Chinese "Friendship Farms" has been used in countries ranging from Gabon, Ghana, and Guinea to Mali, Mauritania, and Tanzania to lock up smaller acreages and thereby stay well below the political radar.

The Merchant-dizing of Africa and Latin America

In addition to a flood of Chinese farmers, there has been wave after wave of Chinese merchants washing over both Africa and Latin America. Some come with the flood of Chinese goods into major cities like Kinshasha, Kampala, Lagos, Lima, and Santiago. Others— a new breed of even more adventurous Chinese merchants—disembark from ships and planes to service the far-flung boom towns that inevitably spring up around the Chinese construction projects that crisscross the African and South American continents.

As for China's émigré prostitutes, we are not kidding here. And just like their predatory pricing manufacturing brethren, the Chinese ladies of the night who come to staff the inevitable bars and brothels that spring up around the colonial trade quite literally use cheap tricks to push the locals out. Here's what the authors of *China Safari* had to say about the economics of hooking in the timber-rich nation of Cameroon: "Chinese prostitutes will turn tricks for as little as 2000 CFA ($4.25), whereas the locals...won't get into bed for less than 5000."

And here's yet another laugh-out-loud data point that tells us all we need to know about the economic pressures driving much of Chinese emigration: When the police tried to rescue a group of Chinese women brought by human traffickers for prostitution to Congo-Brazzaville, these hookers insisted on staying in the country. That's because the money and treatment they were getting was better than anything they could receive in their home province of Sichuan. Apparently, it's better to perform unnatural acts in a Congolese brothel than commune with nature on a peasant farm in Dragonland.

China Exports Its Killing Floors and Toxic Waste Dumps

Chinese firms pay their labor forces very little and have them work long hours; how can one expect them to behave differently overseas? With 6,700 Chinese coal miners dying from accidents every year (17 a day)..., how can one expect Chinese ventures to do better in other parts of the world?...China has severely damaged its own ecological system during its rapid modernization process; how can one expect it consciously to implement Western-style environmentally friendly measures elsewhere?

—Wenran Jiang, University of Alberta

Whether it's construction workers, merchants, prostitutes, farmers, or a flood of cheap goods to shut down local businesses, China is effectively exporting its own economic and unemployment problems to its new colonies while driving the indigenous population deeper into the welfare lines or to outright begging on the street. But these are hardly the only noxious exports.

China is also exporting the same utter disregard that it demonstrates on its own domestic soil for both worker safety and environmental protection. As Professor Wenran Jiang has waxed eloquent upon, no one should be surprised. For if Beijing's central planners won't even protect their own flesh-and-blood workers and their own environmental treasures, why should anyone expect China to behave any better or different in the cobalt mines of the Congo, the forests of Gabon, the silver mines of Peru, or the copper mines of Zambia?

In fact, the brazenness with which China ravages the land of its colonies seemingly knows no boundaries. Just consider what happened when one of China's biggest state-owned enterprises—Sinopec—rolled into Gabon to explore for oil. The back story here is that in 2002, Gabon's government had the foresight to designate fully a fourth of the country—mostly virgin forest—as a nature preserve. However, upon its arrival in Gabon, Sinopec promptly began prospecting for oil right in the middle of this preserve. It carved roads willy-nilly through the forests while wantonly dynamiting portions of the park—and only wound up with a slap on the wrist from the government.

And just as "blood diamonds" have helped pay for Chinese weapons in places like the Congo to slaughter innocent civilians and arm teenagers, China's imports of Liberian timber have helped finance and arm combatants in a staggeringly bloody civil war.

Where's That Pale Rider When You Need Him?

[I]n Namibia, on taking issue with their ill treatment, workers were told to "suffer now so that future generations can enjoy." In [Kenya, a] community blocked road construction works demanding that they be provided with water for domestic use and for their livestock. This was at the height of a severe drought and the Chinese contractor had denied the community access to the only borehole with water within a radius of the road work.

—Africa Review

Regarding worker health and safety, there is nothing but fear and loathing in the factories and mines that Chinese bosses run in Africa and Latin America. For just as in China, it is a tale of long hours, low pay, unsafe working conditions, and incredibly abusive bosses—along with all manner of dumping of mining wastes into the adjacent environment.

Need some gory details here? Well, try this little cry-out-loud atrocity: When laborers at the Collum Coal Mine in Southern Zambia presented their grievances over poor pay and unsafe conditions, two of their trigger-happy Chinese bosses responded by downing 11 of the miners with shotgun blasts. Where is Clint Eastwood's "Pale Rider" when you need him?

And this shooting wasn't an isolated event. Just a few months before at another Zambian mine, a strike turned into a riot when a Chinese manager fired into the crowd. Of course, a Foreign Ministry official in Beijing promptly called the massacres a "mistake." Ya think?

China's Amoral Code Undercuts the West

Of the 640 million small arms circulating in the world, it is estimated that 100 million are found in Africa.
—Baffour Dokyi Amoa, *Pambuzaka News*

Given all the dire consequences associated with Chinese colonialism, it is an open question as to why so many African, Asian, and Latin American nations are welcoming China with such open arms. In fact, there are many answers to this question, but any one particular answer depends on the kind of country we are talking about.

One type is personified by the swath of Africa's dictatorial hell holes that are ruled by military juntas, charismatic mass murderers, or putatively "democratic leaders" elected by stuffed ballot boxes or at the point of a gun. Rogue regimes such as Angola, the Sudan, and Zimbabwe are always at the top of this list.

In these and many other African and Latin American countries featuring weak democracies or military strongmen, China's colonial rule is rooted in this chilling slogan first mouthed by Chinese President Hu Jintao to the Gabon parliament: "Just business with no political conditions."

By adhering to this amoral code, China will do business with any foreign government no matter how ruthless, repressive, or corrupt. In doing so, it will utter nary a word of criticism and offer nary a clause to condition trade on such trifles as human rights or financial transparency.

Now, right off the bat, you should see that Beijing's amoral approach to foreign policy provides it with an incredibly strong advantage over the truly civilized nations of the world like the United States, Great Britain, France, and Japan. These nations, either individually or through bodies like the United Nations, try to use diplomatic weapons like trade embargos and the withholding of bank credit and foreign aid as sticks to beat despots into line. However, when these civilized nations try to exert such pressures, enter the Dragon—typically secretly through the back door.

Indeed, when the United States cuts off trade to the Sudan because its Arab military junta is killing black Africans in Darfur, or when the UN imposes an arms embargo on the Ivory Coast or Sierra Leone, or when Europe tries to pressure Eritrea or Somalia, or when virtually the entire world tries to force the dictator Robert Mugabe of Zimbabwe into a power-sharing arrangement to honor the results of an election, Beijing's amoral opportunists spring into action. They offer these repressive regimes access to anything they want—from small arms and advanced fighter jets, to computers and sophisticated telecommunications systems.

Here's just one firsthand account of the "blood for oil" carnage almost entirely perpetrated with Chinese weaponry in Darfur from the BBC documentary, *The New Killing Fields*:

> *Thousands of women and children are being systematically raped in Darfur while their husbands, brothers, and sons are murdered in cold blood.... The government planes bomb African villages and then send their men in on camels, horses, and trucks.... Villages are attacked five times over. One woman called Kalima...tried to call to her husband when her village was attacked. But the militia men had killed him, and her son clinging to her in fear was taken away by Arab militia and burnt alive—the boy was 3 years old. Kalima was herself then raped by these men.*

In these ways, while we in the free and democratic nations of the world take the moral high ground, an opportunistic China plows the fields of commerce. Through this process, the Dragon has helped arm thousands of African children with AK-47s in places like Liberia, Nigeria, and Sierra Leone—while its construction equipment helps plow hundreds of thousands of corpses under the killing fields of far-off places like Darfur.

Et Tu, Australia? Then Falls the World

China Guangdong Nuclear Power Holding Co...offered 83.6 million Australian dollars...for control of Energy Metals Ltd., adding to a wave of Chinese investment in Australia's natural resources. State-owned CGNPH's offer to buy 70% of the...Bigrlyi uranium project in Australia's Northern Territory also signals China's first significant corporate move into one of the world's biggest uranium producing nations.

The offer comes amid a low point in relations between China and Australia following the detainment last month of four employees of Anglo-Australian mining giant Rio Tinto Ltd., including Australian citizen Stern Hu, on charges of bribery and infringing on state secrets. It also comes as disquiet grows among some politicians and commentators about the amount of Chinese investment in Australia's mining sector.

—The Wall Street Journal

Perhaps what is most startling about Chinese colonialism is how even countries with well-developed economies and strong demo-cratic institutions, like Australia, Brazil, and South Africa, are likewise succumbing to China's checkbook charms.

Consider, for example, Australia. This is a country with a well-educated population, a highly skilled workforce, and virtually all the natural resources it needs to become an industrial powerhouse. But instead of developing industries to process its natural resources and then use these resources to manufacture goods, its short-term think-ing leadership simply lets China come in and buy its resources, dig this extraordinary wealth out of the ground, and ship it off on the cheap to Chinese factories.

In the last few years alone, companies like Yangzhou Coal Mining, China Minmetals, Hunan Valin Steel & Iron, China Metallurgical, and Shanghai Baosteel have pulled off mega-deals for raw materials. While this has been a boon for a few hundred of Australia's elite families, it's a long-term recipe for poverty once China hollows out Australia's mines.

Even in the near term, Australia is getting the short end of the colonial stick. That's because when China sends finished goods made with Aussie raw materials back Down Under, Australia runs an ever-larger trade deficit with China—despite its vast natural resource wealth!

Both Brazil and South Africa are in similar—and even leakier—colonial boats. Both countries sit upon an incredibly diverse array of treasures. Both countries have a budding middle class and a great opportunity to join the league of industrialized nations. But both nations are surrendering far too many of their natural resources to China—and running large trade deficits in the process.

For example, in Brazil, China has poured over $7 billion into the oil industry alone, while the ubiquitous Sinopec managed to buy a large chunk of Brazil's prodigious oil reserves in the Santos Basin. Nor is this Sinopec's first dance in Rio: It loaned Brazil's state-owned company Petrobras $10 billion in exchange for the rights to 10,000 barrels of oil a day for the next decade—at bargain basement prices. John Pomfret of *The Washington Post* has painted this literally bigger "Chinamax" picture:

> *Here along the golden sands that grace the Atlantic coast-line 175 miles north of Rio de Janeiro, China is forging a new economic reality. Just past a port where workers are building a two-mile-long pier to accommodate huge vessels known as Chinamaxes that will transport iron ore for China's ravenous steel industry, past berths for tankers to*

lug oil to Beijing, a city of factories is sprouting on an island almost twice the size of Manhattan. Many of the structures will be built with Chinese investment: a steel mill, a shipyard, an automobile plant, a factory to manufacture oil and gas equipment.... The investments in Brazil reflect China's "going out" strategy, which seeks to guarantee natural resources for development purposes and to shield the country's state-owned enterprises from slower growth at home.

Said a worried South African President Thabo Mbeki about colonial gambits such as these in his home country, "If Africa just export[s] raw materials to China while importing Chinese manufactured goods, the African continent could be condemned to underdevelopment."

Whether it's a civilized Australia, a war-torn Congo, a nation in transition like South Africa, or a dictatorial basket case like Zimbabwe, what all of these nations share in common is this: China is systematically stripping these countries of their treasures. And once these treasures are cut down, shoveled out, and depleted, these colonies will be hollow shells, bereft of the industrial capacity and job creation ability that they would otherwise have enjoyed in a non-colonial future.

The American Eagle Has Become the World's Biggest Pigeon

The Manufacturing Dragon is voracious. The Colonial Dragon is relentless. The American Eagle is asleep at the wheel.

—Ron Vara

The bottom line for all of this is that while China has a resource acquisition strategy to keep its factories humming, the rest of the world does not. While China's million-man army marches across

Africa, Asia, and Latin America implementing its strategy of locking down resources, locking up markets, and locking out the rest of the world, the American Eagle remains grounded, Europe is stuck in perennial denial, and Japan is simply paralyzed with fright. This was not always so—at least for America.

Indeed, the United States used to be a master at projecting "soft power" around the globe through aid missions, diplomacy, and military assistance. Now, however, the American Eagle has turned into the world's biggest pigeon; and we are down to running Peace Corps missions in countries that have smaller national debts than ours and hunkering down in armed garrisons in countries where we don't belong. But it's long past time that we and the rest of the world first wake up—and then stand up against—the budding colonial empire in our midst. Again, as Peter Finch so eloquently suggested, the civilized world needs to throw open its East-facing window and shout, "I'm mad as hell and I won't take it anymore."

For if we do not, the de facto natural resource embargo that China is placing on the world through its colonial strategy will eventually act as a noose around the necks of all the world's economies. Over time, as China's rising colonial empire gains ever-more control of the Earth's most precious resources and as its appetite continues to grow, the noose will steadily tighten around the soft necks of America, Europe, Japan, Korea, and others.

Part III

We Will Bury You, Chinese Style

8

Death by Blue Water Navy: Why China's Military Rise Should Raise Red Flags

All power flows from the barrel of a gun.
—Mao Zedong

The last time most Westerners took full notice of the Chinese military was on June 4, 1989. That's the day the Dragon's tanks rolled over bodies and bicycles around Tiananmen Square and trigger-happy shock troops took target practice on protesters pinned against the walls of the Forbidden City.

Since that bloodshed more than two decades ago, China's leaders have not softened their attitudes one bit toward political dissent. What has changed considerably is their military arsenal.

In fact, China's Army, Air Force, and especially its Navy have all taken Great Leaps Forward toward becoming the most formidably equipped in the world. Unfortunately, much of this shiny new weaponry is now aimed squarely at us.

A weapons of mass destruction case in point is the Dongfeng (DF) or "East Wind" 31A. This is a mobile-launched, long range, intercontinental ballistic missile (ICBM) that is hard to track, harder to spot, and more than ready to deliver a 1-megaton nuclear warhead right to your doorstep in Des Moines or Decatur.

Or how about the Jin class nuclear missile submarine with its Jù Làng-2 ICBMs? These "Giant Wave" missiles can be armed with multiple warheads capable of frying any city in the United States or Europe.

And speaking of submarines, did you know that on the tropical island of Hainan, China's southernmost province, the Navy has built a James Bond–style underground hideaway? This base's clear purpose is to shield the comings and goings of China's growing submarine fleet from Western satellites—a fleet that now regularly intrudes into Japanese territorial waters and just as regularly stalks U.S. ships on the high seas.

As for control over those high seas, there is also the DF-21D ballistic anti-ship missile—a true naval warfare game changer. It's a mobile-launched, Mach 10, solid fueled demon expressly designed to drive America's Pacific Fleet from the Taiwan Strait and Sea of Japan right back to the beaches of Hawaii; and this sudden screaming death has just one target—aircraft supercarriers like the *USS George Washington*, which house crews of over 5,000 American sailors and aviators.

What do these armaments have in common? They are distinctly *offensive* weapons geared not toward territorial defense but rather toward what Chairman of the Joint Chiefs of Staff Mike Mullen has described as "expeditionary" campaigns. Indeed, this weaponry is part of a rapidly expanding arsenal that could be used effectively against the likes of India, Japan, or Vietnam in regional conflicts. It could be used equally effectively to take on the United States over control of such strategic chess pieces as world shipping lanes—or to finally take Taiwan in an ultimate *mano-a-mano* blitzkrieg.

Here's how Admiral Mullen has framed the growing contradiction between what civilian leaders like Premier Wen Jiabao insist is a "peaceful rise" and what, in reality, has become the most rapid military buildup of a totalitarian regime since the 1930s:

> *[China's] heavy investments of late in modern, expeditionary maritime and air capabilities seem oddly out of step with [its] stated goal of territorial defense. Every nation has a right to defend itself and to spend as it sees fit for that purpose. But a gap as wide as what seems to be forming between China's stated intent and its military programs leaves me more than curious about the end result. Indeed, I have moved from being curious to being genuinely concerned.*

Just how much should all of us *outside* the Pentagon be concerned? And what exactly is the truth behind China's alleged peaceful rise?

The only way to correctly answer these questions is to analyze what China's military forces are *doing*—not by swallowing whole what its civilian leaders are saying. That's why over the course of the next four chapters we are going to drill down into the impressive set of military capabilities a rising China is developing.

We begin in this chapter with a wake-up call overview of China's traditional brute-force military branches—the Army, Air Force, and Navy. Chapters 9 and 10 then move to an even more alarming analysis of China's growing capabilities in modern espionage and "asymmetric warfare." To complete our assessment, we will look closely at the astonishing rise of China as a space power—and come to better understand why the People's Republic sees control of the heavens as the ultimate strategic high ground.

By the end of these four chapters, it should be clear that we in America do not just need a "Sputnik moment" as President Barack Obama has called for to jump-start our economy. We—along with Europe, Japan, and the rest of the world—also need a "Winston Churchill moment" that wakes us to the growing dangers of a heavily armed, totalitarian regime intent on regional hegemony and bent on global domination.

The "Chosin Few" Meet Chinese "Hordes"

Yes, we all have our memories of buddies killed, of the hordes of Chinese assaulting our frozen lines, and the long, danger- ous walk out, but I truly believe the uppermost thought in our minds, when we think of that campaign, is the cold! Those long nights in a ditch, or a foxhole, with the thermometer hanging around 40 degrees below zero, will long be remem- bered.

—Korean War veteran Lee Bergee, USMC

Since the days of Mao Zedong, China has relied on a military strategy grounded in the use of overwhelming force. Today, even as China is moving toward a far more modern view of warfare, it contin- ues to maintain the world's largest standing army. This army is a "horde" 2.3 million strong; and its boots on the ground far outnumber the combined forces of Canada, Germany, the United States, and the United Kingdom. Moreover, China's ground troops are exceedingly well supplied with the world's largest inventory of tanks, artillery, and personnel carriers.

On the tank front alone, China's 6,700 dwarf Taiwan's 1,100, South Korea's 2,300, and Vietnam's 1,000 or so. Even the U.S., in the middle of fighting two Asian land wars, only runs about 5,000 tanks.

Emblematic of the Red Army's rapid shift to new technologies is the "Type 99" main battle tank, which is the vanguard weapon today for China's modernized ground force. Its design is largely stolen from the venerable Soviet T-72. This high-tech killing machine incorporates everything from laser-guided missiles and satellite navigation to explo- sive reactive armor that can repel armor-piercing projectiles.

All in all—and it's a whole lot of "all"—the Red Army is a formi- dable expeditionary force. It remains eminently capable of the same kind of quintessentially old-school human wave attacks that the world already bore stark witness to in conflicts ranging from China's 1962 surprise attack on India to its 1979 unprovoked assault on Vietnam.

And with the machinations and threats of a lunatic North Korea remaining ever in the news today—and with China North Korea's biggest ally and protectorate—let none in the United States ever forget the People's Republic's role during the Korean War. This 1950s bloodbath should have been a quick mop-up of poorly supplied North Korean troops by United Nation forces. Instead, in the pivotal battle of the war, China's human waves turned Chosin into a frozen Hell; and thousands of young Americans, Brits, Australians, and Koreans bled out in cold mud under ruthless Chinese fire. Let's not forget, too, that this was a relentless war that Mao Zedong pitilessly extended for two more years. He even sacrificed his own son to the pointless cause while doing it—only to doom at least three generations of North Koreans to virtual slavery and starvation.

The Best Air Force the Dragon Can Buy, Steal, or Scrounge

Wargaming, including an extensive simulation by Rand, has shown that the U.S. would generate a 6-1 kill ratio over Chinese aircraft, but the Americans would lose.
—Aviation Week

While China's Red Army relies on sheer numbers, its Air Force is becoming one of the best that the Chinese can buy with our "Walmart dollars" or that its spies can steal.

Consider the Shenyang J-11B and the J-15 "flying shark." The first, a twin-engine jet fighter, is a carbon copy knockoff of the Russian Sukhoi Su-27. The second, an aircraft carrier-capable plane, is the equally counterfeit twin of the Russian Su-33.

Now here's what so darkly comic about these counterfeit planes. With each, China first signed a purchase and licensing agreement with Russia. However, once China got delivery of a plane or two, it simply reverse-engineered the Russian technology and then backed out of the deal—which just goes to show you there is no honor between a thief and a thug.

In response to getting ripped off not once but twice, an angry Russian Defense Council Member, Colonel Igor Korotchenko, discounted the Chinese knockoffs by claiming in the Russian International News Agency that: "The Chinese J-15 clone is unlikely to achieve the same performance characteristics of the Russian Su-33 carrier-based fighter." Then he added, "I do not rule out the possibility that China could return to negotiations with Russia on the purchase of a substantial batch of Su-33s." Well, don't hold your breath, Colonel.

As for other noteworthy aircraft flying in Chinese formations, there is the J-17 "Thunder." This plane grabs your attention not so much because of its offensive capabilities—it features impressive air-to-air and air-to-ground missiles. Rather, China's development of the J-17 illustrates yet another of the many covert ways that the People's Republic is acquiring sensitive military technologies. In this case, China used the backdoor vehicle of a phony "joint venture" with Pakistan—and some opportunistic French intervention—to magically create a path to circumvent the European Union's weapons ban on China.

And, speaking of magic, the Chinese Air Force recently pulled out of its collective hat a diverse array of technologically advanced, remote-controlled, and self-guided "drones." These are the same kind of unmanned craft that America has used with great effectiveness in both Afghanistan and Iraq.

To rub its newfound (and newly pirated) capabilities in America's face, China not only debuted a radical new *jet-powered* drone at a Chinese air show in Zhuhai. The exhibitors also included a video simulation of the drone targeting a U.S. aircraft carrier so its crew of 5,000 American souls could be more accurately slaughtered by an incoming Chinese missile. Peaceful rise indeed.

30 Minutes over Tokyo, 10 Minutes to Taipei

Of all the airplanes in the hangars of the Chinese Air Force, the most provocative has to be the Chengdu J-20 "Black Eagle" stealth fighter. In a finely tuned insult to the United States—and perhaps as a rare display of the Dragon's dark military humor—the Chinese Air Force successfully completed the J-20's first test flight during an official state visit by the U.S. Secretary of Defense, Robert Gates. Of course, Gates was the perfect foil for Beijing's little diplomatic joke—and poke in America's eye. For it was Gates, doing his best impression of Neville Chamberlain, who had publicly insisted that China could not possibly produce such a fifth-generation plane before 2020.

What is not so amusing about this radar-evading plane is that it is clearly designed for air-to-ground attacks on China's regional neighbors. Indeed, this Chinese Black Eagle exceeds its American stealth counterpart, the F-22, in a variety of performance factors that clearly value *offensive* bombing missions over territorial air defense. These factors include both a high fuel capacity and the runway clearance required for a heavy weapons load. What such factors mean from a strategic point of view is this: While the J-20 probably isn't agile enough to defend China from top American fighter planes, it is an absolutely perfect weapon if the goal is to sneak up on Kyoto, Taipei, or Seoul with a big payload of bombs and missiles.

As to how China so quickly acquired the kind of sophisticated stealth technology that it took America decades to research and hundreds of billions of dollars to develop, this, too, is a chilling story. According to Croatian Military Chief of Staff, Admiral Davor Domazet-Loso, China acquired its basic stealth technology from the carcass of an American stealth fighter shot down over Serbia in 1999. In fact, as soon as the fighter went down, China dispatched a large cadre of spies to crisscross the region and buy up any parts that local farmers and villagers might have scavenged.

As to whether the People's Republic is preparing to use its air force offensively, incursions by the Chinese Air Force are already forcing Japan to scramble its fighters almost 50 times a year—or roughly once a week and twice the rate of Chinese provocations just a few years ago. Nor is Japan alone in getting this sort of probing. India regularly reports Chinese incursions into its air space, particularly in the disputed regions near Kashmir and Arundachal Pradesh. Can you spell *Hegemon*?

Red Sky, Morning Sailor, Take Warning

The Chinese military's future goal is to secure naval supremacy in the western Pacific waters inside the second line of defense from the Japanese archipelago to Guam Island and Indonesia. After that, the Chinese military will vie with U.S. naval forces in the Indian Ocean and in the entire Pacific region.
—*Asahi Shimbun*

While China's army personifies brute force and its air force has the best flying machines it can buy or steal, China's naval buildup ultimately is the most unsettling to Pentagon analysts. Indeed, the People's Republic is moving forward at Manhattan Project speed to develop a blue water Navy capable of challenging the U.S. Navy. Its first goal is to push U.S. aircraft carrier fleets out of the Western Pacific—and perhaps finally take Taiwan—and then to ultimately project hard power across the globe.

At the center of this grand strategic struggle is one of the most iconic weapons in history—the mighty aircraft carrier. The U.S. Navy likes to call these ships "four and a half acres of sovereign and mobile American territory;" and they've been the backbone of a Pax Americana on the high seas ever since the end of World War II.

In fact, as the Dragon knows all too well, directly confronting a U.S. carrier and its accompanying armada is an exceedingly difficult task. Besides having its own flight wing of 75 fixed and rotor aircraft, a typical carrier like the *George Washington* will be closely guarded by an Aegis guided missile cruiser able to repel any surface attacks. The flattop will also be flanked by several destroyers with anti-aircraft missiles and will likely have at least one sub-hunting frigate running point. Meanwhile, beneath the sea, one or more fast attack, nuclear-powered Los Angeles class subs will be silently escorting this formidable surface group; and, at least in the past, any frontal assault by the existing Chinese Navy would not get within 50 miles of such a fleet in open waters.

It is precisely this kind of formidable carrier force that has thus far kept Taiwan free from the mainland's subjugation. It is also the specter of America's carrier-led Pacific Fleet that keeps Chinese strategists worrying about this ultimate nightmare: That one day the American Navy might blockade the oceanic transit point for 80% of China's imported oil—the Strait of Malacca—in retaliation for some form of Chinese aggression.

Slam BAM, Thank You Ma'am

Known among defense analysts as a "carrier killer," the Dongfeng-21D missile would be a game-changer in the Asian security environment, where U.S. Navy aircraft carrier battle groups have ruled the waves since the end of World War II. The DF-21D's uniqueness is in its ability to hit a powerfully defended moving target with pinpoint precision—a capability U.S. Naval planners are scrambling to deal with.

—Associated Press

Because Chinese military strategists clearly see all the implications of a powerful aircraft carrier force, they are now rapidly developing a two-pronged counter-strategy. One prong involves the building of China's own countervailing aircraft carrier group; the other relies on perfecting its game-changing "carrier killer" missile—known not so affectionately in Pentagon circles as the "BAMer," short for ballistic anti-ship missile.

We say *perfecting* the BAMer because it is no small feat to hit even a large ship bobbing along in the ocean from a thousand miles away. That's why China is busy taking target practice at a carrier-sized rectangle set up at a testing range in the Gobi desert. (Check it out on Google Earth; the coordinates are on our website!)

In fact, China's new carrier killer is a "game-changer" in much the same way the advent of airplane-dropped torpedo bombs drove massive battleships from the high seas at the beginning of World War II. That sea change came when a British bi-plane with a single torpedo bomb helped sink the Nazi's giant new battleship—the Bismarck—on its first cruise. That this truly was a game changer was further ratified by Japanese Admiral Yamamoto, who also used deadly torpedo bombs with devastating effect at Pearl Harbor, sending American battleship after battleship to the bottom.

Yet even as China's big stick BAMer may foreshadow the extinction of the American aircraft carrier as a force projection power—and threaten to drive back America's Pacific Fleet to the safe harbor of Hawaii—China is rapidly building its own countervailing fleet of flattops. In fact, China's first carrier is likely to roll out of Dalian harbor sometime in 2011; and its story would be one riveting hour-long special on the Military Channel.

It's a story that begins with China using a front company operating out of Hong Kong to buy an aircraft carrier from the Ukraine. This ship was the *Varyag*—a 67,500-ton flattop that was supposed to be the pride of the Soviet Union's fleet.

With the breakup of the Soviet Union, however, construction of the *Varyag* was never fully completed. Instead, as its hull was gathering rust in a Black Sea Shipyard in the Ukraine, China developed a Hong Kong front group run by a bunch of former Chinese military officers to buy the ship at auction for a mere $20 million under the ruse that it would be turned into a giant floating casino in Macau.

Seeing through that ruse, the U.S. Pentagon got its putative ally Turkey to initially block transit of the ship. At that point, however, China's deputy foreign minister, Yang Wenchang, flew to Ankara with a $360 million "economic aid package"—read: bribe—to trump Pentagon pressure; and the baksheeshed Turks allowed the *Varyag* to pass through the Bosporus.

Of course, upon the *Varyag*'s arrival in China, it was towed not to Macau but rather to Dalian Harbor for extensive analysis and refitting. Recent photos indicate she has been dry-docked, repainted in the colors of the Chinese Navy, had her flight decks resurfaced, and now sports a shiny new radar mast installed on her island. And very soon now, she will be launched and rechristened as the *Shi Lang*.

And here again, we must show our appreciation for the Chinese military's dark sense of humor—and history! In this case, China has named its first flattop after a famous commander of the Manchu Fleet who originally invaded Taiwan during the 17th century and then worked hard to designate Taiwan as a prefecture of the Fujian province. Yep! The Chinese military sure knows how to send a message.

Over the next few years, China will send a much bigger message. It is expected to send a fleet of at least five flattops roaming around the globe—and no doubt running into the U.S. Navy.

The 007 Dragon Plays "Hide the Submarine"

Photographs emerged last night that appeared to confirm fears in Washington that China is building a giant underground nuclear submarine base on a tropical island. Pentagon chiefs are worried that the secret base near Sanya on China's Hainan Island...could threaten Asian countries and America's dominance in the region. The pictures obtained by respected military magazine Jane's Intelligence Review...*show vast tunnel entrances that are thought to lead to huge caverns capable of hiding up to 20 nuclear submarines from spy satellites.*
—The Daily Mail

No aircraft carrier force and blue water Navy would be complete without a strong "run silent, run deep" submarine force, and China has been quietly building what will soon be the largest fleet in the world. In fact, the newest generation of diesel electric subs are so fast and quiet that they have been able to stalk U.S. Navy ships with little or no detection. Indeed, in one confrontation now as infamous in U.S. Navy lore as it was embarrassing then, a Chinese Type 039 Song-class attack submarine boldly surfaced within torpedo range of the *USS Kitty Hawk* after stalking the carrier group undetected for miles.

China's newer Type 041 yuan-class boats are expected to be even quieter and able to operate fully submerged for much longer periods on a new "Air Independent Propulsion" system—read: to better threaten Western shipping in the Western Pacific and critical straits of Malacca, that crucial choke point for oil flowing to Japan, Korea, and Taiwan. Moreover, to secure distant force projection capability, China has built several new Type 094 Jin Class missile subs designed to pull up to the coast of California and lob missiles as far away as Savannah, Missouri or Savannah, Georgia.

In fact, there is at least some evidence to suggest that the People's Republic may already be practicing for Armageddon off the California coast. Thomas McInerney, a retired United States Air Force Lieutenant General, asserts that the Chinese Navy actually conducted such a test launch off Los Angeles in November of 2010—on the eve of a G-20 Summit, no less. An outraged McInerney had these sharp words for the Pentagon:

> *We should get a definitive answer [from Washington]. This is not an airplane because of the plume and the way you see that plume...That is a missile, launched from a submarine. You can see it go through a correction course, and then it gets a very smooth trajectory meaning that the guidance system has kicked in.*

While the Pentagon quickly and vehemently denied Chinese involvement, it still can't identify the specific plane it says made the contrail. But the real story here is that military experts are even debating a possible missile launch off the City of Angels. Such a debate should leave no doubt that China's investment in offensive strategic weapons is progressing rapidly.

Which brings us back to the aforementioned James Bond–style sub base on Hainan Island. Photos by the Federation of American Scientists do indeed reveal 60-foot-high tunnel entrances that have been cut into the island's seaside hills, and anywhere from a half dozen to a full score of nuclear subs will be able to hide in the base's man-made caverns.

Note that this new 007 base also features a high-tech demagnetization pier used to cloak its subs from electromagnetic detection at sea; and China clearly wants its U-boats left alone and undetected. Indeed, in one well-publicized incident, five Chinese ships—both military and commercial—intentionally and repeatedly crossed the bow of the *USNS Impeccable* it was cruising in international waters 75 miles from the Chinese coast. The American vessel was pulling a towed sonar array to monitor submarine activity coming in and out of Hainan Island; and at one point, the attacking Chinese flotilla dumped floating debris in the path of the U.S. ship. This forced the *Impeccable* to come to an emergency "all stop," after which Chinese sailors attacked the *Impeccable*'s sonar array with grappling hooks. Remember that little tête-à-tête the next time you buy your next fix of Chinese products from Walmart.

All Military Power Flows From a Nation's Factory Floor

Quantity has a quality all its own.
—Josef Stalin

While our ever-so-brief review of China's growing military might leave no doubt about its rapidly improving offensive capabilities, at least some China Apologists will be quick to argue this point: In almost every weapons category, America's technology still remains vastly superior.

In fact, in many cases, these Apologists would be right. For example, in a dog fight, the American F-22 fighter would likely down its Chinese counterpart in a New York minute. So, too, would the *USS Ronald Reagan* and its armada almost certainly send any of China's new aircraft carriers to Davey Jones' locker in short order.

But this love affair with American technological superiority misses a much more important point—one that underscores the insanity of allowing a mercantilist and protectionist China to destroy the American manufacturing base and vitiate our economy. This point is best made from the perspective of a particularly·insightful Nazi artillery commander who was captured at the battle of Salerno. Said he about the futility of his precision German weaponry against a horde of American matériel:

> *I was on this hill as a battery commander with six 88-millimeter antitank guns, and the Americans kept sending tanks down the road. We kept knocking them out. Every time they sent a tank, we knocked it out. Finally, we ran out of ammunition, and the Americans didn't run out of tanks.*

The real truth to be told here is that America didn't defeat Hitler and the Nazis so much with its incredibly brave soldiers as it did with its overwhelming industrial might. In fact, in almost every category, the Nazis had technologically superior weaponry in the latter stages of the war. The German Panzer tank, for example, was the finest in the world, the Germans' famous U-boats were the best subs, the *Bismarck* was the greatest battleship ever floated, and in some classes, Germany's weapons literally had no peers as they fielded the world's only long-range rockets—both the V1 cruise missile and the V2 ballistic missile—and deployed the Me-262, the world's first jet aircraft.

What America did have, however, was the world's biggest factory floor. And once this "workshop to the world" was converted to a total war footing after Pearl Harbor, the huge and highly efficient auto factories of Detroit, shipyards of Maine, chemical plants of Ohio, and steel mills of Pennsylvania churned out vastly superior numbers of tanks and planes and guns and bombs. The result was a military juggernaut that promptly trounced the two greatest war machines the world had ever seen.

In fact, no one understood the inevitability of an American victory better than Admiral Yamamoto. He spent the day after his devastatingly successful surprise attack on Pearl Harbor not in jubilation but rather in depression and desperation. For he knew full well that a massive American response would follow; and as mighty as Japanese industry was at the time, it would be no match for the American Heartland.

America's growing military problem today, however, is that the biggest auto plants are no longer in Detroit but in cities like Chengdu, Jilin, Nanjing, and Wuhu; the busiest shipyards are in Bohai, Dalian, Fujian, and Jiangan; and the mills and smokestacks that churn out almost ten times more tonnage a year than American steelmakers are in Chongqing, Hebei, Shanghai, and Tianjin.

This, then, is what both our Pentagon and our modern-day Neville Chamberlains in the White House and on Capitol Hill need to fully understand: China's J-20 fighter doesn't have to be the world's best if it can field 1,000 of them versus our 187 F-22s.

China's Shang class attack subs really don't have to be better than the *USS Los Angeles* class or the British *Astute* class boats if they can fill half the Pacific Ocean with them.

And when it comes to all those rockets on China's launch pads and in China's ballistic missile subs, just how precise does the aiming of a hundred hydrogen bombs directed at Middle America need to be before we are willing to acknowledge the People's Republic's hegemony over Japan, Taiwan, India, and Australia?

This is why we do indeed now need a Winston Churchill moment. As Churchill once said about World War II:

There never was a war in history easier to prevent by timely action than the one which has just desolated such great areas of the globe...but no one would listen, and one by one we were all sucked into the awful whirlpool.

In our new Winston Churchill moment, we must clearly see that to win a traditional military war against a United States that has already surrendered much of its industrial capacity to China, all China needs to do is to develop (or pirate) credible weapons systems and then build them in sufficient quantities to overwhelm our technologically superior forces.

In fact, China has already done the former. It's time to wake up before it does the latter. It's also time for all of us to understand much more clearly the intimate relationship that exists between a nation's manufacturing base and its military power.

9

Death by Chinese Spy:
How Beijing's "Vacuum Cleaners" Are
Stealing the Rope to Hang Uncle Sam

One spy is worth 10,000 soldiers.
—Sun Tzu, *The Art of War*

The primary objective of Chinese intelligence operations targeting the U.S. government and its industries is to collect technical and economic information, with the dual purpose of making the Chinese military-industrial base more sophisticated and the economy more competitive.
—*Intelligence Threat Handbook*

Every day, a loose network of thousands of professional and amateur Chinese spies gather intelligence in the offices, factories, and schools of America, Europe, and nations ranging from Brazil and India to Japan and South Korea. And every minute of every day, hundreds of Chinese hackers use thousands of hijacked computers to batter down the firewalls of industrial, financial, academic, political, and military information systems around the world looking for valuable data and quietly documenting vulnerabilities that can be exploited to devastating effect in the future.

Why do we in America put up with what the U.S.–China Commission has called "the most aggressive country conducting espionage against the United States"? That's a good question that we must ask ourselves—whether we go to work every day at the White House or on Capitol Hill or whether we shop every week for cheap Chinese products at our local Walmart.

In this chapter, we look carefully at the dark and shadowy world of Chinese espionage on American soil—and elsewhere around the world. In the next chapter, we turn to a review of China's arguably even more dangerous and provocative cyberespionage—a form of so-called "asymmetric" warfare that has the capability to reach into every computer, household, business, and bureaucracy on the planet.

By the end of these two chapters, we hope that everyone in America—from Main Street and Wall Street to the halls of the CIA, FBI, and Pentagon—has an epiphany about the naiveté of engaging in unconditional commerce and trade with a country that is using spycraft, both old and new, to systematically strip us of our technologies and probe our defenses for a possible eventual kill.

While We Hunt Bin Laden, the Dragon Runs Wild and Free

Beijing does not favor the classical methods used by other big intelligence services, featuring tight control over a few, deeply buried and valuable agents. Instead, it employs a vast, decentralized network that employs Chinese students, businesspeople, and delegations in the United States, and targets Americans of Chinese ancestry as possible espionage recruits.
—The Christian Science Monitor

As part of its boots on the ground, traditional spycraft, China's government, and many of its state-run industries, actively runs a highly sophisticated three-pronged espionage campaign against many nations around the world—with major rivals like America, Europe, and Japan drawing much of the attention. This three-pronged strategy involves penetrating academia, industry, and government institutions to steal valuable financial, industrial, political, and technological information and prepare for possible disruptive and destructive attacks in the event of a hot war.

In fact, while the United States intelligence infrastructure has been consumed by the War on Terror, Chinese operatives have been allowed to run wild and free in America. Their vehicle is an elaborate "hybrid" espionage network, very different from that of the traditional spycraft of the old Soviet Union.

At the height of the Cold War, the Soviet Union's KGB relied on a relatively small number of professional "secret agents" stationed overseas and a seemingly constant supply of new American traitors they "turned" through bribery or blackmail. While China has its own share of secret agents and turned Americans, it relies far more heavily upon a highly decentralized network of low-level spies, the vast majority of which are ethnic Chinese.

China's cadres of semi-pro spies and amateur informants are typically recruited by agencies such as the Ministry of State Security— China's KGB—as well as by specific industry groups. Some of these spies may be drawn from the Chinese–American community. As noted by the *Intelligence Threat Handbook*, they are typically brought into the network in one of two ways: either by appeals to Chinese nationalism and ethnicity or by coercive threats to family members living in China.

Far more of China's spies are embedded among the roughly 750,000 Chinese nationals who are issued U.S. visas in any given year. They may be reporters for news agencies like Xinhua, students at American universities, touring business executives, guest workers at American corporations or national labs, or simply tourists. In fact, the vast quantities of legitimate Chinese visitors to America every year coupled with the large Chinese–American community make it easy for recruited spies to fly well below FBI radar and do as Mao Zedong once advised: "Swim with the fish."

Free Visas to the U.S. Candy Store

Spying is war without the fire.
—Li Fengzhi

The case of Li Fengzhi is instructive because it illustrates both how easy it is for a Chinese agent to infiltrate the United States and how deep the Chinese espionage network runs. Li was working as an analyst for the Ministry of State Security when he slipped quietly into the United States as a graduate student at the University of Denver in 2003.

According to interviews we conducted with Li, his life started out innocently enough as a son born in 1968 to an educated family in Liaoning Province. Upon graduating from college in 1990, Li joined a provincial intelligence service; and, within a few years, he moved up to the Ministry of State Security where he worked for Beijing as an agent in his home province. According to Li, as a naïve young man, he saw this as a "very good job and a special career working for the government."

As an analyst for China's version of the KGB, Li spent time gathering intelligence on Eastern Europe and Russia while pursuing a PhD in international politics. In 2003, he was chosen to travel to the United States. Instead of spying against the United States, however, Li had an epiphany.

As Li saw more and more of the outside world and what freedom looked like, he, in his own words, "began to see that the Chinese Communist Party was evil and that it had been harming the Chinese people." It was on the strength of this epiphany that Li sought to defect to the United States.

According to Li, when he "left the Ministry of State Security, they had about 100,000 documented agents or informants, not counting the very amateur ones, and a large number of individuals who worked

as spies within other Chinese governmental departments." By comparison, the U.S. FBI has only about 13,000 sworn officers.

Likewise according to Li—and this is his perhaps most damning
revelation—the majority of official Chinese agents are Chinese
reporters, photographers, NGO members, influential Chinese-
American leaders and business people, engineers, and scholars. In
Li's words, while these professional spies "might not have conditions
to get the important information, they will focus on recruiting informants to get that intelligence."

What is remarkable about the Li Fengzhi story besides how easily
he was able to slip into the United States despite his background in
intelligence is how much more of a realistic view he has of China than
most citizens of the United States.

A Veritable Beehive of Vacuuming Activity

So just what exactly does China's spy network do, and how does it
do it? In the industrial espionage arena, this network is constantly
seeking to acquire new technologies, trade secrets, and processes. On
the military front, espionage goals range from the acquisition of new
weapons systems to more detailed information about America's military bases and operations.

In both its industrial and military espionage, the hallmark of Chinese spying is its relentless beehive patience. Decade by decade,
thousands of its "worker bee" spies and information gatherers
painstakingly vacuum up small bits of information from America's
university research facilities, sensitive national laboratories, Silicon
Valley start-ups, and defense-related companies.

In fact, this glacially moving, time-consuming process is totally in
character with China's long-run view of history—and fully consistent
with Sun Tzu's famous dictum that "one spy is worth 10,000 soldiers."

For once enough small bits of information are vacuumed up and fed back to mainland China and compiled, they offer Chinese intelligence agencies and state-owned enterprises a clear composite view of entire technologies, processes, or systems.

As Scott Henderson has stated in *The Dark Visitor*: "Rather than set a targeted goal for collection, they instead rely on the sheer weight of information to form clear situational understanding." That this kind of vacuumed information can be quite valuable is reflected in these famous words of none other than George Washington, the father of America. On the benefits of grassroots intelligence gathering, he astutely observed:

> *Even minutiae should have a place in our collection, for things of a seemingly trifling nature, when enjoined with others of a more serious cast, may lead to a valuable conclusion.*

To date, China's spy network has stolen technologies and processes ranging from subsystems of the Aegis guided missile destroyer, the inner workings of neutron bombs, and naval reactor designs to plans for the space shuttle, Delta IV rocket specs, and ICBM-capable guidance systems. This Communist beehive has been equally effective in vacuuming up details on weapons systems ranging from the B1-B bomber, unmanned aerial vehicles, and submarine propulsion systems to jet engines, aircraft carrier launch systems, and even highly specific U.S. Navy warship operations procedures.

Throughout all these acts of war without fire by China against America, both law enforcement and counterespionage efforts have been extremely lax, our politicians have taken no retaliatory actions, and the American public has been grossly underinformed.

On top of all this, many of America's most elite academic and research institutions have become naïve cheerleaders for the so-called Chinese economic miracle. Part of the problem is a lucrative flood of grant money now flowing in to support various Chinese research efforts. This makes American universities reluctant to "bite the Chinese hand that feeds them." An even bigger part of the problem is the billions of dollars in tuition money that floods in from China's 125,000-plus visiting students to America's universities. While the majority of Chinese students in the United States are among the brightest and hardest working and hopefully will make contributions to America and the world, enough of them are under some level of Communist Party influence to warrant a more serious upfront vetting process.

From a public policy point of view, however, throwing open the doors of American education to any and all Chinese comers is a dangerous game. For as China well knows, much of the technological innovation that has made America great begins in the research facilities of places like CalTech, Harvard, and the Massachusetts Institute of Technology and national laboratories like Argonne, Lawrence Berkeley, Los Alamos, and Sandia. Indeed, it is not for nothing that our nation's universities and national labs—as well as corporate R&D centers such as Silicon Valley and defense companies like Hughes and Loral—have become veritable "candy stores" for Chinese industrial and military espionage.

One Good Turned Agent Deserves Another—and Life Imprisonment

"Mr. Shriver sold out his country and repeatedly sought a position in our intelligence community so that he could provide classified information to the People's Republic of China," U.S. Attorney Neil MacBride said.
—Reuters

While ethnic Chinese make up the bulk of the Dragon's spy network, China's spymasters have at times also been highly successful in "turning" non-Chinese into agents in the old Soviet style.

Consider, for example, Ko-Suen Moo, a South-Korean born sales consultant for Lockheed Martin and other defense firms. This turned agent wound up in a Florida airplane hangar trying to buy an entire GE-manufactured turbofan jet engine specifically designed for the dogfighter *par excellence* F-16. Luckily, in this case, U.S. customs agents shot the plot down; but sometimes America is not so lucky.

Such was the bad luck with another South Korean turned by the Chinese, Kwon Hwan Park. He succeeded in exporting two Blackhawk helicopter engines to China via a Malaysian front. Lightning didn't strike twice, however, as Park was later arrested at Dulles Airport heading to China with a suitcase full of military night vision equipment.

While many of China's spies are quasi-amateurs like Moo and Park, some agents—so-called "sleeper agents"—have been intentionally planted into the United States. That's how Boeing engineer Dongfan Chung collected Space Shuttle and Delta IV rocket designs destined for Beijing. By the time he was caught, Chung had squirreled away a cool $3 million and was found with over 300,000 pages of technical documents in his home, along with notes about how he hoped to help what he referred to as "his motherland."

The case of Chi Mak is equally disturbing. He was caught shipping plans for U.S. nuclear submarine propulsion and naval command and control systems to China. Mak's case is particularly instructive because it illustrates how Chinese handlers routinely provide shopping lists of specific technologies they are looking for. Shredded documents recovered by the FBI urged Mak to "attend more seminars on special subject matters" and micromanaged his spying efforts by listing technologies of special interest that included "torpedoes, aircraft-carrier electronics, and a 'space-launched magnetic levitational platform.'"

And here's the scariest sleeper agent part: Both Mak and Chung were quietly living in the United States for *decades* as naturalized citizens. And little did any of us know, they were on a mission to betray their adopted country and deliver some of America's most technologically advanced weapons systems to the enemy.

In fact, this kind of spycraft is the very definition of high treason and should have made Mak and Chung eligible for the death penalty. However, that charge was never made, and, in a troubling pattern of light sentencing for Chinese spycraft by the U.S. justice system, they were given sentences of 24 and 15 years, respectively.

This is what really puzzles us the most about Chinese spying in America: U.S. judges and juries don't seem to take it seriously—much less recognize we are in an undeclared state of war. Indeed, time after time, the result has been prison sentences for Chinese espionage that offer little or no deterrent to selling out the United States—for example, the aforementioned Kwon Hwan Park landed a laughable 32-month prison sentence for multiple technology thefts that put the lives of American soldiers and the citizens of our allies in Japan, Taiwan, and Korea at extreme risk.

And please take note: It's not just Asians with names like Moo and Park and Chinese-Americans like Mak and Chung that are selling out America to the Chinese. How about Glenn Shriver?

The case of this not-so-favorite son of Grand Rapids, Michigan, illustrates just how aggressive China can be in recruiting foreign agents. Shriver was a U.S. student abroad plucked right off a campus in Shanghai; and he eventually tried to penetrate the CIA while under the direction and pay of his Chinese spymasters. Demonstrating just how cheap treason can be these days, Shriver was given a mere slap on the wrist: a 4-year sentence.

10

Death by Red Hacker: From Chengdu's "Dark Visitors" to Manchurian Chips

Cyber espionage is the great equalizer. Countries no longer have to spend billions of dollars to build globe-spanning satellites to pursue high-level intelligence gathering when they can do so via the web.
—Shadows in the Cloud

While China's human spy network relentlessly "vacuums" whatever secrets it can from whatever American university campuses, businesses, research labs, and government offices its agents can penetrate, China's growing cadres of computer hackers arguably pose an equal, and perhaps even greater, threat.

To date, China's "Red Hacker" brigades have infiltrated NASA, the Pentagon, and the World Bank; hit the U.S. Commerce Department's Bureau of Industry and Security so hard it had to trash hundreds of computers; emptied the hard drives of the Lockheed Martin F-35 Joint Strike Fighter project; and virtually carpet-bombed the U.S. Air Force's air traffic control system. They have also hacked the computers of reform-minded Congressmen as well as the House Foreign Affairs Committee.

During the 2008 Presidential campaign, Beijing's Red Hacker brigades even broke into the email servers of both the Obama and McCain campaigns as well as the Bush White House. And in one of

137

the most brazen breeches of diplomatic protocol, the laptops of the United States Commerce Secretary and several of his staff were kidnapped and loaded with spy software during a trade mission to Beijing.

In addition, while traditional spycraft has often relied on the "honeypot trap"—a Mata Hari mistress to extract secrets during pillow talk or a lady of the night to put potential marks into compromising positions—China's virtual spymasters are now using a new variety of digital "honeypots" to hijack data from computers. Indeed, beyond the usual prostitutes and bugged hotel rooms in Shanghai, China's agents are now offering virus-laden memory cards and even whole digital cameras as gifts. According to Britain's MI5 secret service department, when attached to the victim's computers, these nefarious digital honeypots install software that allows hackers to take control.

In fact, being a hacker in China is "sort of like being a rock star," says China-hacking expert and author of *The Dark Visitor*, Scott Henderson. It's even a career that reportedly up to one-third of Chinese school kids aspire to.

Like an online mirror of China's distributed spy network, large cadres of amateurs handle much of the grunt work in what is a massive cyberwarfare effort. Every day, thousands of these so-called "hacktivists" continually probe, vandalize, and rob the institutions of the West—as well as Asian rivals like Japan and India.

In considering the extent of the Chinese cyberwarfare threat, it is first useful to identify the major goals of cyberespionage. The simplest is to disrupt the operations of Western systems by vandalizing websites or by overwhelming the servers with a "denial of service" attack.

A second obvious goal is to steal valuable information: credit card numbers and identities at the individual level; technologies, bid documents, corporate financials, and trade secrets at the industrial level; and weapons systems at the military level.

Still a third goal of cyberwarfare is to corrupt data in a way that causes significant downstream damage. For instance, by compromising stock or bond market trading systems, China's Red Hacker brigades might disrupt trading, manipulate transactions, or skew reports and thereby incite a financial panic.

Finally, hackers can impact the real world by taking control of systems that control physical assets. For example, a team of Chinese cyberpatriots might shut down the electricity grid of New England to "punish" America for an action like welcoming the Dalai Lama to the White House or selling arms to Taiwan.

Beijing's Dark Visitors Salute the Flag

Question: Under what circumstances will you perform a hack?

Answer: If it is a matter that affects us internationally, then we will gather members to perform the attack.

—Chinese Hackers Talk Hacker information security conference

What all the major activities of China's Red Hacker brigades have in common is that they are conducted at arm's length and under the loose supervision of China's Communist Party. Of course, the Party maintains its distance precisely so it can always issue a plausible denial for whatever outrage bubbles up to the surface—a bold hack on the Pentagon, the hijacking of a big chunk of the Internet for 18 minutes, an attack on Google's source code, and so on.

But make no mistake about it. China's so-called "hacktivist" militia would not exist but for the guiding hand of Beijing. As James Mulvenon at the Center for Intelligence Research and Analysis explains, "These young hackers are tolerated...provided that they do not conduct attacks inside of China. They are sort of useful idiots for the Beijing regime."

"Useful idiots" indeed. While Los Angeles has its infamous "Crips" and "Bloods," China's hacktivist militia has organized into thousands of small groups with names like "Green Army Corps," "the Crab Group," and even all-girl ensembles like "Six Golden Flowers." They work together to improve their skills, share tools and techniques, and inflame each other's nationalistic passions. Combined, these cybergangs form an amorphous ideological-driven coalition with colorful names like the "Honkers."

China even has hundreds of "hacking schools" to teach young computer whizzes the dark arts. Large professional ads for cyberespionage training and tools may be found in public places, and, says Wang Xianbing of hackerbase.com, they "teach students how to hack into unprotected computers and steal personal information." Meanwhile, China's central government allows groups like the China Hacker Union to openly operate and even keep business offices while ripping off foreigners—so long as they don't hack into domestic Chinese sites or software.

Lest anyone doubt that China's hacktivists operate under the protection of the central government, consider that China has the most heavily controlled and surveilled Internet in the world. The idea that any rogue hacker could exist for any extended period within China and beyond the reach of Beijing's army of censors is patently absurd.

In fact, whenever a hacker group breaks Beijing's biggest unwritten rule—never attack the Chinese government—retribution is swift and sure. For example, when several members of a hacker group exploited a hole in China's Green Dam censorship software—an important tool used by Beijing to spy on Chinese Internet users—the hackers were promptly arrested. So, too, was a hacker from Hubei Province who, according to the *China Daily*, replaced "a picture of an official on a government website with a girl in a bikini." This cyberprankster got off light by Chinese standards—only a year and a half in prison.

Of course, it is precisely these kinds of occasional crackdowns that keep China's Red Hacker brigades focused on foreign institutions and governments. And these brigades can always be whipped up quickly into a nationalistic frenzy with just a wink and a nod from the Communist Party leadership.

Here's just one "in your digital face" case in point: When Japanese Prime Minister Junichiro Koizumi visited the Yasukuni military memorial—which Chinese nationalists see as a temple for war criminals—Chinese hackers defaced the website of this Shinto shrine with a message signed, "the girl pissing on the Yasukuni toilet." The Honkers Union then followed up with a wave of attacks on a dozen Japanese government sites, including the Fire and Disaster Management Agency and the Defense Facilities Administration Agency.

Now, can you imagine the response from the Chinese government if Japanese hackers had done something like that to China's website for the Olympic games or to the computers of China's Ministry of National Defense? And neither is it just Japan that must endure the periodic wrath of China's cyber über nationalists. When the annual Melbourne film festival in Australia dared to screen a documentary about a Chinese Uyghur leader, Chinese hackers so damaged the website that online ticket sales became impossible.

Beijing's Big League Hackers Take on Techno King Google

If Google with all its cyberresources and expertise is worried about keeping cyberspies out of its crown jewels—its source code—can other Fortune 500 companies reasonably expect to protect theirs?

—The Christian Science Monitor

To see into the devious mind of the Chinese hacker, it's useful to examine more closely the infamous "Operation Aurora." This was the systematic attack on one of the most sophisticated tech companies in the world—Google—along with more than 200 other American firms, from Adobe, Dow Chemical, and DuPont to Morgan Stanley and Northrup Grumman. It was also a hack conducted by what the security firm iDefense called "a single foreign entity consisting either of agents of the Chinese state or proxies thereof."

In Operation Aurora, China's "dark visitors"—a translation of the Chinese term for hacker, "heike"—set up a sophisticated cyberassault. They did so by first befriending employees of target firms via popular social networking sites like Facebook, Twitter, and LinkedIn. After initiating chat sessions, China's cyberspies then lured their new social networking friends into visiting a photo-sharing site that was a front for a Chinese malware installer. Once firm employees took this bait, their computers were infected with viral code that captured and forwarded the employees' usernames and passwords to the hackers. Beijing's hacktivists then used this stolen information to access large amounts of valuable corporate data—including Google's prized source code.

Of course, it wasn't just Google's source code the hackers were after. True to the Orwellian nature of the Chinese state, they also sought to access the Google email accounts of various Chinese human rights activists.

Predictably, the Chinese government denied culpability. However, an analysis of the Internet Protocol addresses of the perpetrators revealed they were from a college closely associated with the Chinese military. As an even more damning indictment of Communist Party complicity, WikiLeaks cables show that the specific attacks on Google "were orchestrated by a senior member of the Politburo who typed his own name into the global version of the search engine and found articles criticizing him personally."

A Pattern of Violence

Beyond Operation Aurora, there have been numerous other instances of highly damaging Chinese cyberattacks. One groundbreaking case in point is the "Night Dragon" affair. This attack was uncovered by the Internet security firm, McAfee, and it was directed against major Western energy firms.

This attack was groundbreaking because it was *not* a typical hacker effort designed to steal credit card numbers or randomly damage servers. Rather, it was a carefully planned and executed plot to gain control of the computers and email accounts of top company executives, with the ultimate targets being critical internal documents on operations, finance, and bidding.

Why did the Chinese government want this information? Because it is of great value to China's numerous state-owned enterprises competing globally against foreign rivals in the energy sector.

To understand the strategic objective of Night Dragon is to understand that China is indeed actively conducting economic warfare across the globe. In fact, hardly a month goes by now without another huge Chinese data burglary coming to light in America, Japan, Taiwan, or Europe.

We can only imagine how many plots have gone undetected and what the cost has been to Western and other Asian economies. And with each new and bold attack, it is becoming extremely difficult to understand why the governments of the United States, Europe, Japan, India, and other virtually assaulted nations don't respond firmly to China's cyberwarfare.

Hijacking the Global Internet for Who Knows What

For 18 minutes in April, China's state-controlled telecommunications company hijacked 15% of the world's Internet

*traffic, including data from U.S. military, civilian organiza-
tions, and those of other U.S. allies. This massive redirection of
data has received scant attention in the mainstream media
because the mechanics of how the hijacking was carried out
and the implications of the incident are difficult for those outside the cybersecurity community to grasp.*

—*National Defense* magazine

Yet another tool that China's Red Hacker brigades have in their bag of tricks is so-called "route hijacking." Using this technique, China has already brazenly demonstrated to the world its ability to seize control of a significant share of the global Internet.

Such route hijacking also illustrates the complicity of China's state-owned enterprises in Beijing's cyberwarfare campaigns. For example, by configuring their domestic Internet routers to falsely advertise a "shortcut" to potential Internet traffic, the state-owned firm China Telecom tricked a huge volume of data outside of China into being routed through its network. Of course, after this now infamous—but lightly reported—18-minute hijacking, the Chinese government coughed up the usual "Who me?" denial.

A DNS SOS on Chinese Hijacking

*If you live outside of China and by chance query a root name-
server hosted in China, your queries will pass through what is
known as The Great Firewall, potentially subjecting you to
the same censorship imposed on Chinese citizens.*

—Earl Zmijewski

Just what is Mr. Zmijewski talking about? It's a problem known as DNS manipulation, and what it means is that China can now even censor Internet users *outside* its Great Firewall.

DNS is short for "Domain Name Services," and it is these DNS entries that make up the "phonebook" of the Internet. DNS manipulation occurs when incomplete DNS data is used to block Internet users in other parts of the world from getting to websites that the Communist party has "unfriended."

To see how China's DNS manipulation has the potential to project its domestic censorship efforts beyond its borders, suppose you are a Facebook user in a country like the United States or Chile. At one point, you try to access Facebook, but you can't get to the site. Maybe you figure there's just too much Internet traffic and you'll try later. But here is what might have really happened: Your query may have been routed to a Chinese server that claimed to replicate a "root" DNS server in Sweden. The problem, of course, is that the Chinese server only replicated the parts of the Internet that Big Brother in Beijing wanted people to see—and that didn't include Facebook.

What such DNS manipulation means is that China's Internet censorship now extends well beyond its borders; and the situation will only grow worse as China tries to claim more administrative authority on the Internet.

Nor is this is a small problem. Because of the global nature of the Internet, on any given day, it is entirely possible that your normal requests for Internet addresses may be routed through China. In fact, over half of the Internet networks worldwide query a Chinese DNS server in any given year. The likelihood of your requested site coming back as "not found" because of Chinese censorship is only increasing. This is because rather than opening the Internet more and more as China claims it is doing, its list of censored websites is actually ever-growing.

As a final observation on the dangers of China's DNS manipulation, it was actively used in response to anti-government protests following the upheaval in Egypt. In fact, during this period of social unrest, DNS manipulation, along with other techniques, was used to block the business social networking site LinkedIn as well as searches and websites containing the words "Egypt," "Jasmine," and the name of the U.S. ambassador to China, "Huntsman."

With tongue firmly in cheek, we strongly suggest China's cyber-cops switch soon from a blacklist of websites to a "whitelist," because the list of sites they allow to be visited might soon be smaller than the ones they block.

Is Hacking the Dalai Lama Bad Karma?

After a 10-month cyberespionage investigation, researchers have found 1,295 computers in 103 countries with software that is capable of stealing information from high-profile targets such as the Dalai Lama and government agencies around the world...The attacks have been traced back to computers in China.

—HotHardware.com

Besides stealing weapons systems from the Pentagon and industrial and military secrets from companies like DuPont, Northrop Grumman, and Google, China's Red Hacker brigades can also be mobilized to help crush any dissent either within or outside of China's borders. Just consider what happened to the computers of the exiled Dalai Lama and his supporters during protests in Tibet. In these attacks, so-called "phishing" emails were sent to both the Tibetan Government in Exile in Dharamsala, India as well as to offices in London and New York. The authentic-looking messages encouraged the recipients to open documents that were infected with a Trojan virus labeled the "Gh0st Rat."

Once opened, Gh0st Rat took full control of the user's Windows environment, replicated itself to other PCs, and began to scan the systems for documents that it then delivered to servers in Sichuan province, China. In some cases, the malware began to monitor the user's keystrokes and may have even commandeered webcams and microphones to record and transmit conversations in the rooms of infected systems.

These Gh0st Rat hacks also infected computers in the foreign ministries and embassies of South Korea, India, Germany, and 100 other nations; and experts analyzing the attacks and working in the dark underground of Chinese hacking forums were able to trace the source to Chengdu and even to particular individuals at the University of Electronic Science and Technology. Of course, the Chinese government took no action to stop the cyberattacks, much less locate the perpetrators. Nor did Beijing offer any response short of the usual denials.

Again, we must ask: Why are the governments of countries like the United States, India, and Japan putting up with these blatant acts of cyberwarfare?

The Manchurian Candidate Has a Chip in His Shoulder

Computer hackers in China…have penetrated deeply into the information systems of U.S. companies and government agencies, stolen proprietary information from American executives in advance of their business meetings in China, and, in a few cases, gained access to electric power plants in the United States, possibly triggering two recent and widespread blackouts in Florida and the Northeast.
—*The National Journal*

Just consider this scenario: A Chinese engineer designs a remote control "backdoor" into a computer's operating system or, alternatively, a "kill switch" into a complex, custom computer chip that is not obviously detectable. China then exports these secretly embedded "Manchurian" chips and backdoors to the United States, where they become part of larger systems that perform their normal functions.

Meanwhile, just as in the movie *The Manchurian Candidate*, these Manchurian devices await some kind of signal that allows Beijing to either shut down or take control of the equipment—perhaps a critical system like an electricity grid, a metropolitan subway system, or a GPS tracking device.

Lest you think this is science fiction, planting such Manchurian chips is remarkably easy to do—particularly by a country that has become the world's factory floor. Planting such bugs in computers is easy because modern software programs can have millions of lines of code. Embedding Manchurian instructions in microchips for our computers and phones and iPods—and security systems!—is equally easy because such chips can contain hundreds of millions of logic gates in which to hide a digital surprise.

Now, if you doubt such things can actually sneak by inspection, we've got news for you. Software engineers and chip designers hide things in their work all the time just for kicks. A classic example is that of a Merlin the magician insert; it pops up whenever an arcane series of actions are taken in Adobe Photoshop. Even the main character from the book *Where's Waldo?* was rendered at a mere 30 microns onto a microprocessor by a prankster engineer.

The broader point is that finding such Manchurian surprises in a source code or computer chip isn't generally part of the quality assurance process used to test subcomponents from China. All inspectors try to do—even military inspectors—is ensure that when you take the product out of the box, it behaves within the specifications that it was designed to operate in. As Princeton electrical engineering professor Ruby Lee has explained, "You don't check for the infinite possible things that are not specified."

The fact that Chinese hackers have the capability to implant Manchurian chips is particularly distressing because most computers today from Hewlett-Packard, Dell, and Apple are now made in China—in fact, most of them are assembled at the same mega-factory in Shenzhen. Moreover, China is where your very own Windows or Mac operating system was most likely loaded—along with many other software application programs you may use.

Again, we want to stress that this is not some *X-Files* fantasy or off-the-wall conspiracy theory. In fact, America itself pioneered precisely this kind of Manchurian chip warfare long ago during the Cold War with the Soviet Union. And here's a classic case in point.

According to the CIA's own website, President Reagan personally informed the CIA of a valuable KGB double agent known as "Farewell" who had revealed how the Soviets were obtaining important Western technology. Instead of simply shutting off the leaks, policy advisor Gus Weiss devised a clever ruse, the result of which was to plant "contrived computer chips" into Soviet military equipment.

That these kinds of contrived Manchurian chips can cause great damage is illustrated by what has been described as the largest non-nuclear explosion in history. It occurred in 1982 when a remote section of the Soviet Union's vital Trans-Siberian Pipeline exploded into a huge fireball. It was subsequently revealed that the cause of this blast was bogus pipeline control software that CIA counterintelligence had first sabotaged and then intentionally left for the Soviets to "steal" from a Canadian firm. How's that for clever?

Writ large, the CIA-engineered Trans Siberian explosion is the poster child for the dark art of escalating cyberdamage into the real world. With more and more computers configured as the semi-autonomous controllers of everything from medical infusion pumps to nuclear power plants, human lives are becoming increasingly dependent on silicon and software.

In fact, Beijing's hacktivists may already have destabilized our national electricity grid not once but several times. According to the *National Journal*, there is evidence that a Chinese hacker may have helped trigger "the largest blackout in North American history," one in which an estimated 50 million people were affected.

More broadly, according to a senior U.S. intelligence official quoted in *The Wall Street Journal*, "the Chinese have attempted to map our infrastructure, such as the electrical grid," and these infiltrations have left behind software "that could be used to destroy infrastructure components." There is no doubt in this official's mind that "if we go to war with them, they will try to turn them on."

Our point, then, is a simple one: Manchurian chips are all too real. With so many American companies moving so much of our computer hardware and software production—and even research and development—right into the heart of China, we may very well be setting ourselves up not just for importing Chinese products but a wide array of Manchurian chips.

In weighing all the ever-mounting evidence on Chinese cyber-warfare and espionage, the ultimate policy question is whether we are going to consider China's "hacks" as the acts of war they really are—or whether we are simply going to keep sticking our heads in the sand and see no Red Hacker brigade evil. In considering that question, please remember the warning of General James Cartwright, the former head of U.S. Strategic Command and former vice chairman of the Joint Chiefs of Staff. To Cartwright, the impacts of a well-executed and broadly based cyberattack "could, in fact, be in the magnitude of a weapon of mass destruction."

11

Death by Darth Liu: Look Ma, There's a Death Star Pointing at Chicago

We are devoted to the peaceful use of space and are ready to extend out cooperation to other countries.

—President Hu Jintao

If anyone wanted to know what the Japanese were planning to do in the 1930s, all they had to do was read their plans and training documents. These plans were then being executed across the Asia-Pacific region. Many in America viewed claims about the increasing threat of the Japanese military as preposterous because they were committed to a peaceful rise. The Chinese are claiming a peaceful rise as well, coupled with a large increase in their armed forces and weapons. All that is needed now, as then, is to take a hard look at the policy and doctrine of the Peoples' Liberation Army...with respect to [their] space capabilities and armed forces and what they plan to do, which is to counter our space superiority.

—Christopher Stone, *Space Review*

Just as with its Earthly adventures, China claims it seeks only a "peaceful rise" into the heavens. However, one of the biggest questions facing the Pentagon right now is whether China's aggressive rise into space may turn out to be the ultimate weapon to bring America to its knees. This is a particularly important question in an era when the country that once sent a man to walk on the moon now has a space program that is at best on hold and at worst in shambles.

Make no mistake about it; China's space exploration program is particularly impressive and aggressive. Over the next several decades, it plans to send missions to both the moon and Mars, while last year alone, China launched 15 orbital payloads. This ambitious launch schedule made it the first nation to achieve launch parity with the United States; and China is on a clear trajectory to surpass America in sheer launch volume at just about the same time the U.S. completes its final Space Shuttle mission and shuts the program down.

As to exactly what China is launching into space, payloads range from observation satellites and additions to its global positioning system to manned space missions and a second lunar orbiter. China is also expected to launch its first space station module for both scientific and military purposes by 2012, while three flights in the next two years are expected to dock with that station. Moreover, by leveraging its manufacturing prowess, China is moving away from custom-designed spacecraft to those produced on an assembly line; and this innovation will allow it to dramatically increase flight rates.

. Even as China has soared, America's NASA space program— upon which so much of our critical national technological edge rests—has spent an entire decade lost in space. The troubled American Space Shuttle program was scheduled to end in 2010, but with flight delays and one added mission, it will retire sometime this year. After that, there is no clear plan for U.S. manned spaceflight. This is because the Obama administration and Congress remain at odds over both what should be the right mission and what methods should fulfill that mission.

What this political gridlock means is that there will be no U.S. government-operated, manned flights for at least 5 years. For the foreseeable future, that means American astronauts must hitch rides to the International Space Station with the Russians—even as China makes its aggressive lunar and space station pushes.

In light of this Tale of Two Space Programs heading in quite opposite directions, we come back to this question: Will this be a peaceful Chinese rise into the Heavens or a race to seize the ultimate high ground while the American space program remains all but grounded?

The Three Musketeers of Space Exploration

In the 2,900 cubic kilometers of [the asteroid] Eros, there is more aluminum, gold, silver, zinc, and other base and precious metals than have ever been excavated in history or indeed, could ever be excavated from the upper layers of the Earth's crust.

—BBC News

In support of the idea that China's space exploration program is merely an extension of its peaceful rise, there are at least three factors motivating China's aggressive program. The first is the development of the many and varied new technologies that invariably accompany space exploration. The second is the future extraction and transport of key energy sources and raw material resources from space to China's factories. The third is to act as a Darwinian safety valve for an overpopulated and rapidly warming planet. Each of these factors constitutes important reasons for civilian space exploration. Together, they can be used to paint a pastoral picture of China's space exploration efforts.

From GPS and Solar Power to CAT Scans

From this pastoral perspective, one of the most important reasons to engage in space exploration is a reason that America has totally lost sight of—the super boost that such exploration gives to the rate of technological innovation and economic growth in a country. What is remarkable here is how quickly America's political leaders have forgotten the role that space exploration provided in stimulating our economy—and improving our quality of life!—over the past 50 years.

Consider that, without NASA and our space program, we would likely not have today the Internet as we know it, our GPS network, all manner of solar power technologies, medical applications ranging from CAT scans and MRIs to needle breast biopsy, miracle plastics and lubricants, and a weather tracking system for hurricanes and wildfires that has saved hundreds of thousands of lives and billions of dollars while significantly boosting crop outputs. Together, these innovations alone have provided our economy with trillions of dollars in benefits. And let's not forget more mundane but no less useful inventions such as the "memory foam" for Tempur-Pedic mattresses.

While America has forgotten the importance of space exploration as an economic catalyst, China totally gets it. In fact, the head of China's lunar program, Ouyang Ziyuan, has explicitly stated that the Apollo moon effort drove the U.S. tech boom; and he frequently uses that as rationale for China going to the moon. It's not just more rapid innovation, however, that China will receive from its space program.

A Mining Cornucopia

What China also seeks in space is the valuable array of precious metals and raw materials that reside in the crusts of both the moon and numerous near-Earth asteroids. This bounty ranges from gold and platinum to extremely rare metals critical to high-tech manufacturing.

In fact, successful mining operations in space would do much to alleviate growing raw material shortages and the pollution associated with resource extraction. Consider, for example, Asteroid 433, otherwise known as Eros. Scientists writing in the journal *Nature* have predicted that in a fortunately distant future, this giant, 34-kiloton chunk of rock is likely to hit our planet and cause a disaster bigger than the impact that wiped out the dinosaurs some 65 million years back. The good news, however, is that Eros is jam-packed with all manner of mineral wealth just waiting for some enterprising space station to extract. Moreover, with its light gravity and a total lack of environmental constraints, extracting raw materials from Eros with freely available solar energy would be relatively simple once the transportation is in place. Nor is this completely sci-fi, as a NASA space probe visited Eros in the year 2000 and landed on it in 2001.

And here's a radical idea that has been proposed by private space entrepreneur Jim Benson for both avoiding the calamity of a collision with Earth and getting Eros's mineral bounty back to our planet: Attach rockets to the asteroid to gently adjust its orbit. In this way, it would eventually be possible to bring Eros into a steady position within our Earth-moon system and thereby eliminate any threat of a collision. Of course, this scenario begs the question as to who will get there first and plant their flag—and steering rockets—on resources like Eros.

Nor is it just raw materials like aluminum, gold, and zinc that China may seek in space. From the Chinese perspective, the even bigger lunar prize in the shorter term may well be realizing the enormous potential of nuclear fusion energy. Unlike the current problematic nuclear fission power plants, fusion energy would be both clean and safe and truly be "too cheap to meter." And here's the lunar connection: An ingredient that many physicists believe could bring fusion within reach is Helium 3—an extremely rare isotope thought to be abundant on the moon.

As China's moon czar has framed the potential of Helium 3: "Each year, three space shuttle missions could bring enough fuel for all human beings across the world." Mr. Ouyang might well have added that the successful development of fusion energy from moon-based materials would be a death blow to the OPEC oil cartel and a magic bullet against global warming.

Chinese visionaries like Ouyang also see the moon as offering a free and virtually nightless environment in which to generate solar power up to eight times more efficiently and then beam it back to Earth. Science fiction, you say? Yes, indeed. Just like walking on the moon or talking to anyone anywhere on Earth from a handheld device.

And speaking of walking on the moon, it is perfectly understandable why the Chinese space program is aggressively targeting the moon with two successful orbital probes and planned robotic and manned landings for peaceful purposes. What is disconcerting, however, to American private enterprise space entrepreneurs like billionaire Robert Bigelow, is that while China is busy preparing to plant flags on the moon, America spins its wheels. As Bigelow warns:

> By the time the Chinese began to systematically do this around the key locations on the moon, it is probably too late for other countries to put together expeditions to head off complete ownership of the water, ice, and all the valuable areas.

A Darwinian Escape

Besides serving as a catalyst for technological innovation and a fecund source of energy and natural resource extraction, space exploration also provides a potentially important safety valve in an era of overpopulation and climate change. If you think this, too, is science fiction, think again. As NASA Administrator Michael Griffin has observed:

> [T]he goal isn't just scientific exploration...it's also about extending the range of human habitat out from Earth into the solar system as we go forward in time...In the long run a single-planet species will not survive. We have ample evidence of that.

This is a sentiment shared by physicist Stephen Hawking as well when he tapped out the following on his computer: "Our only chance of long-term survival is not to remain inward looking on planet Earth but to spread out into space."

Of course, colonizing the moon, Mars, and beyond will take many decades. However, one of the advantages that China has over America is its ability to focus on the long term and think in terms of generations rather than individuals. Because of this long-term view, at this point in time, China has a much higher probability of successfully colonizing the best real estate in space than any other country. The question we come back to is whether China's seizure of the ultimate high ground will be used strictly for peaceful purposes or, instead, to also help subdue rivals. It is a question to which we now turn as we look first at China's growing arsenal of defensive weapons and then its plans for offensive weapon capabilities.

China's Space Warfare Epiphany—The Best Defense Is a Good Defense

Outer space is going to be weaponized in our lifetime.
—Senior Colonel Yao Yunzhu, PLA Academy of
    Military Sciences

Perhaps the best evidence of China's intentions to militarize and weaponize space may be found in the surprising abundance of open source literature on space warfare published by various Chinese military officers and strategists. From "plasma attacks against low-orbit satellites" and "kinetic kill vehicles" to "beam weapons" and "orbital ballistic missiles," the common thread of this literature—much of which has been well analyzed by the U.S.–China Commission—is the destruction or subjugation of American military forces through the exploitation of the commanding heights of space.

Here, for example, is the decidedly unpacifist vision of Colonel Li Daguang from his book *Space Warfare*. Besides advocating the

integration of civilian and military uses for China's space programs for
economic reasons, Li sees the optimal military strategy as one that
will do the following:

> *Destroy or temporarily incapacitate all enemy satellites above
> our territory, [deploy] land based and space based anti-
> satellite weapons, counter US missile defense systems, main-
> tain our good international image [by covert deployment and
> keep] space strike weapons concealed and launched only in
> time of crisis.*

The very existence of published writings such as these in a tightly
censored Communist world is curious. Not only do they openly con-
tradict the official position of China's civilian leadership, but they very
much confound the ability of Pentagon analysts to figure out just
exactly what is going on behind the bamboo curtain—and what
America's response should be.

One possibility is that this wealth of literature describing all manner of ways to bring Uncle Sam to its knees is simply a ruse to prod
America into an expensive space arms race. The other possibility is
that the threats made by the likes of Colonel Li are very real; and,
absent an adequate response, America is leaving itself vulnerable to
either a Pearl Harbor-style space attack or a *fait accompli* surrender.

Either way, one thing is clear: The United States unquestionably
still holds the strategic high ground of space today. What is very much
in question, however, is who will hold that strategic high ground in
the many tomorrows that will follow.

From that high ground, both the U.S. economy and the military
depend heavily on a complex network of more than 400 orbiting
satellites that provide everything from reconnaissance and navigation
to communication and telemetry. It is precisely this impressive network that gives America's fighting forces nearly preternatural power
in the eyes of their adversaries.

Using the vantage point of space and its numerous advantages in
high-tech weaponry, the U.S. has been able to fight a number of wars

with decidedly asymmetrical casualties. While 150 Americans died in combat during the first Gulf War in 1991, anywhere from 30,000 to 56,000 Iraqi soldiers were killed. The same kind of asymmetric casualty rates were likewise in evidence in the American-coordinated NATO attack in 1999 during the Kosovo War as well as in the initial invasion campaign for the 2003 Iraq War.

Whatever your own views of these military actions by the United States, the "game changing" domination of space by the Americans has not gone unnoticed by China. In fact, the 1991 Gulf War is generally regarded in Pentagon circles as Beijing's wake-up call about how even the world's largest army, that of China, might be subdued by a numerically far smaller enemy.

To Kill or Blind, That Is the Chinese Question

As long as China's space program is in the hands of its generals, it will largely reflect the People's Liberation Army's strategic requirements. This was the case for the former Soviet Union, where the military also controlled the Soviet space program. As seen by its development of multiple anti-satellite weapons systems, its willingness to make military use of manned space programs, and its outright deceptions, China is increasingly following the Soviet example of seeking military dominance of outer space.

—Richard Fisher, StrategyCenter.net

From the Chinese perspective, there are at least two defensive measures that can be taken to counter the U.S. space advantage. One is to destroy part or all of our satellite constellations. The other— which achieves the same result without the explosions—is to simply blind our surveillance birds. That China is developing capabilities in both areas should be evident to anyone who bothers to look.

In the area of satellite destruction, China has already tested several ways to blow up—or literally kidnap—American satellites. This testing began with a big and messy bang in January 2007 when the Chinese military shot one of its own aging satellites out of the sky.

This apparently "ready for retirement" weather satellite had faithfully circled the globe several times a day for more than a decade; but it was easy prey for a modified DF-21 intercontinental ballistic missile that lifted off from the Xichang launch facility in Sichuan province. The missile threw out a kinetic kill vehicle that took on a collision course with the innocent target; and upon impact, the nuts, bolts, panels, and wires of the satellite together with thousands of fragments and pieces of the kinetic kill vehicle created our galaxy's largest mass of space junk.

Today, that field of Chinese space junk still remains a huge navigational hazard; China is apparently just as willing to pollute outer space as its own rivers and air basins. At risk from disastrous collisions with China's space junk are more than two-thirds of the nearly 3,000 satellites and craft in orbit. In fact, the list of potential victims includes the International Space Station and its crew, which has had to adjust its orbit at least once to avoid a dense part of the Chinese space hazard.

This is hardly the only sign that China is developing antisatellite or "ASAT" weapons capabilities to knock America's GPS out of the sky. In January 2010, Chinese space gunners shot down a suborbital target at an altitude of about 150 miles with a mobile launched, solid fuel missile and a new kinetic kill vehicle called the KT2. And note that the KT2 is a double threat technology—good for either ballistic missile defense or destroying orbital space systems.

Besides these weapons that could cause American satellites to go boom in the night, there is China's innovative new "Space Kidnapper." This weapon was tested in August of 2010 when two Chinese satellites had a secret rendezvous in space. The goal of the test was to see if one satellite could perform what is blandly called a "noncooperative robotic rendezvous" with the other. The world is still waiting to hear from China as to whether the test was a success—although ground observations clearly suggest it was. And if this technology truly works, just imagine a fleet of these kidnappers being dispensed to capture members of the U.S. satellite family.

Blinded by the Light—The Future's So Bright Our Satellites Need Shades

They let us see their lasers. It is as if they are trying to intimidate us.

—Gary Payton, Deputy Undersecretary of the
    U.S. Air Force for Space Programs

Of course, you don't have to obliterate or kidnap an American satellite to render it harmless. One other way that is both more elegant and possibly less provocative is to either temporarily "dazzle" or simply blind the satellite. In this arena, China likewise is developing deadly capabilities.

In fact, China's provocative demonstration of this kind of capability began more than five years ago in the fall of 2006. As reported in the highly respected *Jane's Defence Weekly*, during this time, U.S. spy satellites experienced a "sudden decline in effectiveness" as they "passed over China." At the same time, telescopes at the Reagan Test Site on Kwajelein Atoll, in the South Pacific, were able to detect the reflected laser light to confirm the cause and Chinese origin.

More broadly, *The Economist* magazine reports, "The Chinese routinely turn powerful lasers skywards, demonstrating their potential to dazzle or permanently blind spy satellites." The U.S. response has, however, been muted—in large part because of the budget constraints now facing an American military preoccupied with wars in other theaters.

Of course, for China's neighbors like Japan and Taiwan, the potential loss of the space infrastructure supporting the U.S. Navy's unfettered access to the Western Pacific is simply terrifying.

From Buck Rogers to Beijing's Orbital Nukes

China looks set to pull ahead in the Asian space race to the moon, putting a spacecraft into lunar orbit Oct. 6 in a preparatory mission for an unmanned moon landing in two or three years...The mission, called Chang'e 2 after a heroine from Chinese folklore who goes to the moon with a rabbit, highlights China's rapidly growing technological prowess... China's moonshot, like all space programs, has valuable potential military offshoots. China's space program is controlled by the People's Liberation Army, which is steadily gaining experience in remote communication and measurement, missile technology, and antisatellite warfare through missions like Chang'e 2.
—The Christian Science Monitor

While using outer space as an observation point to track U.S. military movements and disabling the American satellite systems are important *defensive* goals of the Chinese space program, the real prize may be using space as an *offensive* weapons platform. Options run the gamut from boulders hurled off the moon with enough energy to destroy a metropolis on Earth, EMP pulse bombs designed to disable our electronic infrastructure, and directed energy weapons fired from space to orbiting H-bombs and space planes capable of raining nuclear death on any city in the world.

In fact, if China were to drop a nuclear bomb from space, it would be infinitely more effective than lobbing that same warhead from a rocket out of the Gobi Desert. This is because earth-launched rockets have distinctive heat signatures that allow early detection and long trajectories that allow for tracking and interception. On the other hand, an orbital nuclear bomb needs only an undetectable jet of compressed air to drop from the silence of space. It then uses gravity to rapidly cover the short 200 miles or so to the Earth's surface while such an attack route is virtually undetectable—until it is too late.

To support the offensive capabilities of its space exploration program, China is building a massive infrastructure of space assets. These include a growing fleet of huge space tracking ships; new spaceports and ground stations; dozens of new communications, relay, and surveillance satellites; and last, but hardly least, an extremely expensive Global Positioning System of its own.

China's GPS is known as Beidou, and it is named after the Big Dipper Constellation, whose tail has long given mariners an arrow to the North. The fact that China is launching its own GPS to rival that of the United States is strongly suggestive of China's militaristic intentions. After all, the United States offers its GPS free to the world, and there is no reason for any other country to undertake the tremendous expense of developing its own system—unless it intends to destroy the American GPS system or otherwise engage the United States in military conflict.

It's not like we haven't been warned about China's offensive weapons space threat. In January 2001, a space security commission appointed by the House and Senate Armed Services Committees concluded that America is at serious risk of a "Space Pearl Harbor" and that strategic planning to counter developing offensive capabilities in China (and Russia) is urgently required. As with so many other warnings, the recommendations of this report were inadequately addressed in the wake of 9/11, as America's military and intelligence operations refocused toward tactical threats from primitive enemies.

The Taiwan End Game:
Anti-Access/Area Denial

"[The] goal of a space shock and awe strike is [to] deter the enemy, not to provoke the enemy into combat. For this reason, the objectives selected for a strike must be few and precise... This will shake the structure of the opponent's operational system of organization and will create huge psychological impact on the opponent's policymakers."
—Colonel Yuan Zelu, People's Liberation Army

Colonel Yuan has truculently described China's vision of a Space Pearl Harbor for us. He and many of China's more hawkish leaders dangerously view their antisatellite weapons, GPS-blinding lasers, and orbiting nuclear bombs along with their antiship ballistic missiles, extensive submarine fleet, cyber weaponry, and forms of economic warfare as active chess pieces in a game designed to achieve a surprise political checkmate over America while avoiding any retaliation from the qualitatively superior U.S. forces and weaponry.

Taken in their totality, China's growing five-dimensional array of air-, land-, sea-, cyber-, and space-based weaponry supports a strategy referred to in Pentagon circles as anti-access/area denial, or A2/AD. Its goal is to deny the U.S. Navy and Marines access to the coastal waters of China so that China can project its power into the region.

Of course, if China's five-dimensional war machine can drive U.S. naval forces out past the so-called "second island chain," which is an imaginary line running from Japan through Guam down to Indonesia, China's civilian government can pretty much tell Japan, Korea, Taiwan, and Vietnam how things are going to run and how resources are going to be divided up. This is a chilling development, particularly for Taiwan, because once China's A2/AD strategy is fully operational, the little island of free Chinese has little hope of remaining independent from the mainland.

Why? Because current U.S. strategy is all about *preventing* Chinese military forces from taking Taiwan by using our aircraft carrier groups as a deterrent. If America's Pacific Fleet is, in fact, driven back past the second island chain, Chinese military forces will be able to easily overwhelm Taiwan's defenses with their thousands of missiles and massive troop strength. After that, the United States has no real plan or conceivable option to *retake* the island from Chinese forces dug in among the civilians. It's the sort of situation that Captain James T. Kirk once famously described with gallows' humor as: "We've got them just where they want us!"

These kinds of observations bring us back to the question: Is China's rise into space really going to be a peaceful one? A more detailed look at what China is actually sending up into space provides even more fuel for the militaristic fire.

Lock the Doors on the Space Station! The Chinese Are Coming

On September 27th, a Chinese Shenzhou space capsule came within 45 kilometers of the International Space Station, and two of the three crewmen made the first Chinese space walk (going outside the spacecraft in their space suits). Later, a small, 88-pound microsatellite (the BX-1) was released from the Shenzhou. This was supposed to be a science experiment, but the fact that the Shenzhou came so close to the International Space Station, and then released a smaller, maneuverable (via small gas jets) BX-1, indicated another satellite destruction drill. The BX-1 could easily have been directed at the nearby space station, and destroyed it.

—James Dunnigan, StrategyPage.com

Each time China launches one of its manned Shenzhou space capsules, it also puts up a large, cylindrical, autonomously operating orbital module. Each module is about eight by nine feet; and because of an utter lack of transparency in the Chinese space program, the rest of the world has absolutely no idea what these modules contain. Is it nuclear bombs? Spying equipment? Or maybe it's just some more purple space potatoes or an innocuous ginseng plant experiment. Who knows?

Here's what we do know, at least about one of those Shenzhou missions. This incident once again illustrates the kind of in-your-face tactics of a country that would have run over Gandhi with a tank—twice to make its point.

China's Shenzhou 7 mission not only sent up three of its astronauts, or taikonauts; it also carried a "microsatellite" named the BX-1. As part of the mission, the Shenzhou 7—where Shenzou translates as "divine vessel"—pulled a carefully planned but dangerously unannounced stunt typical of the China's war hawks. It was a "drive-by" buzz of the International Space Station by the orbiting space capsule.

Even more outrageous, China's taikonauts also released the BX-1 microsatellite just before that drive-by, presumably so it could do its own little spy run—or perhaps, as analyst James Dunnigan has suggested, conduct a simulated antisatellite weapons test. In the process, China violated the so-called "conjunction box" range where NASA mission controllers would have considered moving the station—if they had known it was coming.

To understand the consternation this caused at NASA, you have to understand that China's astronauts passed just 25 miles below the space station, and the mysterious little BX-1 may have come as close as 15 miles. When you are in an orbit more than 26,000 miles long in a vast 3-dimensional space and traveling at 18,000 miles per hour, that's infinitesimally close—and extremely dangerous.

To put an exclamation point on the possible dangers, China's state TV even announced during the flight that the 40 kilogram nanosatellite "had started drifting away from its intended trajectory." That was hardly comforting for the European and American astronauts sitting in a $100 billion aluminum can watching a Chinese spy satellite and a gaggle of snooping taikonauts get up close and personal.

Going Asymmetric on America's Military Might

A strong enemy with absolute superiority is certainly not without weakness...[Our] military preparations need to be more directly aimed at finding tactics to exploit the weaknesses of a strong enemy.
—*People's Liberation Army Daily*

Before leaving China's emerging threat from space, it's useful to put its growing defensive and offensive space weapons capabilities in a broader strategic context. In fact, the crown jewel of China's carefully laid-out military planning is its focus on so-called "asymmetric warfare."

Asymmetric warfare techniques typically play the weaker but more clever David role to a more physically or technologically superior Goliath. In China's case, faced with a significant technological disadvantage—and despite a huge troop advantage—Chinese strategists are constantly looking for surprising and inexpensive ways to disable, destroy, or otherwise defeat America's greatest technological strengths.

We saw, for example, one typical asymmetric warfare weapon in Chapter 8, "Death by Blue Water Navy." This was a relatively inexpensive antiship ballistic missile capable of sinking an American aircraft carrier—or at least scaring it back past the second island chain. Another example from this chapter is that of antisatellite weapons capable of taking down the American GPS and satellite communications grid. As the great Prussian military strategist Clausewitz once suggested, "If you entrench yourself behind strong fortifications, you compel the enemy to seek a solution elsewhere."

To get an idea how China's cheap weapons could, in the future, take out America's much more expensive technology, consider this gambit offered up in a Chinese military white paper entitled "Methods for Defeating GPS":

> *An ordinary inexpensive weather-monitoring rocket may carry a bomb containing a large amount of small lead shots into a designated orbit. Once exploded, the small lead shots will fly out with a relative velocity of 6.4 kilometers per second and destroy any satellite they encounter. When a few kilograms of gravel are thrown into orbit, they will attack the satellites like meteor showers and incapacitate the expensive GPS constellation.*

It is precisely these kinds of weapons and scenarios that China is developing that expose the lie to its claims of a peaceful rise. All of us outside of China must keep in mind that the very rhetoric of "peaceful rise" is purposely designed as a mask to hide China's true militaristic intentions. Colonel Jia Junming made this abundantly clear when he wrote this:

> *Our future space weapons program should be low profile and 'intense internally' but relaxed in external appearance to maintain our good international image and position.*

As the 2001 U.S. Space Commission warned: "We are on notice—but we have not noticed."

Part IV

A Hitchhiker's Guide to the Chinese Gulag

12

Death to a Big Planet: Do You Want to Be Fried with That Apocalypse?

China's environmental problems are mounting. Water pollution and water scarcity are burdening the economy, rising levels of air pollution are endangering the health of millions of Chinese, and much of the country's land is rapidly turning into desert.

—Foreign Affairs

This soot-blackened city of Linfen in China's inland Shanxi province makes Dickensian London look as pristine as a nature park. Shanxi is the heart of China's coal belt, and the hills around Linfen are dotted with mines, legal and illegal, and the air is filled with burning coal. Don't bother hanging your laundry—it'll turn black before it dries.

—Time

The Chinese people are not generally known for being stupid. But what China's business and government leaders are doing to the air, land, and waters of their country—with the tacit acceptance of much of the population—has to be one of the dumbest, most short-sighted, and self-destructive acts of mass violence against Mother Nature the world has ever witnessed. Whether it is the eye-stinging, throat-scratching, lung-busting toxic air pollution belching up from

171

China's factory floor, or the tsunami of cancerous chemicals and raw feces inundating great rivers like the Yellow and Yangtze, or the ubiquitous heavy metals, pesticide residues, and deadly "e-waste" marinating prime farmland or China's Long March of deforestation and desertification from the westernmost province of Xinjiang to the very gates of Beijing, it's becoming an ever more Silent Spring virtually year round.

Of course, Communist Party officials are wont to excuse their crimes against Mother Nature by arguing that their budding empire is still in a relatively early stage of its economic development. They insist that at least some environmental damage is to be expected before Red China makes the "inevitable" transition to Green China. And at least some "jobs now, environment later" party apparatchiks are quick to point out that when industrial America was first developing over a century ago, Pittsburgh was encased in a coal-encrusted shroud and Cleveland was a city where, if you couldn't walk on the water, you could at least set that water on fire.

Well, we hear that China. But China please hear this: Anything that America has ever done in its environmental history or that Victorian England ever did during the Industrial Revolution or that Brazil or Indonesia or Mexico or indeed any other big country anywhere today is now doing pales in comparison to the wholesale and retail environmental desecration now going on in China. And you don't have to be Al Gore to understand this inconvenient truth: Much of the environmental damage being done is not just irreversible; China's industrial "slash and burn" spillover effects are spreading quite literally like a cancer around the world.

It is because of this last observation that all of us outside of China must ultimately be concerned about the Chinese government's myopic willingness to wantonly trade off its air, water, and soil for 30 pieces of silver and a bigger global market share. For unlike in Las Vegas, "What happens in China *doesn't* stay in China." To bring this slogan right to our doorstep, consider that the toxic gases rising up like locusts from China's factory floor now befoul the air basins not just of Japan, Taiwan, and the Korean Peninsula but also of Los Angeles, San Francisco, and Denver.

Consider also, as Chapter 2, "Death by Chinese Poison," has graphically illustrated, that the bacteria, dioxins, heavy metals, and toxic pesticide residues that pollute the waters and soil of China are winding up in our apple juice, chicken, fish, garlic, honey, vitamins, and other foods and drugs that America imports from China.

And looking into our children's future, as air and water pollution, desertification, over-development, increasing soil toxicity, and climate change increasingly shrink or contaminate the Chinese harvests of key staples like wheat, rice, and soybeans, China will increasingly compete for food supplies from around the world—and prices will spike accordingly, from the village markets of Africa to the supermarkets of Europe to the food aisles of Walmart in America.

For all these reasons and many more—including China's role as the world's most egregious global warmer—all of us around the world need to clearly understand the "Tragedy of the Global Commons" now unfolding and confront China accordingly.

Don't It Make Our Blue Skies Brown

In America, we take city kids out to farms to show them cows and where milk comes from. In China, that's the same kind of trip many adults raised in industrial cities like Beijing, Chongqing, and Chengdu must take to realize that the sky is actually blue during the day and has stars out at night.

I learned this lesson firsthand on a humanitarian mission helping some urban Chinese doctors screen rural children for congenital heart defects and adults for hypertension. When these city mice got out to the countryside, they were amazed to actually see stars.

The funny part was that the air was still so polluted even in the mountains of Yunnan, that rather than witnessing the amazing spectacle of two thousand stars that awes an American child on a camping trip to Joshua Tree or Mount Washington, all we actually saw was the handful of twinkling smudges you'd catch most any night in Los Angeles.

—Greg Autry

Anybody who has traveled to China to see the Forbidden City, the Great Wall, or that great graveyard of democracy otherwise known as Tiananmen Square knows exactly what the problem is: You just shouldn't be able to see, taste—or have to choke on—the air you need to breathe. But that is the daily lot in life for hundreds of millions of chronically coughing Chinese citizens, most of whom really and truly have *no* idea that the sky can be a deep azure blue in the day and twinkle with a billion stars at night.

It's not just a blotted sky, however, that the Chinese people have to worry about when it comes to the ill effects of air pollution. According to a seminal World Bank study, such pollution kills a staggering 700,000 Chinese souls annually. That's roughly the equivalent of choking out the entire population of the city of San Francisco, the states of Wyoming or Delaware, the Canadian province of New Brunswick, or even the entire nation of Bahrain *every single year*.

Now parse this: In quintessential Orwellian fashion, when the World Bank's study first came out, Beijing's censors demanded this 700,000 corpse statistic be suppressed in the printed edition of the final report; these Communist Party hacks didn't claim it was untrue, simply that the grim findings might lead to social unrest. Indeed—and wouldn't it be about time?

And here's another mind-numbing statistic that isn't exactly a state secret either. The world's most populous nation features over 100 cities with over one million people; and virtually every one of these teeming masses of humanity is shrouded in a toxic haze of sulfur dioxide and lung-piercing particulates. Moreover, of the 20 largest cities in the world with the absolutely worst air pollution— Mexico City and Jakarta come achingly to mind—fully 16 of these gas mask-optional metropolises are in China.

Just why is the air in China so filthy? Simply because China relies on coal for 75% of its energy needs—with little serious effort to manage its coal use cleanly. Indeed, throughout China, coal is transported, burned, and disposed of with little pollution control technology and with even less regard for its impact on human or animal life. (One of us has even personally witnessed sites where ton upon ton of coal has slid into the Yangtze River from pathetically constructed cliff-side storage bins—which are then patched up with an equal lack of concern.)

It's not just that coal is China's choice for electricity generation. In many rural Chinese households, raw coal is still burned for cooking and heating—with little or no ventilation. And it is because of coal's ubiquity in the Chinese economy that it accounts for 90% of China's sulfur dioxide emissions—the principal ingredient of smog. High coal dependence is also the reason why China's air is heavily laden with particularly lethal particulate matter, which can deeply penetrate— and often lacerate—lung tissue.

As to why any of us should care if the citizens of China want to choke themselves to death, remember this: For every 100 tons of sulfur dioxide or particulate matter or deadly mercury the Dragon's factories belch into Chinese skies, thousands of pounds of these pollutants eventually reach vulnerable eyes, lungs, throats, and nervous systems in Japan, Korea, Taiwan, and, eventually, North America. It's not for nothing that you can wake up in Carson, California or Seattle, Washington and exclaim, "I hate the smell of China in the morning."

Water, Water Everywhere and Nary a Drop to Drink

America's three great rivers—the Colorado, Mississippi, and Ohio—are so filthy that it is dangerous to swim or eat fish caught in them. Parts of the Ohio River in Pittsburgh are so thick, dark, and soupy it looks like one could walk across it.

—FactsandDetails.com

You don't have to be a card-carrying member of the Sierra Club to know this quotation is phony. But once you replace "America" with "China," substitute the "Yangtze, Pearl, and Yellow" rivers for the "Colorado, Mississippi, and Ohio," and swap "Guangzhou" for "Pittsburgh," the environmental picture painted by the website FactsandDetails.com is all too real.

Nor do you have to be a member of the National Rifle Association to know that if the rivers and waterways in America were even a tenth as filthy as those in China, the good old U.S. of A. would literally be up in arms. In China, however, there is precious little being done to protect the most precious of its resources—water.

Frankly, we find this aspect of China's lack of environmental stewardship to be the most astonishing. With 20% of the planet's population, China has only 7% of the world's fresh water; and vast portions of the country—including over 100 cities—suffer from chronic drought. Despite such water scarcity, China's business and government brain trust has allowed 70% of all Chinese rivers, lakes, and streams and 90% of all Chinese groundwater to become severely polluted. Moreover, in industrial bastions like Shanxi, much of the river water is even too toxic to touch. Jeffrey Hayes offers this brief snapshot of a real movie playing out in rivers and lakes all across China:

Waters that used to teem with fish and welcome swimmers now have film and foam at the top and give off bad smells. Canals are often covered with layers of floating trash, with the deposits particularly thick on the banks. Most of it is plastic containers in a variety of sun-bleached colors.

Such damage is being done by a relentless torrent of *billions* of tons of largely untreated industrial waste, chemical fertilizers, and raw animal and human sewage that spew from everything from chemical factories, drug manufacturers, and fertilizer producers to tanneries, paper mills, and pig farms. Because of this relentless barrage of untreated wastes, a *billion* Chinese citizens must drink polluted water on a daily basis while at least 700 million of these chosen many must endure their potable water "seasoned" with human or animal wastes.

Meanwhile, the Liao River, which is the biggest river in southern Manchuria, is a monument to the maxim that the faster China grows, the further it gets behind in environmental protection. For even though the river's banks feature new water treatment facilities, these facilities have been utterly overwhelmed by ever-increasing pollution levels.

As to why so much pollution winds up in Chinese waters, here's just one typical "fly by night" scenario offered up by one of the "T-shirt kings" of Guangdong Province—Fuan Textiles. As chronicled by the *Washington Post*, Fuan's factory was shut down for illegally dumping 20,000 tons of waste that literally dyed the local river red. However, after unemployment rose, local government apparatchiks quietly encouraged Fuan to simply change its name and move to a new location.

In fact, China's horrific water pollution has added a whole new term to the lexicon of environmental disasters—the so-called "cancer village." Along the Huai River alone, there are more than 100 such cancer villages; and these beleaguered peasant backwaters feature esophageal, stomach, and intestinal cancer rates every bit as high as the death rates faced by American doughboys storming the beaches of Normandy.

And think about this: As recently as Mao's time, the Chinese people were very closely connected to the water. Today, however, even a reincarnated Chairman Mao—who loved to swim across the Yangtze—wouldn't be caught dead in it. In this same tawdry vein, despite easy access to many mountain rivers, the residents of cities like Chengdu and Chongqing don't consider recreational fishing to be an option outside of man-made pools inside "fishing parks." Meanwhile millions of citizens in Shanghai live right on the coast and at the mouth of a great river, but almost nobody dares to bathe or swim in the deadly waters surrounding the city.

To view this environmental shame from an American perspective, consider the plight of Lake Tai. This Chinese equivalent of America's beautiful Lake Placid in the Adirondacks is the third largest lake in China, is home to more than 90 islands, and is famous for its beautiful limestone formations. Today, however, a beleaguered Lake Tai is becoming even better known for its propensity to turn bright green from algae blooms that deplete the lake's oxygen, kill fish, and render the lake's water totally unsuitable for drinking.

And what's an endangered Chinese natural resource like Lake Tai without an environmental activist who has been tortured for trying to protect it? To his credit, Wu Lihong did hold out for five days before the police finally beat a "confession" out of him and sent him off to the Chinese slammer—which in China is truly a slammer.

China's Invisible Scourge—Soil Toxicity

China's arable land, which feeds 22% of the world's population, is facing grim pollution and degradation, warns Zhou Xiansheng, director of the State Environmental Protection Agency (SEPA)... The decline in soil quality has become one of the most worrisome byproducts of China's breakneck economic growth. Heavy metals are accumulating in the soil, hardening the soil surface and reducing its fertility, and

residues from chemical fertilizers and pesticides are showing up in farm products, poisoning both people and livestock. Currently, about 10 million hectares of cropland—10% of the country's total cropland area—has been contaminated.
—Worldwatch Institute

China Environmental Times rightly calls soil contamination the "invisible pollution" because, unlike water and air pollution, it is not very visible to the naked eye. And today, in any given part of China, it truly is "pick your soil poison."

For example, in the electronics manufacturing hub of the Pearl River Delta, the biggest problem is with heavy metals such as mercury, lead, and nickel. However, in the breadbasket of Northern China, it's more like a flood of pesticides while China's prime vegetable growing areas are inundated with carcinogenic nitrates from over-fertilization. Meanwhile, in fruit fields and orchards across China, intensive use of "a copper sulfate compound used in insecticides and germicides has led to widespread contamination of fruit that can cause chronic poisoning." And despite an official nationwide ban on DDT, its continued regular use and long-term impacts are apparent in the insect-free and bird-free world of Western China's farmland.

What's so myopic about so much of this pollution is that it is the malignant outgrowth of an insane "more is better" philosophy embraced by millions of Chinese peasant farmers. Whether it is fertilizer or pesticides for crops or antibiotics for livestock (or lead in our toys and paint), there is no deft chemical touch in China but rather a "pour it on" and "paint it on" mentality that is about as safe as plutonium flakes in potato chips.

Just consider China's over-fertilization epidemic: Chinese farmers use more than 30 million tons of nitrogen fertilizer each year and routinely apply double or triple what crops require. According to soil expert Fusuo Zhang of the China Agricultural University, this surfeit of fertilizer has caused soil pH to plummet, and the resulting soil acidification is cutting crop production by as much as 30 to 50% in some areas.

A similar Rabelaisian appetite for pesticides—together with often improper use—has led to the contamination of over 5% of China's soil while, all told, China's loss of arable land to all toxins adds up to fully 10%. To be clear here, that's over 25 million acres down the toxic tubes; and it is the equivalent of wiping out over 80% of the farmland in Iowa.

This is hardly the end of the story, however. There is also the matter of China's willingness—indeed, its extreme eagerness—to be the dumping ground for one of the most toxic modern concoctions ever created—so-called "e-waste."

Such e-waste is the stuff of dead computers, obsolete cell phones, and other electronic gadgets; and it's a veritable heavy metal concert like no other. As *ScienceDaily* tells it: "Up to 50-million tons of e-waste is generated worldwide each year—enough to fill a line of garbage collection trucks stretching halfway around the world;" and of course it's China backing up its garbage trucks to collect fully 70% of that e-waste.

This is not just West dumps East. It also the fifteenth century meeting the twenty-first century. In this squalid e-waste world, Chinese peasants squat over small charcoal grills to melt lead solder from circuit boards and use only small portable fans to ward off the toxic fumes as they pick bare-handed through the computer chips and capacitors and diodes that will be resold to electrical appliance factories.

It's an ultra-primitive recycling process amidst all the paraphernalia of modern life. And it yields China's factory floor yet another competitive edge over countries like Brazil or Mexico or France or

America that are willing to treat their citizens like human beings rather than as human sacrifices to the godless goal of cheap production.

This is all so disgusting on its face, and all the more so because the toxic dust that results from the recycling process travels for miles into the Chinese countryside. Indeed, in and around e-waste reprocessing ghettos like Guiyu in Guangdong Province, the levels of copper, lead, nickel, and various other toxic heavy metals are 100, 200, and 300 times higher than safety levels.

So what, then, is the grand total cost of all of China's various sources of soil contamination—from chemicals, fertilizers, and pesticides to e-waste? According to China's own scientists, the price tag comes in the form of over 10 million tons of grain lost annually—a number equal to about one-sixth of the U.S. wheat harvest, half the total corn production of Mexico, and almost all of the annual rice production of Japan. So to put this price tag in another way we will all come to painfully understand at the checkout line of our local grocery store, that's over 10 million more tons of grain that China will have to raid from the food supplies of other countries every year because of its lack of environmental stewardship.

The Emperor of Global Warming

The world has never faced such a predictably massive threat to food production as that posed by the melting mountain glaciers of Asia. China and India are the world's leading producers of both wheat and rice—humanity's food staples. China's wheat harvest is nearly double that of the United States, which ranks third after India. With rice, these two countries are far and away the leading producers, together accounting for over half of the world harvest.

—Friends of the Earth

At this point, we think you get the very clear pollution picture—and how China's utter disregard for its natural resources affects us all. Yet there is still one more environmental issue we need to put on the planetary table. This is the very weighty matter of the prodigious contributions of China's factory floor to climate change.

Before we delve into this issue, we know that there are many Americans who do not believe climate change is real, much less a legitimate danger. To those of you in this camp, we merely want to say this:

> The costs of failing to prevent climate change if it is indeed real are likely to be far higher than any costs we might incur to prevent climate change if it turns out to be a hoax. Viewed from this perspective, action on climate change would seem to represent a prudent insurance policy against a phenomenon we do not yet know anywhere near enough about.

So within the context of these observations, we further note that as early as 2006—*years* before any experts thought it would happen—China absolutely sprinted past the United States to claim the mantle of biggest greenhouse gas emitter. Moreover, over the next several decades, if gone unchecked, China's coal-fired-driven growth, working in tandem with a projected swarm of hundreds of millions of new cars on Chinese roads, will lead to an exponential increase in greenhouse gases that will absolutely dwarf that of all other nations combined—including the United States.

Of course, the China apologists will argue that China has a "right" to pollute the world in proportion to its massive population. But that begs the question of exactly who is responsible for China being severely overpopulated in the first place? China certainly can't pin that one on anyone else.

The biggest irony of all of this is that China actually stands to be one of the biggest victims of climate change. To understand why, it's helpful to know that the mighty waters that flow through China's two greatest rivers—the Yellow and the Yangtze—largely originate in the snow pack and glaciers of the Tibetan-Qinghai Plateau. These glaciers are already melting at the rate of about 7% a year, and if Planet Earth does indeed continue to heat up, these glaciers will melt far faster. That, in turn, means China will first face several decades of epic flooding—followed by chronic droughts and famines as its two biggest rivers run all but dry.

Meanwhile, as the polar ice caps continue to melt and sea levels rise, coastal cities like Shanghai and Tianjin will face submersion. That this is a very distinct possibility is validated by this dire warning from the Red Cross's Dr. Peter Walker: "[W]ithin 80 years, 30 million people in China are going to be under sea. We know it is going to happen, so we must look at ways of how to protect the area."

Well, China, how about starting to protect yourself and your neighbor India and the rest of us—rather than blaming the rest of the world for the problem and demanding that America and Europe pay for any solution?

Why China is Killing Itself—and the Planet

> *An industrial city—though China doesn't really have any other kind—Tianying accounts for over half of China's lead production. Thanks to poor technology and worse regulation, much of that toxic metal ends up in Tianying's soil and water, and then in the bloodstream of its children."*
> —Time

To close this chapter, we must answer what should by now be one glaringly obvious question: Why is China's totalitarian government—which *should* be able to control anything it wants within its borders—allowing China to become the dumping ground of the world?

Answering this question is of utmost importance—not the least of which to Chinese citizens. For it is certainly true that China's battering of Mother Nature will ultimately cause far more suffering than anything the Chinese people endured during the 1930s horrific Rape of Nanking by Japanese imperial forces or over the course of the British Empire's ruthless "opium wars" during the nineteenth century. Indeed, these "foreign humiliations" which the Chinese Communist Party are so fond of reminding the world of, while brutal and far reaching at the time, now seem second order small when it comes to the environmental humiliation the Chinese Communist Party is now inflicting on its own people.

So why exactly *is* this Grand Tragedy of the Commons happening? Surely, part of the fault must lie squarely in the board rooms of foreign companies like BASF, DuPont, GE, Intel, and Volkswagen that strategically export their pollution to China. Besides having fallen in love with all of the various illegal subsidies the Chinese government uses to encourage offshoring, the corporate executives of these foreign companies much prefer the fast and loose rules of China's "Environmental Predation Agency" to America's Environmental Protection Agency, Japan's Ministry of the Environment, or the European Environment Agency.

Ultimately, however, the blame for China's "Death to a Big Planet" must lie with the Chinese Communist Party itself for not just accepting its environmental humiliation—but also for engineering and financing it. In fact, the unprecedented willingness of an "any color but Green" China to allow the wholesale trashing of its air, water, and soil ecosystems boils down to three simple factors working in deadly interaction with an almost perfect lack of future vision.

One factor is embodied in the unwritten Communist Party principle that says "pollute and grow now and protect later." From this myopic perspective, it's better to trade off another piece of the Chinese environment to steal a few million more jobs from the

West—and thereby keep the political peace within China—than it is to pay the freight for environmental protection.

A second related problem is that with so many of the enterprises in China owned by the state, the fox is not only guarding the environmental henhouse; it is running the entire chicken and egg business. In fact, China's state-run enterprises are among the very worst offenders when it comes to the wholesale dumping and spewing of pollutants into the waters and onto the land of China.

Still a third source of China's utter disregard for its environment is the Confucian idea that man's role is to conquer nature rather than to live in symbiosis with it. One of the most tragic illustrations of this fantastic Chinese delusion dates back to days of Mao Zedong and the great leap backward during the 1960s. This was the time of Mao's infamous "Kill a Sparrow" campaign—concocted by the Chinese dictator to rid the countryside of rats, mice, mosquitoes, and public pest #1, the lowly sparrow.

This felony dumb crime against nature was straight out of a Chinese revolutionary opera as Chairman Mao mobilized millions of peasants to sing and shout and bang on pans to scare the sparrows from the fields. Mao's goal was to prevent the sparrows from feasting on the seeds of the planted crops—but what the Chairman didn't count on was that as much seed as sparrows might eat, they devour even more insects.

So it was that once China suppressed its sparrow population, China's prime agricultural lands were overrun by hordes of hungry locusts. While the resulting starvation literally killed tens of millions of Chinese, the real long-term tragedy is that the Communist Party hasn't learned a wit about the wisdom of environmental stewardship.

13

Death by Chinese Pogrom: When Mao Met Orwell and Deng Xiaoping in Tiananmen Square

Communism is not love. Communism is a hammer, which we use to crush the enemy.

—Mao Zedong

In China's "worker's paradise," far too often the "enemies" of the Communist Party state are the citizens of China themselves. These citizen-enemies are the real hard-working people in the "People's" Republic who want higher wages and better working conditions, who long for clean water and breathable air, who strive for reasonable health and pension benefits, and who desperately and fervently seek the freedom to express their political and religious views.

In conquered territories like Tibet, Inner Mongolia, and Xinjiang province, these Chinese Communist Party "enemies" are also the indigenous peoples who dare to seek autonomy from Beijing, who demand some rightful share of the prosperity created from the exploitation of the resources in their homeland, and who deeply and viscerally resent a massive influx of the dominant ethnic Han Chinese immigrants imported by Beijing for the express purpose of diluting and "cleansing" their gene pool.

For these hundreds of millions of victims of the People's Republic of China, it's a trifecta of:

- Home-grown repression from a pollution-rife economic growth model run on 50-cent labor
- A rigid, class-based Communist Party theocracy that provides for little upward mobility, and
- An "Orwell on steroids" totalitarianism that watches every little move you make, constricts every breath you take, and brooks absolutely no opposition

In fact, the ironically named "People's Republic" is neither a representative democracy with leaders duly elected at the ballot box by the people nor is it a "republic" where its citizens in any way, shape, or form retain significant control over the government. Instead, the meetings and decision-making processes of the ruling Chinese Communist Party are completely opaque and filtered by a media the party controls with an iron fist.

The Big Lie Begins with China's Name and Is Told by Its Constitution

Citizens of the People's Republic of China enjoy freedom of speech, of the press, of assembly, of association, of procession and of demonstration.
—Article 35 of China's Constitution

Just as the name of China—the "People's Republic"—is a lie steeped in irony, so, too, is the Constitution of the People's Republic a charade laced with absurdities. While Article 35 guarantees rights like freedom of speech, association, assembly, and demonstration, to exercise any one of them—especially demonstration—is to invite either a severe beating or jail, or both.

As for freedom of the press, a prerequisite for a successful police state is its ability to both control information flows and to mold internal and external perceptions of reality through the management of incoming and outgoing communications. This is a two-step process of suppressing real information and replacing it with convincing falsehoods; and China uses its newspapers and electronic media to do this very well. In fact, the latest Press Freedom Index published by Reporters Without Borders ranked China 171 out of 178, putting it just ahead of a half dozen heavily censored black holes like the Sudan, North Korea, and Iran.

As for Article 40 of the Constitution, it reads, "The freedom and privacy of correspondence of citizens of the People's Republic of China are protected by law." This, too, is laughable. Just try to go on the Internet in China and send an email to a friend. Your supposedly "private" missive will be screened by a "Great Firewall" that employs over 50,000 cybercops and censors; and we've personally seen this happen when the police in Shenzhen detained dissidents we had scheduled to meet via email.

To see China's Great Firewall in action, you can also try this: Go to an Internet café in any Chinese city and try typing into your web browser actual phrases like "freedom of speech" or "Tiananmen Square demonstrations." The resulting links will be blocked. Try it again, and your computer shuts down. Do it repeatedly, and you are likely to get a personal visit from one of China's cybercops—or get busted by someone from a network of amateur enforcers who now turn in their fellow Netizens for cash rewards. As Chinese President Hu Jintao has warned:

> [We must] further strengthen and improve controls on the information web, raising our level of control over virtual society, and perfecting our mechanisms for the channeling of public opinion online.

It's useful to add here that, like many things in China, censorship is well integrated into Beijing's economic warfare against its trading partners and competitors. For example, banning Hollywood films from Chinese theaters over claims of cultural and moral objections while tacitly allowing them to be pirated on the streets of Shanghai is clearly a massive trade barrier directed at one of America's great industries.

Similarly, blocking U.S. firms like Google, YouTube, and Facebook from the Chinese market while nurturing Chinese knockoffs like Baidu, Youku, and RenRen is a clear violation of World Trade Organization rules hidden behind a bizarre assumption that censorship is a valid excuse rather than a compounding evil. As *Businessweek* has noted, "If Facebook grew corn or built cars, the cry would go out that China was putting up barriers to trade."

And here's another entry for the irony file: The fact that so many Chinese citizens are hauled off to jail for attempts to exercise the freedoms defined in Articles 35 and 40 clearly suggests that the police in China haven't bothered to read Article 37 of the Constitution. It states

The freedom of person of citizens of the People's Republic of China is inviolable.

In fact, today, there are as many as two million Chinese citizens languishing in more than 300 so-called "Reeducation Through Labor" camps; and tens of thousands of these citizens have been locked up for crimes like being an "unregistered" Christian or for being outed as a member of the Falun Gong religious sect. This, too, is most curious because Article 36 of the constitution clearly states

Citizens of the People's Republic of China enjoy freedom of religious belief.

Of course, when ordinary Chinese citizens are forced to confront the stark contrast between the ideals set forth by their own Constitution and the reality of their everyday Orwellian life, they themselves experience their own severe case of cognitive dissonance. Which raises the question: Just how did a country with such an industrious and intelligent people and such a long and rich cultural and economic history descend into the totalitarian hell it is today? To answer that question, it is useful to look at least briefly into several key historical turning points.

A Mighty Imperial Nation Descends into Isolationist Poverty

A huge [Chinese] fleet left port in 1414 and then sailed westward on a voyage of trade and exploration. The undertaking far surpassed anything Columbus...could have envisioned. The fleet included at least 62 massive trading Galileans, any of which could have held Columbus's three small ships on its decks.

—The Emperor's Giraffe

Much of the innovation and vibrance we associate with China has its roots in the Tang Dynasty (from about 600 to 900 A.D.) and the early Ming Dynasty (from about 1370 to 1450). During both of these periods, China—the inventor of everything from the compass, gunpowder, and multistage rockets to paper money, wheelbarrows, whiskey, and chess—was by far the wealthiest, most powerful, most stable, and advanced civilization on Earth.

During the Ming Dynasty specifically, while Europe slumbered in the dark ages, China developed a robust consumer economy supported by technological innovation and a massive trading empire. It was during this period that the third Ming emperor launched the largest fleets of exploration the world has ever seen—before or since.

As chronicled in Samuel Wilson's *The Emperor's Giraffe,* China's imperial expeditionary fleet consisted of hundreds of massive "treasure ships"—some half the length of a modern cruise ship. They carried tens of thousands of Chinese sailors to India, Africa, and the

Middle East, and they returned with tribute and ambassadors from afar. By comparison, Christopher Columbus's ensemble was a pitiful little group of dinghies, and with this projection of its imperial fleet, China was poised to become an international power that might easily have pushed aside Spain and England in the sixteenth century quest for global supremacy.

China's imperial dream was not to be realized, however. In 1433, powerful court eunuchs abruptly squelched the explorations, destroyed the ships, and even tried to eradicate the records of the voyage. What followed would be a ruinous policy of isolationism during which the once-great nation of China slowly fell into its own dark ages while the West flourished.

Despite its isolationism, in the early 1800s, China still accounted for fully one-third of the world's gross domestic product versus America's meager 3%. Yet at this pivotal point in history, China completely rejected the Industrial Revolution.

Instead, in one of the great boomerangs of history, Chinese technologies such as gunpowder and the compass were weaponized by European nations that eventually came to plunder the once proud and mighty Middle Kingdom. It was during this long period of what the Chinese refer to as the "foreign humiliation" that the emerging powers of the West established colonial beachheads in the port cities of Canton, Xiamen, Fuzhou, Ningbo, and Shanghai. These colonialists came not in peace but to extract China's wealth and ship it back to England, Holland, and Portugal.

It was likewise during this period that Britain launched its Opium Wars to force China to accept deadly opium imports from India so Britain could balance its huge trade deficit with China in goods like cotton, silk, and tea. These wars culminated with the Boxer Rebellion, a Chinese uprising against foreigners that was brutally put down by a joint expeditionary force of European and American armies. It was these foreign armies marching into the Forbidden City and past the tombs of the great Ming emperors that shredded the last bit of Chinese dignity, patience, and, most importantly, cohesion.

In the wake of this foreign humiliation, China slowly disintegrated into full-scale revolution. After the briefest wisp of hope for a republic under Sun Yat-sen in 1912, China was soon embroiled in a bloody, multidimensional civil war between nationalists, communists, and various private warlords. This was a debilitating chaos that invited a crushingly brutal invasion by Japan and climaxed in the rise of Mao Zedong, the founding of the People's Republic in 1949, and the flight of Chinese nationalist forces to the beachhead of Taiwan.

What Mao Did During Woodstock

Nanjing is a big city of 500,000...the number of people executed in Nanjing is too low, more people should be killed in Nanjing.
—Mao Zedong's instructions on the suppression of counter-revolutionaries in Nanjing and Shanghai

To Mao Zedong's credit, he did reunify China under ethnic Chinese or "Han" rule, unconditionally expel all foreigners, and restore Chinese pride. That said, the price the people of China have had to pay in blood, sweat, tears, forced labor, jail, and paranoia for Mao's communist-style liberation has been a very heavy one.

Consider that while Hitler killed or exterminated about 12 million civilians and Stalin about 23 million in his famines and purges, Mao's death toll ranges anywhere from 49 to 78 million. That makes Mao the worst mass murderer of all time—at least according to Piero Scaruffi, who has catalogued history's most horrible genocides.

In fact, during the two-and-a-half decades of Mao's rule, when he wasn't swimming across the Yangtze River for sport, the frenetic Chairman would leap from one mad program or *pogrom* to another.

For example, his "Great Leap Forward" included melting all the steel in the country in useless homemade forges and killing all the sparrows. Economic disaster and widespread famine inevitably followed in the footsteps of Mao's often quite literally insane reforms.

Equally disastrous—and terrifying—were Mao's periodic purges of counter-revolutionaries, intellectuals, and members of his own party he labeled "capitalist roaders." The phenomenon of the 1960s known as the "Cultural Revolution" was particularly brutal; and all those who lived through it are scarred by the experience.

During this Cultural Revolution, while the Rolling Stones and Beatles were emerging from Great Britain to rock the music world and hippies sought peace and love in the fields of Woodstock, crazed vigilantes known as Red Guards roamed the streets of China in search of victims for their peculiar political violence. At the same time, businessmen, intellectuals, and professors were blamed for all of China's ills and were forced into manual labor while citizens lacking revolutionary zeal were routinely rounded up, publicly humiliated, beaten, and locked in labor camps for years. Even as the Chinese economy continued to retreat further into stagnation, the people of China were taught to lie to survive and obey to advance; and this Orwellian pall over the People's Republic remains Mao's most lasting legacy.

State Capitalism Rises from the Rubble of State Communism

It doesn't matter whether the cat is black or white as long as it catches mice.
—Deng Xiaoping

The man who lifted China out of the Mao economic morass was Deng Xiaoping. He was a former revolutionary and purged party leader who had been sent to work in a tractor factory during the Cultural Revolution. After his son was beaten by Red Guards and thrown from a fourth story window, Deng was pardoned and rehabilitated by Hua Guofeng, who became Mao's heir apparent.

Following the Chairman's death, the wily Deng outfoxed Mao's widow and her notorious Gang of Four as well as the man who saved him. While never formally claiming the official party titles of leadership, Deng unofficially seized power, and everyone understood he was the true puppet master.

In truth, Deng Xiaoping is *the* most important figure in the China of today for at least two reasons. First, while the Soviet Premier Mikhail Gorbachev gave in to protestors and allowed the breakup of a Communistic Soviet Union, it was Deng who ordered the Chinese military to slaughter the protestors in Tiananmen Square in 1989—thus preserving the ruthless and repressionary Communist Chinese state.

Equally important, Deng is credited with singlehandedly pushing forward the brand of state-subsidized mercantilist capitalism that is the hallmark of the "beggar thy neighbor" Chinese economy of today. For it was Deng who opened special economic zones to the West and who would ultimately unleash a massive labor force on world markets armed with potent weapons of job destruction like illegal export subsidies and a manipulated currency.

It is this China of today created by Mao and Deng that is as harsh on its own citizenry as it is unfair to its trading partners. In the next chapter, we will catalogue the repression and brutality in all of its Death by China on China inglory. As we do so, you will see how the twin legacies of Chairman Mao and Deng Xiaoping continue to live on in an ever-more-ruthless totalitarian police state.

14

Death by China on China: Shanghaiing the Gene Pool at the Top of the World and Other Earthly Tales

Immersion in sewage, ripping out fingernails, sleep depriva-tion, cigarette burns and beatings with electric prods—these are some of the torture methods used by China's police and prison officers to extract confessions and maintain discipline, a United Nations investigation has found.
—The Guardian of London

Just how does the Chinese Communist Party of today beat, tor-ture, work to the bone, sterilize, jail, and kill its own citizens—and millions of Tibetans, Mongolians, and Uyghurs? Let us count the ways in this chapter; and even a cursory reading of Beijing's brass knuckled brutality should convince you that the problem in China is not with the Chinese people but with a government that regularly runs over its own citizenry.

No Male Child Left Behind—Except for One Tossed in the Trash

It is a serious offense to drown or abandon female infants.
—Sign on a hospital wall in Dai Bu Village, Yunnan Province

China alone stands to have as many unmarried young men—
"bare branches," as they are known—as the entire population
of young men in America. In any country rootless young
males spell trouble...Crime rates, bride trafficking, sexual vio-
lence, even female suicide rates are all rising and will rise fur-
ther as the lopsided generations reach their maturity.
—*The Economist*

It is true, all too true, that China is both grossly overpopulated and the most populous nation on the planet. Yet in many ways, China's "cure" for its overpopulation problem—its "one child policy"—has created far more problems than it solves. Indeed, even as other developing nations like Brazil, India, and Mexico have brought their populations under better control in more humane ways, China's governmental control over reproductive rights remains a chilling study in coercion, forced sterilization, compulsory abortions, and infanticide.

The cornerstone of China's no-choice policy is a punitive fine for having a second child, the hefty amount of which nearly always exceeds the family's annual income. The size of this fine means that most couples who find themselves in a second pregnancy face financial ruin if they decide to have the child. The not unsurprising result is that China has more abortions than the rest of the world combined—close to 13 million a year, and that's a conservative government estimate.

Note, however, that just because a couple may have the money to pay a fine or qualify for an exemption, it still doesn't mean they can actually have a second child. Overzealous local officials, whose promotion chances often rest on the degree of compliance with the one-child policy, have often been known to forcibly round up pregnant women.

For example, *Time* magazine reports how 61 pregnant women were hauled into hospitals in Guangxi, where they were injected with abortion-inducing drugs. The normally pro-China Al Jeezera did a similar feature on Xiao Ai Ying, who was "forced to have an abortion eight months into her pregnancy because she already had a ten-year-old girl." And National Public Radio has described how Christian Pastor Liang Yage and his wife, Wei Linrong, were ordered to a hospital despite being willing to pay the fine for their second child. When the couple refused to sign abortion consent forms, officials just forged their signatures and injected the wife who was seven months pregnant. The next day, Wei went through 16 hours of contractions before giving birth to her dead little boy, who was then tossed into a plastic trash bag by hospital staff.

While Wei Linrong lost her boy, it is mostly girls who suffer from China's one-child policy. In fact, almost all of China's abandoned babies are female, many abortions are sex selective, and female infanticide is still common enough to require public campaigns against the practice. Given that Chinese law bars Chinese couples under 35 and those with kids from adopting, it's no wonder thousands of abandoned little Chinese girls are lucky enough to find loving homes in America, Australia, and Europe—even as China's government-run adoptions bazaar captures more foreign exchange.

At least to journalist Joseph Farah, China's gendercide represents "the biggest single holocaust in human history." Whether you agree, what is true is that Chinese gendercide has resulted in a socially destabilizing gender imbalance. In fact, China now has 119 baby boys registered for every 100 girls, while in some provinces the ratio is as high as 130:100.

Today, as a result of the perverse effects of China's one-child policy, more than 100 million Chinese men are unable to find wives. These "bare branches," as they are referred to in China, total more than the male populations of Japan and South Korea combined or the entire population of young men in America.

The inevitable result has been a dramatic rise in prostitution (and all that comes with it), sex slavery, and even the kidnapping of women from foreign countries. In fact, *The Washington Post* claims that as many as 100,000 North Korean women have been imported into China as sex slaves. What happens in China doesn't stay in China indeed.

The Three Autonomous Provinces of the Apocalypse

We have been cheated, murdered, raped, violated, deprived, betrayed, discarded, sold and tortured for too long!
—Kekenus Sidik, Uyghur protestor

Forced sterilization isn't confined to Chinese women seeking to have a second child. It's quite literally a standard operating procedure in Tibet, Inner Mongolia, and East Turkestan—three of the so-called and ironically named "autonomous" provinces of China. Here's the bigger ethnic cleansing picture.

Despite Beijing's claim that Tibet, Inner Mongolia, and East Turkestan have nominally been under the sway of China for years, the reality is that these regions maintained their proudly distinct cultures and generally exercised home rule until the Communists' tanks rolled in during the 1950s. During this time, the Red Army chased the Dalai Lama out of Tibet and Mao Zedong split up Mongolia with the Soviets. With the help of Stalin, Mao also managed to engineer a plane crash that decapitated the political leadership of East Turkestan and allowed for easy replacement of that leadership with Chinese puppets.

Today, more than 50 years later, all three of these once-independent territories remain under the jackboot of the Communist Party. They also suffer from a relentless ethnic cleansing campaign aimed at replacing the indigenous ethnic populations with ethnic Han Chinese. This so-called "Hanification" of Tibet, Inner Mongolia, and East Turkestan involves everything from the busing in of millions of ethnic Han Chinese and the busing out (or killing of) the locals to sterilizing the local women or diluting their gene pool through policies that drive marriage to Han men.

To date, such ethnic cleansing has been most successful in Inner Mongolia, where more than 80% of the population is now Han. According to the Inner Mongolia People's Party, to bring about this Hanification, more than a quarter of a million Mongolians were murdered while more than 15 million Chinese were moved into Inner Mongolia to water down Mongolian culture.

As for East Turkestan—known now on the Chinese map as Xinjiang Province—Rebiya Kadeer, a Uyghur leader expelled to the United States from her native Xinjiang, has testified to Congress that 240,000 of her people, mostly women, have been forcibly moved out of their ancestral home. Of these women, many have been compelled to marry Han men to cross-breed, while many others have been used for cheap slave labor and as sex workers. Further, despite exemptions in the one-child law for minorities, thousands of Uyghur women have been subjected to "forced abortions, forced sterilizations, and forced insertions of intrauterine devices."

Resentment in Xinjiang came to a head in 2009 with protests that escalated into open battles between Uyghurs and Han Chinese. In a typically hard-line response, Chinese police rounded up and beat hundreds of these protesters—even as they literally "disappeared" dozens of Uyghur men. A resident of Urumqi described the brutal crackdown to Human Rights Watch:

> They told everybody to get out of the houses. Women and elderly were told to stand aside, and all men, 12 to 45 years old, were all lined up against the wall...They beat the men randomly, even the older ones—our 70-year-old neighbor was punched and kicked several times. We couldn't do anything to stop it—they weren't listening to us.

Tibet has hardly fared better than either Inner Mongolia or Xinjiang. In fact, the introduction of a new high-speed rail line to

Tibet from cities like Beijing, Chengdu, Guangzhou, and Shanghai has merely accelerated the rush of a seemingly never-ending stream of Han Chinese into the Himalayas.

In today's Tibet, Han Chinese now own most of the shops in the capital of Lhasa and likely already comprise the majority of the capital's population. Meanwhile, the Tibetan language is being taught as a second, "foreign" language while Mandarin is the only speech allowed in high school.

Rural Tibet is under a similar Hanification siege. In some cases, entire villages have been evacuated and then flooded with Chinese-built dams while nomadic people have been herded into concrete camps and their livestock confiscated. One camp inmate explained the plight of his people: "They have no jobs and they have no land. The only way they can fill their empty stomachs is by stealing."

And here's a Tibetan version of Catch-22: Some local farmers have been reduced to renting their lands to Han Chinese to pay back loans on the new homes they were forced to buy to begin with because of a government policy that required them to relocate. Of course, Chinese bankers have been executing the rental agreements.

For all these reasons and more, Tibetan anger overflowed several years ago as rioters threw stones at police, attacked Han Chinese on bicycles and in taxis, and set fire to Han businesses. As expected, the protestors were brutally repressed—while hundreds of monks who began the unrest with a peaceful protest were rounded up, kicked, and beaten.

Meanwhile, to keep its repression under wraps, Beijing has severely restricted the access of journalists to Tibet. Moreover, *any* foreign visitors must receive special approval, and in recent years such permits have been completely banned near the anniversary of the protests. Those who have snuck in have been horrified—as was British filmmaker Jezza Neumann working on the documentary *Undercover in Tibet*. He has noted, "I haven't met anyone who had been arrested who wasn't tortured."

The filmmakers also relay reports that the Chinese have swept into Tibet with mobile sterilization vans and are forcibly inserting permanent IUDs into Tibetan women as well as performing tubal ligations without anesthesia. One victim describes the process:

> *I was forcibly taken away against my will. I was feeling sick and giddy and couldn't look up. Apparently they cut the fallopian tubes and stitched them up. It was agonizingly painful. They didn't use anesthetic. They just smeared something on my stomach and carried out the sterilization.*

Meanwhile, the Dalai Lama hangs out at his home in exile in India, helpless in his efforts to move his people toward true autonomy from Chinese rule. And in a park near the sacred Potala Palace where the Dalai Lama once lived in winter residence, his followers hide his forbidden image in their pockets and pray while government loudspeakers blast propaganda messages like this: "We are part of a Chinese nation contributing to a great future—we are Chinese people."

Now here's a cry-out-loud ode to both the zealousness and thoroughness of the jackboots of Beijing: They have managed to take two steps to ensure that the next Dalai Lama will be one of their puppets and not an independent voice like the current Dalai Lama. First, they long ago "disappeared" the six-year-old reincarnation of the Panchen Lama, Tibetan Buddhism's second highest religious figure. This world's youngest political prisoner has not been seen since 1996.

Second, and this is as much laugh-out-loud as cry-out-loud, Beijing has banned Buddhist monks in Tibet from reincarnating without the government's permission. *The Huffington Post* has explained the hidden agenda behind this seemingly absurd law: "By barring any Buddhist monk living outside China from seeking reincarnation, the law effectively gives Chinese authorities the power to choose the next Dalai Lama, whose soul, by tradition, is reborn as a new human to continue the work of relieving suffering."

Charles Dickens Does Dongguan

Chinese entrepreneurs have five-star factories that meet the ethical standards of the big companies they cater to. [Alexandra] Harney [in her book The China Price*] takes the example of a Walmart executive who went to visit a factory that sold goods to Walmart. "Her job was to determine whether the factory was producing according to Walmart's ethical standards—which include a strict ban on child or slave labour and rules on occupational hazards, working hours and payment of minimum wages." What the Walmart executive was inspecting...was a five-star factory...[But] the real production takes place in a shadow factory..."Tucked away in a gated business park, the [shadow] factory is not registered with the Chinese government. Its 500 employees work on a single floor, without safety equipment or insurance and in excess of the legal working hours. They are paid a daily rather than a monthly wage. No one from Walmart has ever seen this factory, though Walmart buys much of the factory's output."*
—*Daily News & Analysis*

While Tibetans, Mongolians, and Uyghurs suffer under the boot of Chinese Communist Party rule, workers don't fare a whole lot better. In fact, while Chinese officials love to take Westerners to so-called "five star" show factories that offer guided tours of clean facilities with state-of-the-art safety and environmental protection equipment, they are rarely allowed to see the truly unbearable shadow factory conditions behind the ubiquitous electronic gates and guard shacks that surround virtually all Chinese plants. As a worker in a South China factory where Microsoft Xboxes are assembled has explained: "It is only when the foreign clients show up that management turns on the air conditioning."

Laboring in sweltering sweatshops is just one of the many quasi-slave labor conditions that millions of Chinese workers face; this is true even in factories ostensibly under the direction of large American firms like Microsoft and Walmart. Consider, for example, the

Yuwei Company in the southern city of Dongguan. It makes metal and plastic components for auto parts like brakes, doors, and gear shifts, and the Ford Motor Company accounts for 80% of its business. In addition, Yuwei services companies like General Motors, Chrysler, Honda, and Volkswagen; and as part of its American connection, Yuwei even has a U.S. office and warehouse in Ann Arbor, Michigan.

Now here's what life is like for workers at the Yuwei facilities according to a 2011 investigative report entitled "Dirty Parts/Where Lost Fingers Come Cheap: Ford in China." As this report reveals: Yuwei workers toil 7 days a week in 14-hour shifts and regularly operate equipment with safety devices that have been intentionally disabled. One result is a remarkably high production rate; the other is an equally remarkable high rate of cut, mutilated, or severed fingers and limbs. As the "Ford in China" report describes this carnage:

> Twenty-one year old Worker "A" had three fingers and several knuckles torn from his left hand when it was trapped in a powerful punch press, or stamping machine. He was making "RT Tubes" for export to Ford at the time of his accident. Management deliberately instructed the worker to turn off the infrared safety monitor device so he could work faster. "We had to turn it off. My boss did not let me turn it on," said Worker A. He had to stamp out 3,600 "RT Tubes" a day, one every 12 seconds.

So what's the loss of, say, three fingers, worth in China? About $7,000 in compensation pay—and the loss of the mutilated worker's job and future career prospects. And, by the way, any worker who misses one day's work at a Yuwei facility is docked three days' pay. In fact, getting fired for becoming injured is a standard labor practice in China. As a friend of ours who sells supplies to a Shanghai factory told us, "If there is an accident, even a death, there is no investigation. A second accident at the same task, no investigation. A third time will probably be investigated." Please remember all of this if you ever consider buying a Ford supposedly "Made in America" but put together with a bunch of Chinese parts.

Ain't Nothing "Quasi" About This Slave Labor

Among the 10- to 14-year-old children, the working rate is
11.6% in China. Many companies prefer child labor because
children are cheap, obedient and agile enough to maneuver in
small machine-cramped work areas.
—IHS Child Slave Labor News

They took advantage of my brother because he has a mental
disability. They forced him to work, beat him, tortured him,
and then when he was too weak to take it anymore, they
threw him out on the street.
—Liu Xiaowei

Not surprisingly, in particularly hellish jobs like brickmaking and
low-skilled, numbingly repetitive jobs like toy making, it is difficult to
recruit adequate workers. In such industries, many factory managers
see labor shortages as an open invitation to human trafficking; and
both children and the mentally handicapped are always at the top of
the trafficker's list.

In some cases, the children or mentally handicapped are tricked
or coerced by phony recruiters who sell them to factories. In other
cases, they are simply kidnapped, often by the factory owners themselves. Either way, they wind up in unspeakable working conditions.

Such was the fate of poor Liu Xiaoping, a mentally challenged 30-
year-old. He was taken from his family by one of China's new-age
slave dealers and sold to a brick kiln—notorious for being among the
most brutal of China's many labor hells.

When the kiln was done with Liu, it tossed the broken, but still
alive man out onto the streets with what the *Los Angeles Times*
described as "hands as red as freshly boiled lobster from handling hot
bricks from a kiln without proper protective gloves." Along with these
lobster hands, this man-child in a land of broken promises had chain

marks on his wrists and burns on his legs where the foreman placed scalding bricks as punishment. Where's Charles Dickens when you need him?

And, by the way, even in the most worker friendly of China's factories, often unbearable stresses are created from having to live hundreds of miles from home with strangers while enduring long hours and the grinding monotony of assembly work. One of us (Autry) saw this firsthand on a visit to the highly secretive Foxconn City in Shenzen. This is the world's largest factory with 350,000 workers making products like Apple's popular iPad.

As Chinese factories go, Foxconn's Taiwanese-run facility is far better than most. During his visit, Autry saw dorms, kitchens, and work areas that were first-rate, at least by Chinese standards. There were even game rooms, gyms, and pools. However, the most ubiquitous "amenity" at Foxconn is the string of safety nets protruding from the second story of every building. These nets were put in place to halt a rash of worker suicides. And that's sadly representative of China's solution to intolerable working conditions—don't improve them, just make it harder to kill yourself by jumping out a building.

Don't Bother Checking for the Union Label

Of course, one big reason Chinese companies can so thoroughly exploit their workers is because organizing a *real* trade union in China's "worker's paradise" is effectively illegal. Meanwhile, the official government-backed All-China Federation of Trade Unions is simultaneously a puppet for the companies it serves and a tool for management to spy on and control workers.

China's slave labor situation is further compounded by this abiding fact of Chinese labor relations: Most organized attempts by workers are ruthlessly crushed by either the cops or hired thugs—with the hiring of thugs for beatings and intimidation a common practice in China.

One graphic case in point is offered up by the fate of the 2,000 workers at the KOK Machinery factory outside Shanghai. They had the temerity to organize a strike to protest unbearable conditions— including working with hot rubber in rooms up to 122 degrees Fahrenheit. One female worker described what happened when their protest spilled over into the streets: "The police beat us indiscriminately. They kicked and stomped on everybody, no matter whether they were male or female."

Even filing a grievance within the rules of the system can get you into serious trouble. For example, Li Guohong, an oil worker in Henan, earned 18 months of "Reeducation Through Labor" in one of China's infamous forced labor camps. His crime? Filing petitions and lawsuits in protest of being laid off.

Of course, being sent to a forced labor camp wasn't exactly how Mr. Li envisioned getting back to work. But he has now joined the fraternity of more than 50 million Chinese citizens over the past 50 years who have passed through (or died in) China's more than 1,000 forced labor camps. Today, these camps—known infamously in China as the Laogai (or Laojiao)—contain as many as 7 million Chinese citizens, many of whom are guilty of nothing more than attempting to exercise some freedom to speak, worship, assemble, or organize.

And here's a final observation on the right to strike in China: The only circumstance that the government will allow such strikes to flourish is when they help Chinese enterprises beat foreign competitors.

A case in point is that of a series of strikes and public protests that shut down several Honda automobile factories. Rather than intervene, the usual riot police simply stood by and finally walked away. That left Honda thousands of cars short of production goals. The lack of the usual police strikebreaking also forced Honda to negotiate higher wages with its angry Chinese workers. Of course, this makes Japan's Honda less competitive against Chinese car companies like Chery and Geely.

How Chinese Cops Bring Chinese Parishioners to Their Knees

The persistent desire to control the most intimate area of citizens' lives, namely their conscience, and to interfere in the internal life of the Catholic Church does no credit to China. On the contrary, it seems to be a sign of fear and weakness rather than of strength.

—Communique of the Vatican Holy See

Communism is a secular faith that can brook no dissent, and the Chinese Communist Party does its best to follow Marx's edict to abolish religion. To that end, the Party requires that all religious activity be conducted through state-approved churches, while *unregistered* religious activity can result in severe punishment.

Just consider the case of Yang Xuan. This pastor of the unregistered Linfen Church in Fushan received a sentence of three years for building an illegal church. Then his wife, Yang Rongli, was first severely beaten for organizing a protest of her husband's detention and then slapped with seven years imprisonment. As you read this description of what happened at the Linfen Church, imagine for the moment that Linfen is a church in your own neighborhood:

In the early morning hours of Sunday, September 13, Linfen Church members were jolted awake by rowdy, screeching intruders. A mixed mob of 400 police officers, local government officials, and hired thugs beat the church members who were sleeping at the construction site of their new church building. Heavily bleeding, more than 20 members were severely injured and hospitalized. Local officials instructed the hospitals not to give the victims blood transfusions, forcing them to be relocated to regional hospital care.

As for access to the Holy Bible, copies may only be printed by the officially approved "China Christian Council"; and quantities are limited by the government. Moreover, unapproved printings and distribution of Bibles or Christian literature can result in arrest.

Of course, it's not just Christians and "closet Catholics" who risk the ire of the Chinese Communist Party. It's also quasi-religious groups like the Falun Gong—whose members regularly experience the tip of the Chinese sword.

In many ways, the extreme antipathy of the Communist Party toward the Falun Gong is puzzling. Falun Gong practitioners follow a peaceful philosophy based on Buddhism and Taoism, and they practice a series of physical exercises derived from traditional Chinese Qigong. These exercises are designed not to overthrow the Chinese Communist state but rather to align one's breath, physical nature, and consciousness with the central tenants of Truthfulness, Benevolence, and Forbearance.

In the late 1990s, this then-fast-growing sect attracted the attention of the Communist security apparatus and propaganda system, which promptly labeled it a "dangerous cult." The Falun Gong reaction was, in hindsight, a huge political miscalculation. When 10,000 adherents gathered in silent protest outside the walls of the Communist leaders' compound at Zhongnanhai, this frightened President Jiang Zemin; and he ordered the Communist Party to crack down hard.

In the months following the protest, Vice-Premier Li Lanqing reported that over 35,000 Falun Gong members were rounded up; and since that time, the persecution of members has been as brutal as it has been relentless.

Of course, the Communist Party's harsh response has produced some serious blowback in the form of a Falun Gong led anti-Communist Party campaign that features a worldwide newspaper and satellite television service. In China, however, the repression of this sect continues unmercifully; and thousands of its adherents have been shipped off to the Chinese Laogai gulags for beatings and torture.

Falun Gong practitioners are also often sequestered in so-called "psychiatric" ward extensions of the Laogai where all manner of brainwashing is attempted. According to the Congressional testimony of Ethan Gutmann: "Falun Gong comprises between 15 to 20% of the Laogai system. That's about half a million to a million Falun Gong in detention on average, representing the largest Chinese Security action since the Maoist period."

Just as with the other forms of slave labor that produce collateral damage to workers around the world, the repression of the Falun Gong likewise has its global labor market implications. To see these implications, we end this chapter with this description of a typical day in the life of a Falun Gong prisoner from the Falun Dafa Information Center:

> *Mr. Wang Jiangping is handicapped and can't knit as fast as the others. It's almost 2:00 a.m. and the Division Six prisoners have been working since dawn. They have to meet the deadline. His fellow Falun Gong practitioners nod off only to be wakened by guards stabbing them with scissors. Mr. Wang is exhausted. The guards throw bricks at his chest. The Changji Labor Camp has to meet Tianshan Wooltex's quota of Kashmir sweaters, or the guards won't get their bonus. The Chinese "reform through labor" camps have become privatized. They are small enterprises that sign contracts with big companies and export products to overseas shopping malls.*
>
> *It is a place where torturers get rich, and where Falun Gong practitioners slave to pay for the purchase of the electric batons that will shock them if they slow down. These are places where persecution drives profit. These are places where sleep and food deprivation, filth, stench, beatings, heat, cold, and toxic odors are daily routines. These places are where products for export are made by the slave labor of prisoners of conscience: doctors, teachers and students abducted from their homes for practicing Falun Gong.*

Part V

A Survival Guide and Call to Action

15

Death by China Apologist: Fareed Zakaria Floats Away

China's growth has obvious and amazing benefits for the world, and in particular for America.
—Fareed Zakaria

Hey Fareed, would you like a little mustard with that hyperbole? And after you finish gushing about China, could you please answer this question:

> How can any American journalist, business executive, consumer, politician, pundit, or scholar credibly defend a totalitarian regime that knowingly sells products that maim and kill us, hacks our computers to pirate our intellectual property, launches mercantilist attacks upon our economy to steal our jobs, uses planet Earth like a giant ashtray, treats its own workers like a bunch of slaves, and is arming itself to the teeth so it can sink our Navy and shoot our satellites out of the sky and have its way with the world?

That is a very good question. And it has no defensible answer. Yet every day across America a surprisingly large number of Apologists and Appeasers—from the likes of Fareed Zakaria, James Fallows, Tom Friedman, and Fred Hiatt to Nicholas Kristof, David Leonhardt, and Joseph Stiglitz—vigorously defend China against those who would press for long-overdue reforms.

In fact, the very existence of this unofficial "China Apologist Coalition" within America's borders has an important political implication: We as a nation cannot effectively confront the Chinese government until we first clearly identify the Apologists and then fully refute what has become a veritable Tower of Babel against meaningful change in the U.S.–China relationship.

That's the overarching purpose of this chapter, and, to begin, here's a list of the six major players in the China Apologist Coalition. They are in no particular order and include the following:

- The "Democratize and Tame the Dragon" Liberals
- The "Damn the Mercantilist Torpedoes, Free Trade Ahead at Any Costs" Conservatives
- The Wall Street Banker Expat Spin Doctors
- The Washington Power Elite Appeasers
- The "World Is Flat" Globalization Gurus
- The Panda-Pandering Think Tanks

The "Democratize and Tame the Dragon" Liberals

President Clinton will close years of political and economic debate Tuesday and seal a major achievement of his administration by signing off on normalized trade with China...The move is designed to open China's mammoth market to U.S. businesses and pave the way for China's entry into the World Trade Organization...Clinton argued that bringing China into the global trade regime will help make Beijing a more responsible and accountable member of the world community.

—CNN

Distilled to its essence, the "Democratize the Dragon" Liberal argument for supporting China's rise is this: We must "engage" the Dragon to tame it.

In this view, all that a Totalitarian China really needs to become a Democratic China is time—and a hefty dose of economic prosperity. By becoming more affluent, the argument goes, "they" will become just like "us"—that is, a civilized democracy that respects free speech, human rights, intellectual property, the rules of free trade, and the sanctity of the ballot box.

It is precisely this misguided argument that represents the tap root of America's current economic problems with China. This is because the Clinton administration used it relentlessly in the late 1990s to support its policy of "engagement" with China and to press forward all the Congressional legislation that was needed to shoehorn China into the World Trade Organization in the year 2000.

Of course, history on this particular issue has proven to be a harsh mistress for President Clinton. For over the last decade, America has gotten just the opposite result promised by his administration's policy of "engagement" with China.

Indeed, the more wealth that China's economy has generated for its budding middle class, the more Chinese citizens have been willing to buy into the idea that totalitarianism is both necessary and desirable to keep the miracle growing. Professor Ming Xia has described the American Liberal's total misread of the Asian neo-conservative mindset:

> In the West, liberal Democrats often expect that the emerging market economy will create a sizeable middle class, who then will become the backbone of civil society and the driving force for democratization. But many Asian specialists have found that the dog does not bark in East Asia: Under the state-guided capitalism in East Asia, the middle class often depends on the state for employment (state functionaries and professionals) and resources (business people) and therefore is not active in opposing the state. This is the case in China, too. Not surprising, the middle class has been sided with neo-conservatism in China since the 1990s.

To put this in plain terms, far too many of the people of China seem far too willing to give up their free speech and human rights in exchange for the right and wherewithal to buy BMWs and Big Macs. That's why Harvard Professor Samuel Huntington warned Liberals in the mid-1990s not to fully buy into the concept of engagement. Huntington's warning is paraphrased in the *Taiwan Review*:

> *The essence of Western civilization is the Magna Carta, not the Magna Mac. Indeed, the Chinese may eat Big Macs or even drive cars, but still not care to introduce popular sovereignty into their politics, particularly when they have thrived under government-driven, authoritarian capitalism.*

In thinking through this problem, we want to make one thing abundantly clear: There is nothing inherently "Chinese" about totalitarianism and nothing that prevents the Chinese people from prospering in free societies. Indeed, Taiwan, Hong Kong, Singapore, and the worldwide Chinese Diaspora has proven this over and over.

In fact, the success of the Chinese people in other, more democratic systems is the result of pride, a strong work ethic, and a great respect for education. Sadly, however, the Communist Party's propaganda machine has falsely convinced a significant portion of China— and much of the world—that it is the Communist Party's "inspired leadership" that has produced China's wealth.

So the next time you hear liberals insist we must engage the Dragon to tame it, remind them that engagement only works if China is willing to play by Western rules—not make up its own.

The "Damn the Mercantilist Torpedoes, Free Trade Ahead at Any Costs" Conservatives

As if the world economy wasn't fragile enough, politicians in the U.S. and China seem intent on fighting an old-fashioned currency war. The U.S. is more wrong than China here, and

it's important to understand why, lest the two countries send the world back to the dark age of beggar-thy-neighbor currency protectionism.
—*The Wall Street Journal*

Lest anyone think we are picking unduly on the Left, guess what? At least one segment of America's Right Wing is equally to blame.

The hallmark of these "Damn the Mercantilist Torpedoes, Free Trade Ahead at Any Costs" Conservatives is a blind faith in the principle of free trade no matter what kind of mercantilist and protectionist policies America's trading partners adopt. However, as we painfully learned in Chapter 4, "Death to America's Manufacturing Base," free trade only benefits *both* trading partners if *both* play by the rules. Otherwise, and as is very much the case with the lopsided U.S.–China trade relationship, one country wins at the expense of the other's income, jobs, manufacturing base, and prosperity.

What is perhaps most disconcerting about the "Free Trade Ahead at Any Costs" Conservatives is that it is virtually impossible to reason with them. These self-righteous ideologues seemingly condone any violation of free trade rules by China even as they insist that America continue to abide by those rules. Indeed, nowhere in this ideological mindset is the intellectual flexibility to distinguish, for example, between bad protectionist tariffs and quotas designed to close markets to foreigners versus legitimate measures of self-defense like countervailing duties in the presence of illegal Chinese government subsidies.

Just who exactly are we talking about here? A useful starting point is the editorial pages of *The Wall Street Journal.* For as the excerpt leading off this section illustrates, any time the topic of trade reform comes up, *The Wall Street Journal* and its stable of editorialists and Op-Ed thoroughbreds go on the attack using a tried-and-true propaganda formula.

This formula always begins with branding any defensive action taken against China as "protectionism." After dropping the emotionally charged "P-word," *The Wall Street Journal* then follows up with a dire warning of an impending trade war if the U.S. tries to defend itself against Chinese predation.

Of course, if real reform is a possibility, *The Wall Street Journal* will really try to scare us by referencing the role of the Smoot-Hawley tariffs in triggering the Great Depression. It's all so much cow manure, but it is undeniably potent propaganda that has served *The Wall Street Journal*'s "Free Trade Ahead at Any Costs" agenda well over the years.

Which is not to say that *The Wall Street Journal* is alone among the elite members of the financial press in its bashing of would-be China reformers. Regrettably, two other major global players—the daily *Financial Times* and the weekly *Economist* magazine—suffer from a similar ideological disposition to ignore China's unfair trade practices for fear that cracking down on such practices might somehow undermine the global free-trade regime.

We would also be remiss if we did not include in this particular Apologist camp various conservative academics and members of several of the nation's conservative think tanks. For example, Dan Griswold at the Cato Institute and Ed Feulner of the Heritage Foundation can be frequently heard playing this free trade tune. And Harvard's Greg Mankiw and Stanford's Ronald McKinnon can likewise be counted on to run up the free trade flag at the first sign of Congressional bills on topics like currency reform. However, what all these brittle ideologues don't seem to realize is this:

> China is doing far more harm to free trade as a long-term global proposition than any defensive crackdown on Chinese mercantilism and protectionism would ever entail.

The Wall Street Banker Expat Spin Doctors

The combined resources of Goldman Sachs, GSGH, and Gao Hua represent the largest team among international investment banks in China.
—Goldman Sachs website

While we do not question either the integrity or the motives of the "Democratize and Tame the Dragon" Liberals or "Free Trade Ahead at Any Costs" Conservatives—they fervently embrace their positions based on an ideological commitment—the same charitable assessment cannot, however, necessarily be granted to our third member of the China Apologist Coalition. These Wall Street Banker Expat Spin Doctors represent all the various big banks and financial services companies that have put up large shingles in China and that are now making money hand over fist—often at America's expense. Of course, the signature strategy of this group is to use public interested arguments to advance their own financial interests.

Arguably, the worst offenders in this group are financial giants like Goldman Sachs and Morgan Stanley. They have set up some of the largest American shops in China, regularly hobnob with Chinese officials, and want to make sure that nothing rocks their golden boat.

Toward that end, they have employed two of the highest profile hired guns in the China debate—Jim O'Neill, chairman of Goldman Sachs Asset Management, and Stephen Roach, former chairman of Morgan Stanley Asia. Like *The Wall Street Journal's* editorialists, each is quick to brand anyone who seeks reform with China a "protectionist" or "China basher"—and both enjoy rock star status in the government-run Chinese media. But what most distinguishes these two heavy hitters from the crowd is their own clever use of economic arguments and tortured use of statistics.

Consider, for example, Jim O'Neill. On the eve of a critical decision by the U.S. Treasury Department on Chinese currency manipulation, the *Financial Times* gave O'Neill a column to make the incredible claim that, "the renminbi [another term for the Chinese yuan] is very close to the price that it should be." Right, Jim. And Mao Zedong was a capitalist.

Or how about this fear-mongering excerpt from the Beijing-run *China Daily*, which is ever-quick to give Stephen Roach some of its blood-stained ink:

> *Morgan Stanley Asia chairman Stephen Roach said Friday it was ironic for the US to blame China's currency for its high unemployment rate and trade deficit, and trade sanctions on China would have a disastrous outcome for the United States...The US-China bilateral trade deficit has very little to do with the renminbi. It reflects the fact that America does not save and countries that do not save have to import surplus savings from abroad.*

Wow. In a single paragraph, Roach shifts the entire blame to America for its huge trade deficit with China, uses fear-mongering to raise the specter of some vaguely defined "disastrous outcome," and, most incredulously, claims that China's undervalued currency is not really a factor.

Nor is there anything subtle about Roach. In response to a Nobel Laureate's harsh criticism of an undervalued renminbi, Roach barked: "I think we should take out the baseball bat on Paul Krugman."

Of course, when we read stuff like this, we always wonder why China is so unwilling to fairly value its currency if, as Roach claims, it really doesn't provide a big boost to China's economy. As for the claim, "America does not save," Roach refuses to acknowledge the important role that China's currency manipulation process plays in artificially suppressing America's interest rates and thereby its savings rate.

What is perhaps most irksome about the likes of O'Neill and Roach is their willingness to torture statistics until they will say anything they want. Consider this claim Roach made in an interview in *Barron's*:

> *Last year the U.S. ran trade deficits with 90 countries. China was the largest, but there were 89 others that account collectively for a lot more than our trade deficit with China.*

Oh really, Mr. Roach. In fact, China alone accounts for a full 45% of the U.S. trade deficit in goods, leaving Roach's other 89 countries to divide up the remaining 55% for an average of less than 1% each.

Even more to the point, China accounts for fully 75% of the U.S. deficit in goods when petroleum imports are taken out of the equation. Yet as the "Lee Atwater" of Dragonomics, Roach gets away with claiming other countries are a "lot more" responsible for America's trade deficit when nothing could be further from the truth.

The broader point, of course, is that when you see Wall Street advocates like O'Neill and Roach arguing against meaningful reforms with China, just remember who they are working for and where their rice is being fried.

The Washington Power Elite Appeasers

I believe it is peace in our time.
—Neville Chamberlain

I absolutely believe that China's peaceful rise is good for the world, and it's good for America.
—Barack Obama

Over the last decade, as China has had its way with the American economy, it hasn't seemed to matter who sits in the White House, runs the Treasury Department, or holds the majority on Capitol Hill.

Regardless of which political party is in power, the Washington Power Elite consensus has been to appease rather than confront the Dragon.

With President George Bush, the problem was largely ideological—as a free trader, he just couldn't fathom the damage being done to the American manufacturing base by a mercantilist and protectionest China. Add to this Bush's distraction with the war in Iraq, the War on Terror, and his obsession with the "evil doers," and we wound up with eight years of a "see no China evil" policy from the most powerful man on the planet.

And here we must make a confession. Both of us had very high hopes that once we had a "regime change" in Washington in the 2008 election, America would move briskly down the road of meaningful reforms with China. However, with President Barack Obama, it has become all too clear that we have merely traded one Washington Power Elite Appeaser for another.

What is most troubling about all of this is that President Obama seems totally incapable of connecting the increasingly obvious dots between America's economic malaise and China's Weapons of Job Destruction. Perhaps it is because he believes he needs to keep borrowing Chinese money to finance his massive fiscal stimulus and budget deficits. Perhaps it is because he has surrounded himself with pro-China Cabinet members and advisors like the White House's Jason Furman, Commerce Department Secretary Gary Locke, National Security Council Senior Director Jeffrey Bader, Treasury's Lael Brainard, and State Department officials James Steinberg and Kurt Campbell.

Most ominously, perhaps it is that President Obama really and truly doesn't understand the intricacies of global macroeconomics and, as a modern-day version of Neville Chamberlain, "absolutely believe(s)" that China's "rise" will be "peaceful" and "good for America." But either way, we in America have not been served well on the China question by the last two occupants of the White House.

And, given this tale of two presidents, it's not surprising either that we have a similar tale of two Treasury secretaries—Bush's Henry Paulson and Obama's Timothy Geithner. Despite numerous opportunities—and overwhelming evidence!—both men have repeatedly refused to take one of the most important and direct steps this nation could possibly take on the way to meaningful trade reform with China, namely, to brand China a currency manipulator.

Of course, nobody really expected Hank Paulson to crack down on China's currency bombings. After all, before becoming Treasury secretary, Paulson was one of the most important ringleaders of the Wall Street Banker Expat Spin Doctors. Indeed, as chairman and CEO of Goldman Sachs, Paulson made over 70 trips to China. Paulson's China connection helped earn his firm hundreds of millions of dollars; and no way was this Wall Street insider going to bite the Beijing hand that had fed his Goldman Sachs comrades so well.

As for how Timothy Geithner turned so quickly into a China apologist, this is much more of a mystery. And boy, do we mean *quick*. In a "now you see it, now you don't" New York minute, Geithner went from China reformer promising to brand China a currency manipulator during his confirmation hearing to China appeaser as soon as he sat down in the Treasury secretary's office.

The "World Is Flat" Globalization Gurus

So far, America's economic relationship with China has been successful and beneficial—and beneficial for both sides....

A factory work shift [in China] is typically 12 hours, usually with two breaks for meals (subsidized or free), six or seven days per week. Whenever the action lets up—if the assembly line is down for some reason, if a worker has spare time at a meal break—many people place their heads down on the table in front of them and appear to fall asleep instantly.

—James Fallows

How can an American intellectual like James Fallows reconcile his first statement with his second observation? This, too, is a good question; but if America's Globalization Gurus are good at anything, it is the ability to sweep contradictions under the rug with Through the Looking Glass-like tales such as China's heavy reliance on sweatshop labor somehow being "beneficial" to America and its workers.

As for who the Globalization Gurus are, they are the men (and occasional women) who write artful prose and inhabit the pages of prestigious national magazines and newspapers like the *Atlantic Monthly*, *The New York Times*, and *Time* magazine. Besides Fallows, they go by names like Tom Friedman, Nicholas Kristof, and yes, the aforementioned Fareed Zakaria.

What these Pied Pipers of a Despairing Flat World have in common is the misbegotten belief that American workers and the companies that employ them no longer have the capability to be cost competitive with developing nations like China.

This council of despair is both a curious and counterfactual one because historically the United States has always been able to compete with lower-wage nations through its superior productivity advantage. With such an advantage, it doesn't really matter if workers in Shenzhen or Saigon are earning 50 cents an hour and American workers are earning 30 times that if American workers—armed with newer technologies and superior capital equipment—can be 30 times more productive.

Of course, America's problem today with China is that it doesn't just have to compete with low wages. As we discussed at length in Chapter 4, American companies and their workers must also overcome China's illegal export subsidies, currency manipulation, and numerous other Weapons of Job Destruction. Yet no American should ever doubt this abiding economic truth:

Given a level playing field with China or anybody else, American companies and their workers can compete with anyone in the world.

It is because of this abiding truth that real trade and currency reforms with a cheating China are so critical at this juncture in our history. Still, the Globalization Gurus refuse to acknowledge this truth and instead insist that American workers need not apply for manufacturing jobs because these jobs are all "inevitably" going to countries like China.

Our beef with these Globalization Gurus is not just that they are dead wrong. It is also that they use their positions of privilege and power at the top of the journalism food chain to mislead and, in some cases, outright lie to the American public in promotion of their globalization agenda. Consider, for example, this Fareed Zakaria rant against Chinese currency reform from his privileged perch at *Time* magazine:

> *On Sept. 29, the House of Representatives passed a bill [that] would punish China for keeping its currency undervalued by slapping tariffs on Chinese goods. Everyone seems to agree that it's about time. But it isn't. The bill is at best pointless posturing and at worst dangerous demagoguery. It won't solve the problem it seeks to fix. More worrying, it is part of growing anti-Chinese sentiment in the U.S. that misses the real challenge of China's next phase of development.*

In fact, Beijing's propaganda machine could not have churned out a more artful dodge. By arguing that the proposed currency reform bill would "punish China," Zakaria first sets up China as a poor victim to be "slapped" by tariffs rather than as a mercantilist predator that America must defend itself against. Earth to Fareed: It's against free trade rules to undervalue your currency by 40% simply to beggar your trading partners.

Zakaria next asserts that imposing countervailing duties to offset China's undervalued currency "won't solve the problem it seeks to fix." Oh really? If the problem is getting China's currency to fair value, of course such countervailing measures will work, and such duties would conveniently generate some badly needed revenues for the U.S. government until China gives up or plays fair.

Note also that the "it takes one to know one" Zakaria cleverly seeks to label anyone who supports trade reform as a practitioner of "dangerous demagoguery." And what would a pro-Dragon Zakaria rant be without the assertion of China bashing and the rise of a "growing anti-Chinese sentiment."

This is indeed masterful propaganda—and Time Warner pays Zakaria handsomely for it. But the bigger problem with pundits like Zakaria is that they simply don't do real research to bolster their pro-China assertions.

Consider, for example, Zakaria's characterization of the alleged sources of China's cost advantage over American manufacturers in that very same *Time* magazine article. To Zakaria, it's not just low wages. It's also other factors such as "hospitality to business, compliant unions, and a hard-working labor force."

Of course, there are all sorts of *little* things wrong with Zakaria's analysis. In the "hospitality to business" category, Zakaria must believe that rampant corruption in China somehow improves the business climate. As for Zakaria's term "compliant unions," that's certainly putting lipstick on a pig; Chinese labor unions exist in name only and God (and a waiting team of doctors) must come to help any labor organizer who tries to form a real bargaining unit. And regarding China's "hard-working labor force," if you mean that Americans are unwilling to work 12-hour days, 6 days a week with regulated toilet breaks in sweat shop conditions, yep, Fareed, you got us there.

But these are relatively *little* quibbles with Zakaria's analysis of China's production cost advantages. The really big problem with his argument is that he makes no mention whatsoever of the *real* sources of China's competitive edge. These, of course, are the aforementioned weapons of job destruction that violate virtually every rule in the free trade book. Again, as documented in Chapter 4, they include China's massive illegal export subsidies, its rampant currency manipulation, its blatant counterfeiting and piracy, its illegal policy of forced technology transfer, and so on. And in that "so on," let's not forget the cost advantage the Dragon's factories gain from using China's rivers and streams and the world's atmosphere as giant waste disposal sites.

Just why does Zakaria choose to omit the most important sources of the Dragon's competitive advantage besides its cheap labor? There are really only two possibilities.

The first is that Zakaria understands the power of these Weapons of Job Destruction but purposely chooses to ignore them. That raises issues of integrity.

The second possibility is that Zakaria truly doesn't understand the economics of the U.S.–China trade relationship. That raises issues of credibility—and the real possibility that this ultra-light weight hot air pundit might truly float away some day.

Of course, at this point you may think we are picking on Fareed Zakaria, but we do so only because we believe he is not just one of the most influential of the Globalization Gurus but also its most irresponsible. To illustrate this last point, it is useful to evaluate one last argument of the Globalization Gurus that Zakaria has helped make popular. Here's Zakaria's argument in all of its Marie Antoinette "Let Bombay eat cake glory": Even if China were to abandon its mercantilist ways, the rise in the cost of China's exports would not reduce the U.S. trade deficit or increase the number of U.S. manufacturing jobs. Rather, such a level playing field would merely, in Zakaria's words, "help other low-wage economies like Vietnam, India, and Bangladesh, which make many of the same goods as China."

Of course, based on our own economic analyses, we believe Zakaria is dead wrong about this. As we have said, we believe the American companies and workers can compete with any in the world on a level playing field, particularly in manufacturing where automation and ingenuity often trump manual labor.

But suppose Zakaria is actually right. What he is saying is that America shouldn't crack down on Chinese mercantilism because it really wouldn't help us. It would only help a bunch of other Third World countries that nobody (or at least Fareed) presumably cares about—places around the world badly suffering from China's beggar-thy-neighbor policies, like our good neighbor Mexico and Zakaria's home country of India. Well, Fareed, that's just plain cold. Have you forgotten your own roots and the slums of Bombay?

The Panda-Pandering Think Tanks

Those who would build a Great Wall of America to fend off China's influence could end up jeopardizing everyone's long-term peace and prosperity while doing little to improve prospects for political change in China.
—Albert Keidel, Atlantic Council

As a final member of the China Apologist Coalition, there are the various Panda-Pandering Think Tanks within and outside the Beltway that regularly thrust themselves into the middle of the China debate. We are not sure exactly why these think tanks are so predictably pro-China; and we don't mean to question either their integrity or their motives. We do, however, want to identify the "usual suspects" in this group, if for no other reason than when you encounter their claims in the media, you can appropriately discount the data or opinion based on their sources.

Here, then, in no particular order, is our "short list" of the think tanks and analysts that we have found wanting on the perspicacity and insightfulness of their China coverage:

- Albert Keidel of the Atlantic Council
- Peter Bottelier and Doug Paal of the Carnegie Endowment
- Kenneth Lieberthal, Bob Rubin, and John Thornton of (and just about anyone else associated with) the Brookings Institute
- Charles Freeman of (and just about anyone else associated with) the Center for Strategic and International Studies
- Almost anyone associated with the Council on Foreign Relations (with Elizabeth Economy a notable exception)
- Ed Gresser of the Progressive Policy Institute

Again, we do not wish to impugn the motives of these analysts or their institutes. We simply say, "Reader beware!"

Summarizing the China Apologist Coalition's Playbook

To end this chapter, it's useful to summarize the major "talking points" of the "China Apologist Coalition." Whenever you see one or more of these arguments made in an Op-Ed article, editorial, speech, TV debate, or think tank report, you can be rest assured that the perpetrator is out to block meaningful reforms with China. Here, then, are some of the popular cons of the China apologists:

- **The *sine qua non*** —Accuse anyone who criticizes China of being a "China basher."
- **The Joe McCarthy**—Brand anyone in favor of trade reform a "protectionist."
- **Let's play on our fears**—Warn that any attempt to defend America against Chinese Mercantilism and Protectionism will lead to a "trade war."
- **Make it a Stephen King horror novel**—Reference the role of Smoot-Hawley tariffs in the Great Depression to create the impression a trade war with China will wreck the global economy.

- **Reverse-reverse psychology**—Warn that if you try to pressure Beijing into undertaking reforms, it will simply backfire.
- **Stall for time after time**—Insist "now" is not the time to undertake reforms—and keep making that argument year after year.
- **Play the Walmart "poor people" card**—Claim that any harm to the American manufacturing base is more than offset by the gains to consumers from the lower prices of cheap Chinese goods.
- **Use Stephen Roach's shell game**—Claim that our trade deficit problem is a "multilateral" problem with the world rather than primarily a bilateral problem with China.
- **Engage in self-loathing**—Blame America's low savings rate for the U.S.–China trade imbalance and not China's mercantilist practices.
- **Can I sell you the Brooklyn Bridge?**—Claim that China's currency really isn't that undervalued—or not undervalued at all.
- **Use the Marie Antoinette–Fareed Zakaria defense**— Claim that trade reform with China won't help the United States but just move trade to other low-cost countries like Bangladesh and Vietnam.

Well, fool us once with these misrepresentations, then shame on the China apologists. But fool us repeatedly, and shame on us.

16

Life with China:
How to Survive and Prosper
in the Dragon's Century

One ship sails East,
And another West,
By the self-same winds that blow,
Tis the set of the sails
And not the gales,
That tells the way we go.
—Ella Wheeler Wilcox, "The Winds of Fate"

We promised at the outset of this book to provide you with both a survival guide and an action plan. We now keep that promise by including in this chapter a set of individual choices, executive decisions, and government policy actions that can be taken to protect you and your family from unsafe Chinese products and to bring about the kind of constructive changes we need to make our relationship with China a prosperous, rather than a perilous, one.

Our underlying belief is that real change in the U.S–China relationship can only bubble up from the grassroots. That's why our primary goal has been to inform every citizen of the world about the broad range of threats that a rising China poses to us all. Our fervent hope is that once the public fully understands the scope of the world's "China problem," the stage will be set for the kind of peaceful political change we need to bring about constructive policy reforms in

Washington—as well as in Berlin, Tokyo, Sao Paulo, and other capitals around the world.

Before we list our proposed individual choices, executive decisions, and policy reforms, we would like to offer some words of wisdom from some of the world's most astute thinkers. To all the policy makers who read this book, we echo Betty Williams' admonition about inaction: "Let's have no empty talk from this assembly, let's get something done."

To those who may think we have been too hard on China or who may let their optimism about a "democratizing" China outweigh the real evidence of its totalitarian nature, please remember the moral imperative from Albert Camus that led off this book: "It is the job of thinking people not to be on the side of the executioners."

Finally, to any American citizen at the grassroots who feels powerless to fight back, please take heart from these words of William James: "Act as if what you do makes a difference. It does." And every day, try to follow Theodore Roosevelt's credo: "Do what you can, with what you have, where you are."

Avoiding Death by Chinese Junk and Poison

We go to a big box retailer like Costco, Target, or Walmart or to a retail drug outlet like Walgreens or CVS or to a grocery store like Kroger or Safeway, and it is virtually impossible to buy China-free products. This is not just frustrating; it's insane. As we have illustrated, far too much of the Chinese junk and poisons that cram America's retail shelves is flat-out deadly. Here are some concrete steps all of us can take to protect ourselves.

#1: First, Let's Change Our Attitude—"Cheap" Isn't Always the Cheapest

We can't change our buying behavior until we fully embrace the principle that seemingly "cheap" Chinese products really aren't that cheap. Besides the price you pay on the tag, you also have to factor in the risks of injury or death, the increased chance you or someone you know will lose her job because of the unfair trade practices involved in delivering that Chinese product to market, and the various regulatory and taxpayer costs that Chinese product failures entail. So if it's "Made in China," put that product back down unless you absolutely, positively need it and can't find a reasonable substitute.

#2: Find the Label—Then Read It Carefully!

We also can't stop buying Chinese products unless we know they have been made in China. Therefore, we all must do a much better job of carefully reading product labels.

Unfortunately, while "country of origin" labeling is required on all products by U.S. Customs regulations, finding the "Made in China" disclosure on a product can be like playing "Where's Waldo?"—and sometimes even requires a magnifying glass. (We are not kidding here.) That's why labeling regulations must require standardized, easy-to-find, and easy-to-read information, similar to the useful nutritional labeling on our nation's food products.

Label subterfuge is, however, not the only problem we face in trying to wean ourselves from Chinese products. This observation leads to our next action.

#3: Tighten Up the Cyberloophole on "Country of Origin" Labeling

In the traditional retail environment, "country of origin" labeling gives sharp-eyed consumers the opportunity to make choices about their purchases. However, as more and more consumers move to the Internet, this ability to use one's discretion is being lost, much to the benefit of unscrupulous Chinese manufacturers.

To understand the problem, just go for a browse on Amazon's website. For any given item, you can see every product detail *except* where the product is manufactured. This is clearly a loophole that needs to be tightened. Federal law should require all online retailers to clearly display the country of origin labeling information for all of their products.

#4: Demand "Country of Origin" Ingredient Labeling

As we have learned, some products are not wholly "Made in China," but rather many of the ingredients or parts in the products are of Chinese origin. For example, if multivitamin capsules are blended for packaging in the United States, producers can still slap on a "Made in the U.S.A." label despite substantial Chinese ingredients. A similar problem exists for products like putatively "American" cars that may have mission-critical parts like brake pads or tires manufactured in China.

Because of the dangers this labeling loophole poses, we urgently need tougher ingredient and component labeling legislation. For example, Congress should require all food and drug producers to clearly label the countries of origin for *all* major ingredients that go into a product—and do so in a standardized and legible manner. As Jerome Krachenfelser has aptly put it: "If you put it in your body, you deserve to know where it's from."

#5: Let Your Favorite Retailers Know You Prefer China-Free

If retailers like Walmart, Target, and Nordstrom know you would prefer China-free alternatives, they will change the way they stock their shelves. So do take the time to talk with all the salespeople and managers at the stores that you typically frequent, and let them know you would be a much more loyal customer if the store offered more alternatives.

To put further pressure on the big box and mall retailers that are so addicted to artificially cheap Chinese products that inflate their profits, you may also want to go online and look for websites that offer China-free products.

Likewise, you should feel free to write a letter or send an email to the customer relations division of both the manufacturers and the retail stores. Tell Apple and Best Buy that "Designed in California" simply doesn't cover up "Built in Guangdong." Once retailers get the China-free message, they will start competing for your business not just on price but on country of origin.

Finally, it is important to view this not as a "Made in the USA" statement but rather as a "Made in the Free World" campaign. *Real* free trade without the kinds of mercantilist and protectionist practices that characterize China can be a good thing. Great products coming from our real free trade partners like Japan, Mexico, and Germany improve our lives and contribute to our mutual prosperity. We need these countries on board the "real free trade" agenda and ready to share the burden of sanctioning a mercantilist and protectionist China whenever that becomes necessary.

#6: Beware of Big Ticket Items from China Bearing "Foreign" Brands

One major way that China plans to penetrate America's markets—particularly "big ticket" items like that of automobiles—is to sell their products under the name of familiar foreign brands that create the illusion of China-free. A case in point is Volvo. This nominally "Swedish" auto firm is now wholly owned by China's Geely Automotive, and its CEO, Stefan Jacoby, has recently stated that the company is considering exporting Chinese cars to the United States under the venerable Volvo moniker. Note also that Honda has been selling a Chinese car, the Jazz, into Europe since 2005. So again, buyer beware. Cash-rich Chinese firms—particularly state-owned enterprises—are going to be snapping up major Western brand names like there is no tomorrow, and you will have to pay attention to the financial press to learn about these deals.

#7: Tort Reform That Makes China and Its Middlemen Truly Liable

We are not even *small* fans of big lawsuits. However, we do believe it's just plain wrong that Chinese manufacturers can't be held accountable in American and international courts of law, while their American, European, and Japanese competitors are.

It's equally absurd that American companies that import dangerous Chinese drugs, foods, and products can't be held more accountable either. The current situation actually reduces the motivation for real tort reform by giving American firms this Chinese escape clause: Move your production to some mysterious broker in Guangzhou, and then pretend you don't know exactly where your products come from. Don't laugh; this happens. That's why we need much tougher laws that clearly assign blame to any American wholesaler or retailer selling a Chinese product that ultimately harms someone here in

America. More accountability will force retailers to find a way to push the liability back to where it actually belongs *or* make other choices when they stock their shelves. So let the White House, Capitol Hill, and your own State House know that it's well past time to crack down on the American middlemen purveying China's junk and poisons.

Disarming China's Weapons of Job Destruction

America's politicians need to get a whole lot smarter about the box that a mercantilist and protectionist China is putting us in—because it looks more and more like a coffin every day! That's why Congress and the President must tell China in no uncertain terms that the United States will no longer tolerate its anything-but-free trade assault on our manufacturing base.

If China refuses to lay down its Weapons of Job Destruction—which violate every rule in the free trade book—the President and Congress will have no other choice than to take swift action. Here's how America can unilaterally disarm these Chinese weapons.

#1: Pass the "American Free and Fair Trade Act"

The simplest and most effective legislative cure for China's mercantilist and protectionist ways—and one that avoids direct confrontation because it need not mention China directly by name—is for Congress to pass the "American Free and Fair Trade Act." This Act would set out the following ground rules—with appropriately tough sanctions for failing to play by them:

> *Any nation wishing to trade freely in manufactured goods with the United States must abandon all illegal export subsidies, maintain a fairly valued currency, offer strict protections for intellectual property, uphold environmental and*

*health and safety standards that meet international norms,
provide for an unrestricted global market in energy and raw
materials, and offer free and open access to its domestic markets, including media and Internet services.*

By passing such legislation, Congress can both safeguard the
international system of free trade and ensure the long-term prosperity of the American economy. Such legislation is not "protectionist"—
as the China apologists will no doubt leap to brand it. Rather, it is
simply common sense and a legitimate *self-defense* in the face of Chinese economic aggression.

#2: Global Cooperation and Coordination Is the Watchword

To quote the great American patriot, Ben Franklin: "We must all
hang together, or assuredly we shall all hang separately." That's why as
a companion action to passage of the Free and Fair Trade Act, the
United States must partner with Europe, Brazil, Japan, India, and
other victims of China's mercantilism and protectionism to petition
the World Trade Organization for full compliance of its rules by
China. Only by strength through numbers will the U.S. and others
succeed in bringing a now "beggaring thy neighbor" China into a true
community of free trading nations.

#3: A Secret Currency Manipulation Mission

If we were asked to identify the single most egregious problem in
the U.S.–China relationship, we'd have to call out the yuan peg to the
U.S. dollar. A floating currency is fundamental to automatically
adjusting trade flows and prevent the sort of chronic trade surpluses
that China runs with so many of its trading partners.

We do agree, however, with the China apologists that the Chinese
government doesn't respond well to direct pressure. That's why, at

least on the currency question, the first best option to bring about a fairly valued Chinese currency may be found in some top secret "shuttle diplomacy."

To this end—and this is an extremely urgent matter!—the White House should immediately send a secret emissary to inform the Chinese Communist Party of this: The United States will have no other choice than to brand China a currency manipulator at the next biennial Treasury Review and impose appropriate countervailing duties *unless* China strengthens its currency to fair value on its own.

In this discussion, America's emissary should make it clear that the United States would much prefer that currency reform be "China's idea," not that of the United States; and that in no way does the United States wish for China to "lose face" on this issue. In fact, that is why this mission must be conducted in total secrecy.

America's emissary must be clear, however, that after more than seven years of debate on this issue, patience has run out in the United States politically, and time has run out economically. Of course, if China fails to act in a timely manner, the Department of the Treasury must follow through on branding China a currency manipulator and impose appropriate defensive duties to bring the Chinese yuan to fair value.

#4: Recognize the Real Corporate Risks of Chinese Offshoring

Far too many American executives who decide to strategically offshore production and jobs to China invariably fail to adequately assess a range of risks. Obvious risks include the loss of a company's intellectual property either through outright theft or via China's policies of forced technology transfer and forced relocation of research and development to Chinese soil.

Beyond the loss of a company's intellectual property, other risks range from endemic corruption, severe pollution, and looming water shortages to the need to scale China's Great Walls of Protectionism. In any comprehensive corporate risk assessment, executives must also acknowledge this reality:

> If there is any one country the United States is likely to engage in military conflict with over the next several decades, it certainly is a rapidly militarizing China. And if you were an American business executive contemplating an offshoring decision, would you really want all of your company's eggs in the China basket when such a conflict arises over Taiwan or Tibet or territorial rights in the South China Seas or access to oil in the Middle East?

It follows that American executives offshoring to China must remove their rose-colored glasses and do a far more comprehensive risk assessment. Such a sober look at the *real* risks associated with offshoring to China should help, in turn, power a new "reshoring" tide that brings jobs back to America, Brazil, Japan, Europe, and emerging markets outside of China.

#5: Be Like Nucor Steel's Dan DiMicco—Not GE's Jeffrey Immelt

If American corporate executives want to better understand the art of fighting back against Chinese mercantilism and protectionism, they need look no further than Nucor Steel and the example set by its CEO, Dan DiMicco. Besides running one of the most successful and technologically innovative companies in the world, DiMicco spends considerable time in the public arena lobbying for real trade reform with China. In this way, DiMicco provides a sharp counterpoint to the naïve or even turncoat behavior of CEOs like GE's Jeffrey Immelt and Westinghouse's Jack Allen.

#6: Stop Forced Technology Transfer and the Hijacking of U.S. R&D

As the U.S.–China Commission has strongly recommended, the U.S. government must "help U.S. companies resist attempts by Chinese authorities to mandate or coerce foreign high-technology firms to reveal sensitive product information as a quid pro quo for market access in China." The U.S. government must likewise help companies resist the forced relocation of their research and development facilities to China as a condition of market entry. We, as a nation, are dooming ourselves to decades of stagnant growth by surrendering our technology to the Chinese, and this must be stopped! Because of the importance of this issue, we must also consider legislation that would prevent our firms from entering into deals with China that require any such technology transfers as a condition of market access.

#7: Stop the Use of Censorship as a Non-tariff Trade Barrier

Many of America's greatest exports are from our best-in-the-world entertainment, media, and Internet firms. China's heavy-handed use of censorship in movies, television, and the Internet combined with tacit support of rampant piracy is a massive assault on free trade. While Facebook is totally blocked in Shanghai, its Chinese counterpart RenRen is receiving a grand welcome in the United States and a $500 million listing on the NASDAQ. This is just so very wrong!

To ensure that China does not benefit from such predatory economic warfare, Congress should pass legislation that blocks any Chinese media and Internet firms that engage in censorship from raising funds from the U.S. stock markets.

#8: Prohibit Chinese State-Owned Enterprises from Buying Private Firms

We must stop pretending that a giant national oil, telecom, or mining firm with the backing of the Chinese state that buys up a competitor in America, Canada, or Australia will ever create any real value for our consumers or shareholders. Instead, we must recognize that China's state-owned enterprises are nurtured in a monopoly environment, fed with profits from unfair trade practices, have access to massively subsidized state bank financing, and are all run by members of a communist party elite intent on locking up markets and locking down resources around the world. While some American CEOs have been happy to sell off our national treasures to Beijing's cadres of state capitalists to pocket a quick buck, such transactions are not even remotely in our national interest.

And let's be crystal clear about this: China would *never* allow a Western company to buy any Chinese firm in a "strategic industry"—which includes aircraft, autos, energy, finance, technology, natural resources, and just about anything more sophisticated than peddling burgers or fried chicken.

Because of the strategic threat from foreign governments gaining control of American private industries, the U.S. Congress should pass legislation preventing domestic private firms from entertaining offers from state-owned enterprises, whether they are Chinese, Russian, or otherwise.

#9: We Need a President with *Both* Brains and a Backbone

Much of the blame for the destruction of the American manufacturing base through a massive wave of offshoring can be laid directly at the White House doorstep. From 2001 to 2008, President George

W. Bush certainly had the backbone to stand up to China. Unfortunately, his ideological blinders didn't allow him to understand the difference between free versus fair trade. As a result, the fiddling Bush administration did nothing but fixate upon the war on terror while a mercantilist and protectionist China systematically took apart our economy job by job and company by company.

In sharp contrast, President Barack Obama certainly has the intellect to understand the problem—he campaigned on a platform of cracking down on Chinese mercantilism and certainly knows the issue. Obama's problem, however, is that he doesn't appear to have the backbone to take the actions necessary.

Forgive our bluntness here, but what we really need now is a leader with *both* brains and a backbone—a Winston Churchill, not a Neville Chamberlain. Barack Obama could fit the bill if he got the message—but if he doesn't, the 2012 election will certainly provide America with another opportunity to find a president who will lead us out of the post-industrial wasteland that America is becoming under the onslaught of China's weapons of job destruction.

Drawing a Hard Line in the Sand on Chinese Espionage and Cyberwarfare

We have seen that China operates the most aggressive espionage network in America and that its Red Hacker brigades regularly assault our personal, corporate, and government computer networks. We must recognize the clear and present dangers these various forms of "war without fire" pose and rise up to counter them. We must also keep asking ourselves: Why are we trading so heavily with a country that so aggressively spies on us?

#1: Beef Up Chinese Counterintelligence Efforts

A lion's share of the resources available to the American intelligence community—the CIA, FBI, and other bulwarks such as the National Security Agency—continue to be devoted to the seemingly endless war on terror. This is hardly surprising as the threat of some Islamic fundamentalist group getting its hands on a weapon of mass destruction is a frightening possibility.

That said, we must also face this incontrovertible fact: Even as a rapidly militarizing China is accumulating hundreds of nuclear weapons, it is waging a relentless war of espionage and cyberattacks against our nation. To counter this equally clear and present danger, we must radically staff up and beef up our dedicated China counterintelligence efforts—and coordinate this work with our allies in Asia, Europe, and Latin America.

While any additional expenditures will be difficult to authorize in an age of severe budget constraints, in the end, we will get what we do or don't pay for. In considering such expenditures, we must recognize that the losses to our economic well-being from China's industrial espionage alone surely dwarf the woefully inadequate sums we are currently spending on countering the Chinese threat.

#2: Aggressively Prosecute and Penalize China's Spies

A spy who contributes to China's ability to develop advanced weapons systems is every bit as dangerous as any Chinese soldier pulling the trigger on those weapons. That's why our courts, our juries, and our prosecutors need to take Chinese espionage a whole lot more seriously; and *any* form of spying should be aggressively prosecuted.

As for appropriate penalties, spying for China by an American citizen is treason—the highest crime against our country. It should be punishable by life imprisonment and, in cases involving military and defense secrets, it should result in execution.

Moreover, if any Chinese agents are caught here in America, they should be locked up and the proverbial key thrown away—for only such harsh penalties will deter spy activity on our soil. And please note here that any American spy caught on Chinese soil would experience a far more brutal fate than anything our justice system could mete out.

#3: Increased Scrutiny of Chinese Visitors and Visas

The Chinese government clearly does not allow tourists, students, or business executives to roam freely throughout China, and it puts severe constraints on many types of visitors, including journalists and documentary filmmakers. Yet America allows virtually any Chinese citizen who asks for a visa to run wild in our country. This must stop now!

Therefore, as part of our enhanced counterespionage efforts, there must be far greater scrutiny of anyone from the People's Republic of China applying for a visa. While the vast majority of Chinese visitors come in peace, there are more than enough secret agents in this bunch to warrant far greater precautions.

Is this "racial profiling"? Absolutely not. It is "country of origin" profiling, and it must be done precisely because China has proven to be the most aggressive nation in the world when it comes to exporting spies to U.S. soil.

#4: Declare Cyberattacks to Be Acts of War—and Respond Accordingly

The Obama administration has called for a more comprehensive cybersecurity policy, and that is all to the good. The cornerstone of this policy must be to treat any state-sponsored cyberattacks as acts of war subject to immediate economic, political, and, if necessary, military retaliation. Moreover, we must be completely honest about where these cyberthreats are coming from and deal with them directly.

In this regard, for far too long, we have allowed the Chinese Communist Party to hide behind the absurd excuse that the computer hacking originating from the most heavily censored and monitored Internet in the world is outside the Party's control. Trust us: If these hackers were distributing videos of Chinese atrocities in Tibet or pro-democracy meetings in Shanghai or Falun Gong worshippers in Chengdu, China's cybercops could and would find them and stop them—quite permanently. So let's end this charade and call a Chinese hacker a state-sponsored Chinese hacker!

We also believe that economic restitution to the victims of Chinese hacking must be part of any comprehensive cybersecurity policy. Accordingly, the American Congress, along with the European Union, the Japanese Diet, and other legislative bodies around the world should pass legislation providing for such restitution to citizens, firms, and government agencies that suffer from foreign hacker attacks. To make such restitution meaningful, such legislation should provide for strong mechanisms to attach the assets of companies found to be involved in such cyberhacking—a case in point being the role of a major Chinese telecom firm in an attack we described in Chapter 10.

#5: Develop a "China Kill Switch" for the Internet

From a strategic perspective, there is no real difference between a power plant destroyed by a Chinese missile or one disabled by a Chinese hacker. Both threats are real. Both have to be anticipated and defended against.

Given the repeated attacks and probes of Chinese hackers on American institutions during what is supposed to be "peace time," it is critical we develop a "China Kill Switch" that can disconnect America's Internet from all Chinese Internet Protocol addresses in the event of a full-scale cyberwar. But that's not all.

Many Chinese cyberattacks are launched from servers and personal computers outside of China that have been hijacked by the Red Hacker brigades. This means a second-level kill switch is needed that can completely isolate key pieces of our infrastructure—utilities, banks, defense firms—from the Internet entirely.

The political discussion of this badly needed defensive system will no doubt include well-meaning arguments over free speech and civil liberties. Obviously, any solution must be designed for minimal impact on civilian communications and in no way limit access to media. However, the external threat to our freedom is unfortunately much more real than some imagined domestic conspiracy; and if we trust our government with a huge nuclear arsenal, we also need to be able to trust that same government to make the right call on protecting our nation from a massive external cyberattack.

#6: Call Beijing Out for Its Reckless Espionage and Theft

Just as we need to call a Chinese hacker a Chinese hacker, we need to call a spy a spy and publicly chastise China for its hostile espionage behavior. We must also make it clear that America, Japan, Korea, Taiwan, Australia, India, and the European Union are not going to continue to look the other way while Beijing's agents steal our technologies, sabotage our institutions, and prepare for a future apocalyptic cyberwar. If the People's Republic of China wants to do business with us, it will have to behave like it belongs in the same club of free and fair trading nations.

Confronting and Countering the Rising Chinese Military Threat

We cannot turn our backs on this truth: China's rapid economic growth at the expense of the American manufacturing base is financing an even more rapid Chinese military escalation. It is a multidimensional buildup of an air, land, sea, cyber, and space war machine that will soon threaten the global supremacy of the American military. We must both acknowledge and confront this threat; and as we do so, we must keep asking ourselves this question: Why are we buying so many Chinese products when the profits are being used to build weapons that are increasingly aimed at us?

#1: We Can't Overwhelm the Chinese with Our Industrial Might

As a first strategic principle, America must recognize that China is putting the United States in the same role that Germany played facing Roosevelt's America in World War II. The United States beat the Nazis not with superior technology but with the overwhelming might of its industrial machine.

Today, the shoe is on the other foot because it is now China that can churn out hordes of ships, tanks, and planes on its factory floor. Because China's superior *quantity* of weapons can ultimately bury America's superior *quality* of weapons—just like America's matériel overwhelmed the Nazis—we must be ever more clever and strategic in our military strategy.

As a first rule, we absolutely must get more "bang for our buck" out of our moribund, cost-plus military industrial complex. The current weapons procurement system creates spectacularly expensive weapons systems that are constantly over budget, always behind schedule, and often trouble-plagued.

At the same time, we must recognize that as China rapidly arms, our vulnerabilities will only increase. Therefore, if we are ever going to confront the Chinese on this silently escalating cold war, the time is *now*. We need to publicly call them out on their anything but peaceful rise and seriously ask ourselves if "most favored nation" status really belongs to a nation hell bent on being our top military threat.

#2: We Can't Be Lured into an Arms Race and the "Reagan Trap"

From a strategic perspective, America's political and military leaders must also recognize that a cash-flush Beijing would love to put the United States in the same role that the Soviet Union played facing President Ronald Reagan's America in the 1980s. As China well knows, the Reagan administration buried the Soviet Union by luring it into an arms race that eventually bankrupted the Soviets—and triggered the worldwide fall of communist regimes.

Here, again, the shoe is on the other foot. China, with its trillions of dollars in foreign reserves, booming economy, and rapid militarization, would love to lure a fiscally precarious United States into an arms race that could ultimately break America financially. Again, this reality demands that America be both more clever and strategic in its approach—as well as more aggressive in acting to preempt China's lightning-quick military rise.

#3: Honestly Assess Our Vulnerabilities

Following the recommendation of the U.S.–China Commission, the Pentagon should be required to report annually on the ability of the U.S. military to withstand a Chinese air and missile assault on its regional bases and list a set of specific steps that can be taken to survive such an assault. The Commission has also urged our military to "strengthen its interaction with allies in the Western Pacific" and "expand its outreach to other nations in Asia to demonstrate the U.S.'s continued commitment to the region." Building up strong alliances with three of China's likely future targets—Japan, India, and Vietnam—represents an important part of this strategy.

#4: We Must Disarm China's Weapons of Job Destruction If We Are to Prevent China's Massive Military Buildup

It was the famous Prussian military theorist Karl von Clausewitz who once said, "War is an extension of politics, but by other means." Today, in a similar vein, we must recognize that China's rapid military buildup is a direct extension of its economic growth, and that far too much of that growth is coming at America's expense.

That's why ultimately we must come to understand that the best argument for disarming China's weapons of job destruction is not to "save our jobs"—as important as that might be. Rather, the best argument for confronting China's unfair trade practices is one of national defense:

> If we surrender our manufacturing base to Chinese mercantilism while we continue to finance China's rise by buying Chinese products and running massive trade deficits, all we are doing as consumers is ensuring our own eventual demise.

Countering the Colonial Dragon

As we have illustrated in great detail, Chinese boots on the ground are marching all across the African continent and into Latin America looking to lock up energy and raw materials for China's industrial machine. So far, this budding colonial empire has gone virtually unchallenged.

Stemming this tide of Chinese colonialism certainly won't be easy. But just as every journey begins with one small step, there are at least some steps we can take to meet this global Chinese challenge.

#1: Stop China's UN Veto Abuses Now

Here is one of the most important moral questions of our time that each of us as American citizens must continually ask ourselves and our political leaders: How can America's President, Secretary of State, and United Nations Ambassador remain silent as a "rug merchant" China continues to use its United Nations veto power as a bargaining chip to obtain natural resources and raw materials from rogue nations like Iran and dictatorships like those in the Sudan and Zimbabwe? This crass commercial behavior by China to build its colonial empire must be roundly condemned not just by the United States but also by countries around the world—from Europe and Asia to Latin America and especially Africa, which bears much of the brunt of China's bloody and barbaric veto strategy.

#2: Rebuild Our Diplomatic Missions with a Counter-China Focus

We need to beef up and staff up the institutions that have typically helped the United States project "soft power" around the world. These institutions include government agencies like the Foreign Service, the U.S. Agency for International Development, the Peace Corps, and the many branches of the U.S. military that provide services in regions where American forces are deployed.

As part of a revival of U.S. diplomacy, we also need to carefully monitor Chinese activities around the world. Such monitoring must be conducted at the global grassroots; thus, in every one of the almost 300 embassies, consulates, and other diplomatic missions the United States maintains around the world, we should deploy one or more China specialists. More broadly, this focus will help build up a core of China analysts in the American diplomatic and intelligence communities.

Nor should possible corporate contributions to the projection of America's soft power be overlooked. The fact here is that many American CEOs view themselves as patriots, and we need to engage their firms in getting their operations abroad to act as ambassadors for our nation.

#3: Get America's Message Out to the World

Both of us have listened to radio broadcasts from the Voice of America in far-flung places around the world, and we both know first-hand the power of such information. We also know how important facilities like American centers offering libraries and cultural programming can be in swaying "hearts and minds" in developing countries.

Regarding the Voice of America, it is useful to note that satellite TV is extremely popular in rural China, where even 200-year-old adobe brick farmhouses are sprouting big dishes. For this reason, we think it important to expand Voice of America satellite TV service beamed into China; and this can be done on existing Asian positioned geo-sync satellites. If the Chinese protest, we should tell them it's our way of getting some of that "market access" they agreed to when they signed on with the World Trade Organization.

The West might also consider ways to actively provide free Internet proxy server services to Chinese citizens. Such services would allow Internet users behind China's Great Firewall to freely venture into the "real virtual world."

In considering such options, it is useful to remember that America is still by far the media and marketing king of the world. In light of our capabilities, it is amazing that we have completely failed to leverage that ability to effectively sell our democratic values abroad.

#4: Replace French and German with Mandarin in Our High Schools

We are all for multilingualism in today's world, but we find it extremely myopic that in this new twenty-first century, many junior high schools and high schools continue to require students to meet their foreign language requirements with courses in French and German but do not offer classes in Mandarin Chinese. In fact, Mandarin should be offered beginning in elementary school. This is a case where we have met the enemy, and it is our school system. So lobby your school boards accordingly. (While you're at it, have them replace cursive handwriting instruction with keyboarding.)

Stopping Death on China by China

Immediately upon assuming the position of Secretary of State, Hillary Clinton informed the world that America would no longer pressure China on human rights. No more imprudent words have ever been spoken on this subject.

The fact is: We need a "jasmine revolution" in China—peaceful or otherwise—to either rid the people of China of Communist Party rule or have Communist Party leaders loosen their totalitarian grip on the world's most populous nation. Turning down the rhetoric and pressure on human rights abuses as Secretary Clinton has done moves China in exactly the wrong direction and gives the rest of the developing world the impression—hopefully incorrect—that the West tacitly approves of the regime in Beijing and its brand of totalitarian state capitalism.

#1: Reinstitute Human Rights as an Element of U.S. Foreign Policy

The United States and other countries around the world must continue to exert pressure on China to respect basic human rights, including freedom of speech, association, assembly, and worship, along with freedom to organize in the workplace and reproductive self-determination.

America must also be willing to stand up for the rights of indigenous populations like those in Tibet, Inner Mongolia, and Xinjiang Province; and that includes calling for an immediate halt to the ongoing ethnic cleansing campaigns now taking place in these anything-but "autonomous regions" of China.

#2: Divest, Don't Invest

The "Divestment" campaign against South African firms was highly successful in bringing down that country's racist oligarchy. We suggest the same tactic would be just as effective with a country as dependent on foreign investment as China. Do your part by *not* investing in Chinese firms, Chinese mutual funds, or even "developing nation" growth funds that are chock full of Chinese stocks. Frankly, you'll be doing yourself a favor by reducing your exposure to a risk-filled, corrupt, and nontransparent economy plagued by asset bubbles. If you want to play the China growth card, at least do it one step removed by considering investments in the firms and currencies of resource-rich countries like Australia and Brazil that boom as China booms.

#3: Restrict Exports of Internet Censorship Tools

Far too many of the virtual "bricks" that have been laid down to construct China's "Great Firewall" have been made in America by some of our best-known companies—with Cisco being a poster child for this problem. It is far past time we put a halt to this kind of complicity and duplicity. Congress should therefore immediately pass legislation to restrict the export of any software or hardware products that may be used by totalitarian regimes to censor the Internet and telecommunications systems.

Meeting the China Space Challenge

Of all the areas we've discussed, the competition to establish dominion over the high frontier may have the biggest impact on our children's future. Ensuring that our children are free from President Lyndon B. Johnson's nightmare of "sleeping by the light of a communist moon" requires prompt and immediate action. With America's public space program in disarray and the federal budget in crisis, bold new ideas are certainly needed.

#1: Leverage America's Private Industry Advantage to Drive Down Costs

Government support was critical for jump starting our space program after Sputnik. However, since the success of the Apollo program, the moral hazard of cost-plus accounting coupled with pork barrel politics has created an incestuous oligopoly of inefficient aerospace giants and left us with a space exploration bureaucracy that timidly goes where man has gone many times before—and at great expense.

The time has now come to turn the government's space monopoly over to real private industry and let both civilians and our military benefit from the market forces that have always served our nation well. The West was won by miners, ranchers, wagon trains, and railroads, not by Custer's cavalry. A single container full of government astronauts floating closer to the Earth than the distance between Boston and New York is not how you conquer the last frontier.

In fact, reducing the costs of space exploration is something that exciting new companies like SpaceX, Scaled Composites, Sierra Nevada, and XCOR are already doing. Even better, this sort of free-thinking, barnstorming aerospace design is something that China's giant state-owned enterprises can never replicate and China's control freak leadership will never allow—although Chinese spies and hackers will surely try to steal the resulting technologies. We must, therefore, leverage America's private industry advantage in this critical dimension.

For these reasons, NASA administrator Charles Bolden has called for private firms to quickly take over the more mundane "space trucking" functions and thereby provide "reliable, routine, access to low Earth orbit." Delegating these more mundane functions to private enterprise would allow NASA to move back into more exciting exploration challenges. This goal has been backed by President Obama's budget, which includes $6 billion in additional NASA funds specifically allocated to contracting for private launch services. Congressional efforts to sink this plan, backtrack on privatization, and return NASA to a sleepy socialized jobs program must be stopped!

#2: Promote STEM Education

China is producing ten or more times the amount of scientists and engineers as the United States; and we as a country are falling far behind in these fields. We must redouble our efforts at the individual, family, corporate, and government levels to close this widening gap by encouraging our new generations to become engineers and scientists, and by providing appropriate funding, facilities, and opportunities.

Accordingly, scholarships, student loans, and educational grants should be disproportionately tilted to Science, Technology, Engineering, and Math—the so-called STEM subjects. At the same time, parents need to encourage their children to pursue STEM careers. The media can do its part here, too, by generating positive messages and role models about bright kids who do great things that move civilization forward. Corporations can likewise make a point of publicly rewarding their top engineers in the same way they massage the egos of their star salespeople with awards' dinners and trips to the tropics.

#3: Claim the Moon Before China Does

After reading this book, do you really expect that China's space program will be dedicated to the good of all the world? The fact is, we have to anticipate that China is going to start snapping up space resources exactly the way it is carving out the whole South China Sea as a sphere of influence and claiming resource-rich Japanese territorial waters as an exclusive Chinese domain.

That's why the United States must start laying claim to valuable space resources like the moon while we still have a strong position to do so. We must also start laying out our claims to resource-rich asteroids like Eros and potentially colonizable spots like Ceres, Mars, and the Lagrange points. When other countries yell and scream about our "land grabs," pull them to the table and create an equitable system that will allow free enterprise, free thinking, and free people to carry mankind's legacy to the stars rather than a harshly repressive, totalitarian, and state capitalist China.

Concluding Thoughts

While each of the individual actions, executive decisions, and government reforms outlined in this chapter will significantly improve the prospects that the U.S.–China relationship will be a prosperous rather than a parasitic one, what is perhaps most needed around the world is a wholesale attitude adjustment.

For far too long, we in the West have waited for a growing Chinese economy to somehow magically transform a ruthless totalitarian regime into a free and open democratic nation. We have waited through the massacre at Tiananmen Square; the ethnic cleansing campaigns in Inner Mongolia, Tibet, and Xinjiang; the development of the world's most sophisticated propaganda machine and stifling Internet censorship; the unleashing of a flood of lethally dangerous products onto world markets; the gutting of America's manufacturing base; the wholesale polluting of the global commons; the repeated assaults of an elaborate espionage network on military and industrial targets; and the emergence of a five-dimensional expeditionary military force capable of one day enforcing all of its absurd territorial claims around the globe—and no doubt one day in space.

We must wait no longer. Indeed, it is well past time for all of us to confront China—even as we confront our own false hopes that somehow, despite all the evidence to the contrary, China's rise will indeed be peaceful.

And it should also go without saying here that as we move forward on issues ranging from Chinese mercantilism and product safety to climate change, human rights, and military cooperation, working with China at any level will require constant vigilance. It will also require a strict adherence to this variation on Ronald Reagan's cold war advice about negotiating with the Soviet Union. For based on China's abysmal track record to date, with Beijing, we must appropriately "mistrust and constantly reverify."

Epilogue

Back in 1984, I had the task of writing speeches for Ronald Reagan's trip to China. This was the first such outing by an American president since Richard Nixon established relations with the Communists in 1972, and it came during a period of great promise and significant progress in Chinese politics.

At the time, China's leader Deng Xiaoping appeared to be sincerely moving Mao's isolationist prison state toward the community of modern, democratic nations and away from conflict with the West. In response, American companies like Coca-Cola, KFC, and Proctor and Gamble were beginning to plant roots in China, and Chinese exports to the U.S. were growing—yet at this point offered no cause for alarm.

As long as that process of democratic and economic liberalization in Chinese continued, America was right to respond with further engagement. However, as you have just read in this book, that liberalization process ended abruptly in June 1989 with a parade of tanks and a bloody showdown in Tiananmen Square.

Since Tiananmen, a ruthless and reactionary Chinese Communist Party has used any means necessary to remain firmly in power. Today, behind the façade of a "peaceful rise," a far too trusting American nation has been maneuvered into a highly dysfunctional trade relationship with China that is inexorably destroying our manufacturing base and rapidly degrading our ability to defend ourselves from China's rising military threat.

Despite the growing threat from China—and in a remarkably misplaced case of bipartisan support—American presidents from Bush I and Clinton to Bush II and Obama have continued to pursue engagement with Beijing as though the relationship were quite normal. And that is the fundamental flaw in Sino–U.S. relations: Our politicians continue to treat China's leaders as if they were our democratic friends from Europe or Japan, when in fact this is a murderous gangster regime no better than Ahmadinejad's Iran or Gadhafi's Libya and every bit as brutal as Stalin's Russia.

I can assure you that if Ronald Reagan were president today, he would stand up to the totalitarians in Beijing as he once did to the Soviets. There would no "most favored nation" status and no crippling reliance on China to finance our government budget. There would be swift justice for Chinese spies, strong sanctions against Chinese cyberwarfare, and zero tolerance for mercantilist practices such as currency manipulation. There would also be repeatedly expressed diplomatic outrage at China's crass commercial use of its UN veto power to acquire key natural resources from rogue nations. And just as Ronald Reagan insisted to Mr. Gorbachev to "tear down that wall," he would proclaim to the Chinese people, "We are on your side, not the side of your oppressors." And he would assure American workers that, "We are not going to ship your job to Guangzhou for products made more cheaply because of slave labor, illegal export subsidies, blatant piracy, and an undervalued yuan."

In fact, history has already taught us the harshest of lessons about what can happen when we in the community of democratic nations allow ourselves to be seduced by the "economic miracle" of a rising totalitarian power. Indeed, during the Depression-ravaged 1930s, many American business executives were lured to Germany by a seductive mix of cutting-edge technologies, ultra-nationalism, and state capitalism eerily similar to that available in today's China.

During Germany's earlier version of a "peaceful rise," brilliant but naïve conservative businessmen like Henry Ford invested huge sums and built large factories in the Third Reich. Of course, the German government first chipped away at Ford's control with everything from domestic content requirements to the ethnic cleansing of management. Eventually, the company was renamed Ford-Werke, put under complete government control, and used to quite literally transport the German war machine during the blitzkriegs of neighbors ranging from Poland, Denmark, and Norway to the Netherlands, France, and Greece.

At about this same time, "enlightened" liberals were flocking to tour the then-new Soviet Union, and muckraking journalist Lincoln Steffens famously came back announcing, "I've seen the future, and it works!" Caught up in the excitement, Henry Ford ran to build a new auto plant at Gorky to participate in this brave new market. Of course, this, too, was a totalitarian sham, and Ford was ripped off again.

In light of this history—and the profound portrait of today's China so accurately painted in this book—business and political leaders from Detroit and Washington to Paris, London, and Tokyo should all be having a serious sense of déjà vu about what is happening now. So as you finish this book and prepare to respond to its urgent call to action, please remember two things:

First, every day, tens of millions of successful Chinese individuals from San Francisco and Toronto to Singapore and Taipei demonstrate that the Chinese people and Chinese culture can thrive in free societies. When people are beaten, tortured, or killed to hold onto power or when foreigner investors and business partners are lied to and their trade secrets and technologies are pirated, that isn't "Chinese." It is simply wrong.

Second, each of us would do well to carefully consider the implications in the following exchange between Chinese Premier Zhou En Lai and U.S. Secretary of State Henry Kissinger in a 1973 meeting during the genesis of normal relations with Communist China:

> **Zhou:** *Perhaps it is the national character of the Americans to be taken in by those who seem kind and mild.*
>
> **Kissinger:** *Yes.*
>
> **Zhou:** *But the world is not so simple...*

Indeed...

—**Congressman Dana Rohrabacher**,
46th district (Rep, CA)

Endnotes

3   *To feed its manufacturing machine*   www.commodities.xorte.com/0,14,China-Dominates-the-Global-Aluminium-Industry,9751.html; www.icsg.org/index.php?option=com_content&task=view&id=57&Itemid=60; www.editgrid.com/user/nerdsofsteel/Worldsteel_Association_Short_Term_Forecast%2C_April_2010; www.business-standard.com/india/storypage.php?autono=410308; www.chinadaily.com.cn/bizchina/2009-03/02/content_7527574.htm; http://cementamericas.com/cement_newsline/2009-global-cement-0730/

   Moreover, by the year 2035   www.transportation.anl.gov/pdfs/TA/398.pdf; http://oilprice.com/Energy/Energy-General/A-look-at-Chinas-Growing-Demand-for-Oil.html

4   *In exchange for Sudanese oil*   Maggie Farley, "U.N. puts Darfur death toll at 300,000," *Los Angeles Times* (April 23, 2008). http://articles.latimes.com/2008/apr/23/world/fg-darfur23

7   *the People's Republic annually executes*   www.amnesty.org/en/library/asset/ACT50/001/2010/en/17348b70-3fc7-40b2-a258-af92778c73e5/act500012010en.pdf

9   *Chinese espionage activities in the United States*   "China spying 'biggest US threat,'" *BBC News* (November 15, 2007). http://news.bbc.co.uk/2/hi/americas/7097296.stm

   Chinese hackers and spies   Stéphane Lefebvre, "The PRC's Compromise of U.S. Government Information and Technologies," *International Journal of Intelligence and CounterIntelligence* 22, 4 (2009): 652-666.

16   *Fully 10% of all the restaurants*   Li Wenfang, "Illegal cooking oil made from kitchen waste," *China Daily* (November 17, 2009). www.chinadaily.com.cn/china/2009-11/17/content_8986419.htm

18   *I've completely lost confidence in milk powder*   Fox Hu, "Global Dairy IPO Soured by Melamine Scandal Memories," *Bloomberg Businessweek* (October 29, 2010). www.businessweek.com/news/2010-10-29/global-dairy-ipo-soured-by-melamine-scandal-memories.html

   Before melamine, the dealers added rice porridge   Jim Yardley and David Barboza, "Despite Warnings, China's Regulators Failed to Stop Tainted Milk," *New York Times* (September 26, 2008).

19   *The dairy scandal raises the core question*   Ibid.

21 *According to business professor Luo Yadong*   Luo Yadong, "A Strategic Analysis of
    Product Recalls: The Role of Moral Degradation and Organizational Control,"
    Management and Organization Review (July 2008) 4(2): 183-196.

    There reaches a point where I think it's clear   Andrew Martin, "F.D.A. Curbs Sale
    of 5 Seafoods Farmed in China," *New York Times* (June 29, 2007).
    www.nytimes.com/2007/06/29/business/worldbusiness/29fish.html

22 *But one reason is that Chinese orchards*   Tom Marshall, "Arsenic in apple juice:
    How much is too much?" *St. Petersburg Times* (March 14, 2010). www.tampabay.
    com/news/health/article1079395.ece

    tea leaves out on a huge warehouse floor   Richard Knox, "As Imports Increase, a
    Tense Dependence on China," *NPR.org* (May 25, 2007).
    www.npr.org/templates/story/story.php?storyId=10410111

23 *Maybe 30% of farms that put the organic label*   Jordan Calinoff, "China's new
    organic industry," *GlobalPost* (February 19, 2009). www.globalpost.com/
    dispatch/china-and-its-neighbors/090217/chinas-new-organic-industry

    Consider what happened when one Japanese   "Tainted beans from China sicken
    three," *Japan Times Online* (October 16, 2008). http://search.japantimes.co.
    jp/cgi-bin/nn20081016a1.html

24 *Our waters here are filthy*   "In China, Farming Fish in Toxic Waters," *New York
    Times* (2007). www.nytimes.com/2007/12/15/world/asia/15fish.html

25 *Along the Yangtze's route*   Richard Stone, "On China's Beleaguered Yangtze, A
    Push to Save Surviving Species," *Yale Environment 360* (August 23, 2010).
    http://e360.yale.edu/feature/on_chinas_beleaguered_yangtze_a_push_to_
    save_surviving_species/2311/

    The reservoir waters glow an eerie   "Three gorges dam will turn fast flowing
    Yangtze stagnant polluted reservoir," *Probe International* (1999). http://
    probeinternational.org/three-gorges-probe/three-gorges-dam-will-turn-fast-
    flowing-yangtze-stagnant-polluted-reservoir

    [T]he conditions that aquacultured seafood is grown under   Chenglin Liu, "The
    Obstacles of Outsourcing Imported Food Safety to China," *Cornell International
    Law Journal* 43 (2010): 302.

26 *Indeed, this type of "pink primping"*   Stephen Newman, "Carbon monoxide in
    tilapia processing," *SeafoodSource.com* (May 25, 2010). www.seafoodsource.
    com/blogs.aspx?id=4294993601&blogid=4295004787

27 *Certain Chinese companies are now mass producing*   Ethan A. Huff, "Chinese
    companies mass producing fake rice out of plastic," *Natural News* (February 15,
    2011). www.naturalnews.com/031344_plastic_rice.html

    As noted by an official from the Chinese Restaurant Association   Mr. P, "China
    Makes Fake Rice from Plastic? Vietnam Reacts," *Very Vietnam* (January 22, 2011).
    http://veryvietnam.com/2011-01-22/china-makes-fake-rice-from-plastic-vietnam-
    reacts/

28 *Each year, farms grow only 800,000 tons of Wuchang rice*   "Fake high quality rice
    allegedly produced using additives," *Global Times* (July 14, 2010). http://china.
    globaltimes.cn/society/2010-07/551672.html

29 *Amber Donnals was sitting on her porch* "Foreign ATVs may be new danger," *St. Louis Post-Dispatch* (August 3, 2008). http://business.highbeam.com/435553/article-1G1-182177845/foreign-atvs-may-new-danger-hazardous-imports-chinese-made

30 *enemy of the state* Paul Midler, *Poorly Made in China*, (Hoboken: John Wiley & Sons, 2009).

31 *importing defective products* Ibid.

32 *Consider that in 2009* 2009 Annual Report of the European Commission, http://ec.europa.eu/consumers/safety/rapex/docs/2009_rapex_report_en.pdf

   18% for China versus 13% for the United States Eurostat, 2010, http://trade.ec.europa.eu/doclib/docs/2006/september/tradoc_122529.pdf

   Despite vigorous attempts by the European Union 2009 Annual Report of the European Commission, ibid.

33 *China still managed to outdo itself* Ibid.

   The responsible Chinese manufacturer Ibid.

   When Bill Morgan, a retired policeman Leslie Wayne, "Thousands of Homeowners Cite Drywall for Ills," *New York Times* (October 7, 2009). www.nytimes.com/2009/10/08/business/08drywall.html?_r=3&pagewanted=all, 2009

34 *Florida is hypersensitive to hurricanes* Ibid.

35 *Even the head coach of the New Orleans Saints* Ibid.

   To investigate the scandal Investigation of Imported Drywall, Status Update (September 2010). www.cpsc.gov/info/drywall/sep2010status.pdf

   while the IRS had to create a special deduction "IRS Provides Relief for Homeowners with Corrosive Drywall," (September 30, 2010). www.irs.gov/newsroom/article/0,,id=228402,00.html

   One night I found him with blood all over his face Paul Bracchi, "This baby was burned red raw by a sofa giving off toxic fumes," *Daily Mail* (June 21, 2008). www.dailymail.co.uk/femail/article-1028097/This-baby-burned-red-raw-sofa-giving-toxic-fumes-As-investigation-reveals-hundreds-victims.html#ixzz1JKTImWcU

36 *This "DMF" is an extremely powerful chemical* T. Rantanen, "The cause of the Chinese sofa/chair dermatitis epidemic is likely to be contact allergy to dimethylfumarate, a novel potent contact sensitizer," *British Journal of Dermatology* 159, 1 (July 2008): 218-221. http://onlinelibrary.wiley.com/doi/10.1111/j.1365-2133.2008.08622.x/abstract;jsessionid=7A66688E885C626E7065B13AAB906EE4.d02t01

   suffered severe skin or eye complaints Anna Lewcock, "Payout for 'toxic sofa' victims," *Chemistry World* (April 27, 2010). www.rsc.org/chemistryworld/News/2010/April/27041002.asp

   In a heart-wrenching twist Ibid.

37 *On August 2, Mattel recalled about 1.5 million* Associated Press, "Mattel issues new massive China toy recall," MSNBC.com (August 14, 2007). www.msnbc.msn.com/id/20254745/ns/business-consumer_news/

38   *In talking about lead, we would be remiss*   Based on in-person interviews and
     email correspondence from November 16 to 24, 2010 with an anonymous source
     who was the purchasing manager of the U.S. firm.

39   *Walmart said Wednesday it is pulling*   Associated Press, "Walmart pulls Miley
     Cyrus jewelry from shelves," *Portland Press Herald* (May 20, 2010). www.
     pressherald.com/news/walmart-pulls-miley-cyrus-jewelry-from-shelves_2010-05-
     20.html

40   *too difficult to test products already on its shelves*   Ibid.

     In this same year, Walmart was busted   Associated Press, "Walmart Pendants
     Recalled as Disney Bans Cadmium," *ABC News* (January 29, 2010). http://
     abcnews.go.com/Health/wireStory?id=9698836

     It is generally understood that the primary consumer   Associated Press, "Feds dis-
     miss need to recall lead drinking glasses," *Yahoo! Health* (December 10, 2010).
     http://health.yahoo.net/news/s/ap/us_cadmium_lead_glassware

     A major customer complained that our bottles   Paul Midler, ibid.

42   *Hangzhou Zhongce has refused to tell*   Andrew Martin, "Chinese Tires Are
     Ordered Recalled," *New York Times* (June 26, 2007). www.nytimes.com/2007/
     06/26/business/worldbusiness/26tire.html

43   *waited more than 2 years to pass on their suspicions*   Ibid.

     In the ensuing recall of close to half a million tires   "Recalls of Chinese Auto Parts
     Are a Mounting Concern," *New York Times* (May 19, 2008).

     http://wheels.blogs.nytimes.com/2008/12/19/recalls-of-chinese-auto-parts-are-a-
     mounting-concern/; David Welch, "An Importer's Worst Nightmare," *Bloomberg
     Businessweek* (July 23, 2007). www.businessweek.com/magazine/content/
     07_30/b4043005.htm

     In its Hidden Hazards series   Maurice Possley, "Missteps delayed recall of deadly
     cribs," *Chicago Tribune* (September 24, 2007). www.chicagotribune.com/news/
     chi-070922cribs-story,0,1739695,print.story

44   *The side of the crib had come off*   www.cbsnews.com/video/watch/?id=3290580n,
     2007.

     Despite 55 complaints, seven infants left trapped   Maurice Possley, ibid.

     The problem with China is   Gary Davis, "Graco Stroller Recall is Another Failure
     of Chinese Workmanship: Why Do We Keep Putting Our Children at Risk?,"
     Yahoo! Associated Content (January 10, 2010). www.associatedcontent.com/
     article/2613585/graco_stroller_recall_is_another_failure.html

49   *China has become a major financial and trade power*   Paul Krugman, "Chinese
     New Year," *New York Times* (December 31, 2009).

57   *China has intervened on a gigantic scale*   Martin Wolf, "Evaluating the renminbi
     manipulation," *Financial Times* (2010). www.ft.com/cms/s/0/dbc9fa4c-41af-11df-
     865a-00144feabdc0.html#axzz1815jvHMl

61   *China's deadly factory floor*   Gary Roskin, "China's Silicosis Epidemic Triggers
     CIBJO Involvement," *JCK Magazine* (April 2006). www.jckonline.com/article/
     288813-China_s_Silicosis_Epidemic_Triggers_CIBJO_Involvement.php

Yongkang...just south of Shangahi   Joseph Kahn, "China's Workers Risk Limbs in Export Drive," *New York Times* (April 7, 2003). www.asria.org/ref/library/social/lib/031208_NYTimes_sweatshops_inchina.pdf

66 *I really worry about China*   Guy Dinmore and Geoff Dyer, "Immelt Hits out at China and Obama," *Financial Times* (July 1, 2010). http://cachef.ft.com/cms/s/0/ed654fac-8518-11df-adfa-00144feabdc0,dwp_uuid=86be4e0c-53d0-11db-8a2a-0000779e2340.html#axzz1ANArK26I

67 *American workers can compete dollar for dollar*   Eric Lotke, "What Chinese Currency Manipulation Looks Like," *Campaign for America's Future* (November 12, 2009). www.ourfuture.org/blog-entry/2009114612/what-chinese-currency-manipulation-looks

70 *The Chinese government has begun a concerted campaign*   Ambrose Evans-Pritchard, "China threatens 'nuclear option' of dollar sales," *London Telegraph* (August 7, 2007). www.telegraph.co.uk/finance/markets/2813630/China-threatens-nuclear-option-of-dollar-sales.html

74 *We're fed up*   Sewell Chan, "China Says It Will Not Adjust Exchange Rate," *New York Times* (March 24, 2010). www.nytimes.com/2010/03/25/business/global/25yuan.html

75 *First of all, I do not think the [yuan]*   Andrew Batson, Ian Johnson, and Andrew Browne, "China Talks Tough to U.S.," *Wall Street Journal* (March 15, 2010). http://online.wsj.com/article/SB10001424052748703457104575121213043099350.html

77 *General Electric plans to sink more than $2 billion*   "General Electric to sink $2billion into China development as production moves from the U.S.," *Daily Mail* (November 11, 2010). www.dailymail.co.uk/news/article-1328654/General-Electric-sink-2bn-China-development-production-moves-US.html#ixzz1EoBiNLQu

82 *Westinghouse Electric has handed over more than 75,000 documents*   Leslie Hook, "US group gives China details of nuclear technology," *Financial Times* (November 23, 2010). www.ft.com/cms/s/0/fcac14a8-f734-11df-9b06-00144feab49a.htmlUS#ixzz1EoED2nGF

83 *When the Japanese and European companies*   Norihiko Shirouzu, "Train Makers Rail Against China's High-Speed Designs," *Wall Street Journal* (November 17, 2010). http://online.wsj.com/article/SB10001424052748704814204575507353221141616.html

84 *Caterpillar on Tuesday announced plans to lay off*   Daniel Lovering, "Caterpillar to Lay Off 2,454 Workers in 3 States," *Huffington Post* (March 17, 2009). www.huffingtonpost.com/2009/03/17/caterpillar-to-lay-off-24_n_176116.html

   During the past three decades, Caterpillar has grown   "Caterpillar to Build New Excavator Plant in China," *American Machinist* (September 30, 2010). www.americanmachinist.com/Classes/Article/ArticleDraw.aspx?CID=86342

85 *If you can't beat China and can't get the U.S. government*   Richard A. McCormack, "Evergreen Solar Heads To China 'As Quickly As We Can,'" *Manufacturing & Technology News* 17(24): March 4, 2010. www.manufacturingnews.com/news/10/0305/evergreensolar.html

86   *The United States keeps talking about keeping jobs*   Ibid.

     You just can't make this kind of stuff up   At least Rick Feldt still has a job. After
     sending Evergreen offshore, he resigned and signed on as the CEO of Advanced
     Electron Beam.

     A pattern is developing   John Gapper, "China Takes a Short-Cut to Power,"
     Financial Times (December 8, 2010). www.ft.com/cms/s/0/d3da8b78-0309-11e0-
     bb1e-00144feabdc0.html#axzz1EoE7DsUO

87   *I really worry about China*   Guy Dinmore, "Immelt hits out at China and
     Obama," *Financial Times* (July 1, 2010). www.ft.com/cms/s/0/ed654fac-8518-11df-
     adfa-00144feabdc0.html#axzz1EoE7DsUO

88   *On behalf of the undersigned organizations and their members*   "U.S.–China
     Business Council Joint Trade Letter to House Ways & Means Committee
     Opposing H.R. 2378" (September 14, 2010). www.engagechina.com/press/
     contentview.asp?c=52127

91   *To defeat your enemy*   Serge Michel and Michel Beuret, *China Safari: On the
     Trail of Beijing's Expansion in Africa* (New York: Nation Books, 2009). p. 7.

     In the greatest movement of people   Andrew Malone, "How China's taking over
     Africa, and why the West should be VERY worried," *Daily Mail Online* (July 18,
     2008). www.dailymail.co.uk/news/worldnews/article-1036105/How-Chinas-taking-
     Africa-West-VERY-worried.html#ixzz19vjzvYqP

93   *The people of this bewitching, beautiful continent*   Ibid.

94   *When we look at the reality on the ground*   Leslie Hook and Geoff Dyer, "Chinese
     oil interests attacked in Libya," *Financial Times* (February 24, 2011).
     www.ft.com/cms/s/0/eef58d52-3fe2-11e0-811f-00144feabdc0.html#axzz1Ff36d2ST

     The Chinese mortgage on Angolan oil   "Angola secures new China loan," *China
     Economic Review* (March 13, 2009). www.chinaeconomicreview.com/
     dailybriefing/2009_03_13/Angola_secures_new_China_loan.html

96   *Whatever they say, it is a fact that the Chinese*   "China's Policies Draw African
     Nations," *Daily Graphic* (November 11, 2009). www.modernghana.com/news/
     248604/1/china039s-policies-draw-african-nations.html

97   *So there are Chinese to drill the oil*   Serge Michel and Michel Beuret, p. 5.

98   *We have 600 rivers in China*   Serge Michel and Michel Beuret, p. 116.

     With little fanfare, a staggering 750,000 Chinese   Andrew Malone, ibid.

99   *China has snagged over 7 million acres*   Elias Kifle, "Massive Sale of Ethiopian
     Farms Lands to Chinese and Arabs," *Economist* (June 3, 2009).

     formerly white-owned farms for free   Roger Bate, "The Shell Game Comes to
     Zimbabwe," *Weekly Standard* (May 27, 2005). www.weeklystandard.com/
     Content/Public/Articles/000/000/005/657cerfd.asp

100 *Chinese prostitutes will turn tricks for as little as 2000 CFA*   Serge Michel and
     Michel Beuret, ibid.

     That's because the money and treatment they were getting   Saps-dpa, "Chinese
     prostitutes resist effort to rescue them from Africa," *Times Live* (January 2011).

www.timeslive.co.za/africa/article831672.ece/Chinese-prostitutes-resist-effort-to-rescue-them-from-Africa

101 *Chinese firms pay their labor forces very little*   Wenran Jiang, "China's Emerging Strategic Partnerships in Africa," in *China into Africa: trade, aid, and influence*, by Robert I. Rotberg (Baltimore: Brookings Institution Press, 2008), p. 61.

102 *[I]n Namibia, on taking issue with their ill treatment*   "Afro-Chinese labour relations turn sour," *Africa Review* (October 18, 2010). www.africareviewcom/Special%20Reports/Icy%20Afro%20Chinese%20relations/-/979182/1035242/-/15qlmn6/-/index.html

103 *Of the 640 million small arms circulating in the world*   Baffour Dokyi Amoa, "The Role of Small Arms in African Civil Wars," *Pambuzaka News* (Issue 270: September 21, 2006). http://pambazuka.org/en/category/comment/37270

104 *Thousands of women and children are being systematically raped*   "The New Killing Fields," *BBC* documentary, 2004. www.saveourearth.co.uk/soe_article.php?id=49

105 *China Guangdong Nuclear Power Holding Co.*   Ross Kelly, "Chinese Firm Offers to Buy Australia's Energy Metals," *Wall Street Journal* (September 8, 2009). http://online.wsj.com/article/SB125237950076691435.html

106 *Here along the golden sands that grace the Atlantic coastline*   John Pomfret, "China invests heavily in Brazil, elsewhere in pursuit of political heft," *Washington Post* (July 26, 2010). www.washingtonpost.com/wp-dyn/content/article/2010/07/25/AR2010072502979.html

107 *If African just export[s] raw material to China*   "Mbeki warns on China-Africa ties," *BBC News* (December 14, 2006). http://news.bbc.co.uk/2/hi/business/6178897.stm

113 *[China's] heavy investments of late*   "Adm. Mullen's Speech at the 2010 Asia Society Washington's Annual Dinner," *Asia Society* (June 9, 2010). http://asiasociety.org/policy-politics/strategic-challenges/us-asia/adm-mullens-speech-2010-asia-society-washingtons-annual?page=0%2C3

114 *Yes, we all have our memories*   "Korean War: Interview with U.S. Marine Lee Bergee—Chosin Reservoir Battle Survivor and Author," HistoryNet.com (June 12, 2006). www.historynet.com/korean-war-interview-with-us-marine-lee-bergee-chosin-reservoir-battle-survivor-and-author.htm#hide

115 *Wargaming, including an extensive simulation by Rand*   David A. Fulghum, "Chinese Air Force Could Overwhelm Opponents," *Aviation Week* (January 7, 2011). www.aviationweek.com/aw/generic/story.jsp?id=news/awst/2011/01/03/AW_01_03_2011_p21-279384.xml&channel=defense

116 *The Chinese J-15 clone is unlikely*   RIA Novosti, "Russia downplays Chinese J-15 fighter capabilities," (June 4, 2010). http://en.rian.ru/mlitary_news/20100604/159306694.html

117 *China acquired its basic stealth technology*   Associated Press, "Chinese stealth fighter jet may use US technology," *Guardian.Co.UK.com* (January 23, 2011). www.guardian.co.uk/world/2011/jan/23/china-stealth-fighter-us-technology

118 *The Chinese military's future goal*   Kenji Minemura, "China to build two flattops,"
     Asahi Shimbun (February 13, 2009). www.strategycenter.net/research/
     pubID.193/pub_detail.asp

119 *Known among defense analysts as a "carrier killer"*   Associated Press, "China
     Closer on 'Carrier Killer' Missile," *Military.com* (December 29, 2010). www.
     military.com/news/article/china-closer-on-carrier-killer-missile.html?ESRC=eb.nl

122 *Photographs emerged last night*   "Britain's latest weapon against the Taliban?
     'Video diaries' filmed by mobile phone," *Daily Mail* (October 10, 2008).
     www.dailymail.co.uk/news/worldnews/article-1076225/Britains-latest-weapon-
     Taliban-Video-diaries-filmed-mobile-phone.html#ixzz1Epn4qjGZ

123 *We should get a definitive answer*   Hannity, FOX TV News.

126 *There never was a war in history easier*   Winston Churchill, Sinews of Peace
     ("The Iron Curtain Speech"), presented at Westminster College in Fulton,
     Missouri on March 5, 1946.

127 *One spy is worth 10,000 soldiers*   Serge Michel and Michel Beuret, *China Safari:
     On the Trail of Beijing's Expansion in Africa* (New York: Nation Books, 2009). p. 7.

     The primary objective of Chinese intelligence operations   Interagency OPSEC
     Support Staff, *Intelligence Threat Handbook* (June 2004).
     www.fas.org/irp/threat/handbook/index.html

     the most aggressive country conducting espionage against the United States
     U.S.–China Economic and Security Review Commission, 2009, www.uscc.gov/
     annual_report/2009/09_annual_report.php

128 *Beijing does not favor the classical methods*   Peter Grier, "Spy case patterns the
     Chinese style of espionage," *Christian Science Monitor* (November 30, 2005).
     www.csmonitor.com/2005/1130/p01s01-usfp.html

129 *either by appeals to Chinese nationalism*   As noted by the *Intelligence Threat
     Handbook*: "Whatever the reason, ethnic targeting to arouse feelings of obligation
     is the single most distinctive feature of PRC intelligence operations." The U.S. gov-
     ernment *Intelligence Threat Handbook* is an unclassified manual for security offi-
     cers, that has been published by the National Security Agency.

     They may be reporters for new agencies like Xinhua   About 750,000 visas are
     issued a year for these purposes, per State Department data for offices of Beijing,
     Shanghai, Chengdu, Guangzhou, Shenyang, and Hong Kong.
     www.travel.state.gov/pdf/FY10AnnualReport-TableIV.pdf

     Swim with the fish   Some readers may construe our characterization of most
     Chinese spies being ethnic Chinese as being "racist." We do understand the dis-
     comfort some people may feel about this discussion—especially Chinese–
     Americans. However, facts are facts; and we want make it very clear that we have
     no beef with the Chinese people. After all, it is precisely the "Chinese people,"
     whether in countries like Taiwan and Singapore or even at home in Shenzhen, who
     are the biggest victims of China's paranoid espionage apparatus. In fact, one of the
     author's attempts to meet with a group of dissidents in that city ended with Chinese
     security forces hustling our greeting party away at the airport and threatening them
     not to "meet with the American writer," based on information obviously gleaned

from intercepting our email and phone conversations. So let's be both frank and clear here: This discussion of Chinese espionage is not about race. It's about one country recruiting from within its own citizenry and major ethnic group and aggressively spying on themselves and the rest of the world.

130 *Spying is war without the fire* All quotes and facts in this section are from interviews Greg Autry conducted with Li Fengzhi via 28 email exchanges between February 8, 2011 and February 28, 2011.

132 *Rather than set a targeted goal for collection* Scott Henderson, *The Dark Visitor: Inside the World of Chinese Hackers* (2007). www.thedarkvisitor.com

This Communist beehive has been equally effective Stéphane Lefebvre, "The PRC's Compromise of U.S. Government Information and Technologies," *International Journal of Intelligence and CounterIntelligence* 22:4, 652–666.

133 *Mr. Shriver sold out his country* Jeremy Pelofsky, "U.S. man gets 4 years for trying to spy for China," Reuters (January 21, 2011). www.reuters.com/article/2011/01/21/us-usa-china-spying-idUSTRE70K5EZ20110121

134 *Lightning didn't strike twice* "Fact Sheet: Ice Arms and Strategic Technology Investigation," U.S. Immigration and Customs Enforcement (October 2005). www.fas.org/asmp/resources/govern/109th/ICEinvestigationsoct05.htm

attend more seminars on special subject matters Peter Grier, ibid.

137 *Cyber espionage is the great equalizer* Information Warfare Monitor Shadowserver Foundation, "Shadows in the Cloud: Investigating Cyber Espionage 2.0," (April 6, 2010). http://shadows-in-the-cloud.net

hit the U.S. Commerce Department John Rogin, "The top 10 Chinese cyber attacks (that we know of)," *Foreign Policy* (January 22, 2010). http://thecable.foreignpolicy.com/posts/2010/01/22/the_top_10_chinese_cyber_attacks_that_we_know_of

and virtually carpet-bombed Siobhan Gorman, August Cole, and Yochi Dreazen, "Computer Spies Breach Fighter-Jet Project," *Wall Street Journal* (April 21, 2009). http://online.wsj.com/article/SB124027491029837401.html

During the 2008 Presidential campaign Ibid.

138 *And in one of the most brazen breeches* Tom Leonard, "Chinese spies stole US Trade secretary data," *Telegraph* (May 30, 2008). www.telegraph.co.uk/news/worldnews/asia/china/2054874/Chinese-spies-stole-data-from-US-trade-secretarys-laptop.html

when attached to the victim's computers, these nefarious John F. Burns, "Britain Warned Businesses of Threat of Chinese Spying," *New York Times* (January 21, 2010). www.nytimes.com/2010/02/01/world/europe/01spy.html

sort of like being a rock star Venkatesan Vembu, "China's 'hacker babes' on the prowl," *DNA (Daily News & Analysis)* July 14, 2008. www.dnaindia.com/world/report_chinas-hacker-babes-on-the-prowl_1177482

It's even a career that reportedly up to one-third Mara Hvistendahl, "Hackers: The China Syndrome," *PopSci* (April 23, 2009). www.popsci.com/scitech/article/2009-04/hackers-china-syndrome?page=1

139   *Question: Under what circumstances will you perform a hack?*   Dennis Dwyer,
      "Chinese Hackers Talk Hacking," *SecureWorks* (January 4, 2009). www.secure-
      works.com/research/blog/index.php/2009/01/04/chinese-hackers-talk-hacking/

      These young hackers are tolerated   John Vause, "Chinese hackers: No site is safe,"
      CNN Tech (March 7, 2008). http://articles.cnn.com/2008-03-07/tech/
      china.hackers_1_hackers-web-sites-chinese-government?_s=PM:TECH

140   *teach students how to hack into unprotected computers*   Cui Jia, "Training for
      hackers stirs worry about illegal actions," *China Daily* (August 4, 2009).
      www.chinadaily.com.cn/china/2009-08/04/content_8513977.htm

      For example, when several members of a hacker group   Heike, "Chinese hackers
      suspected of breaking Green Dam arrested," *The Dark Visitor: Inside the World of
      Chinese Hackers* (July 14, 2009). www.thedarkvisitor.com/2009/07/chinese-
      hackers-suspected-of-breaking-green-dam-arrested/

      a picture of an official on a government website   Cui Jia, ibid.

141   *the girl pissing on the Yasukuni toilet*   Heike, "Chinese hacker dancing and defac-
      ing = pure awesome!" *The Dark Visitor: Inside the World of Chinese Hackers*
      (August 4, 2008). www.thedarkvisitor.com/2008/08/chinese-hacker-dancing-and-
      defacing-pure-awesome/

      The Honkers Union then followed up with a wave of attacks   Heike, "Chinese
      hackers deface Yasukuni Shrine website...again," *The Dark Visitor: Inside the
      World of Chinese Hackers* (January 1, 2009). www.thedarkvisitor.com/2009/01/
      chinese-hackers-deface-yasukuni-shrine-websiteagain/#more-893

      When the annual Melbourne film festival in Australia   "Chinese hackers attack
      film festival site," *ABC News* (August 1, 2009). www.abc.net.au/news/stories/
      2009/08/01/2643083.htm

      If Google with all its cyberresources and expertise   Mark Clayton, "China cyber
      attacks: Google only one of many US targets," *Christian Science Monitor* (January
      13, 2010). www.csmonitor.com/USA/2010/0113/China-cyber-attacks-Google-only-
      one-of-many-US-targets

142   *a single foreign entity consisting either of agents*   Tania Branigan and Kevin
      Henderson, "Google attacks traced back to China, says US internet security firm,"
      Guardian.co.uk (January 14, 2010). www.guardian.co.uk/technology/2010/jan/
      14/google-attacks-traced-china-verisign

      True to the Orwellian nature of the Chinese state   "Section 2: External
      Implications of China's Internet-Related Activities," www.uscc.gov/annual_
      report/2010/Chapter5_Section_2%28page236%29.pdf

      were orchestrated by a senior member of the Politburo   David Leigh, "US
      embassy cables leak sparks global diplomatic crisis," *Guardian.co.uk* (November
      28, 2010). www.guardian.co.uk/world/2010/nov/28/us-embassy-cable-leak-
      diplomacy-crisis

143   *Rather, it was a carefully planned and executed plot*   Nathan Hodge and Adam
      Entous, "Oil Firms Hit by Hackers from China Report Says," *Wall Street Journal*
      (February 10, 2011). http://online.wsj.com/article/
      SB10001424052748703716904576134661111518864.html?mod=WSJ_hp_
      LEFTWhatsNewsCollection

For 18 minutes in April   "China Experts Have Proof That China Has Hijacked U.S.-Based Internet Traffic," *National Defense* (November 12, 2010). www.nationaldefensemagazine.org/blog/Lists/Posts/Post.aspx?ID=249

144   *Of course, after this now infamous*   Just like in the famous Sherlock Holmes mystery, there was also a curious dog that didn't bark that points to the Chinese government's complicity. In this case, the dog was represented by the fact that almost nobody noticed the redirection at the time.

In fact, such routing errors typically result in many obvious failures because the routes don't complete properly or because the offending networks are overloaded by the unexpected traffic they accidentally ingest. In this case, the misconfigured routers just happened to have enough spare capacity on hand to take on 15% of the entire world's data transfers for the 18-minute gap.

As further evidence of government complicity—and as every frustrated Chinese computer user knows—a great deal of traffic to and from sites outside of China is blocked by the paranoid Dragon's Great Firewall. Yet in this case non-censored Western traffic went into and then out of the Chinese network as though a path had been laid for it in advance. If this was indeed a blunder, as claimed by Beijing, it was a convenient plunder indeed!

If you live outside of China   Earl Zmijewski, "DNS: When Governments Lie," Renesys blog (November 23, 2010). www.renesys.com/blog/2010/11/dns-when-governments-lie-1.shtml

145   *The problem, of course, is that the Chinese server*   Paul Roberts, "Chinese DNS Tampering a Big Threat to Internet Security," *Threat Post* (November 24, 2010). https://threatpost.com/en_us/blogs/chinese-dns-tampering-big-threat-internet-security-112410

146   *After a 10-month cyberespionage investigation*   Jennifer Johnson, "'GhostNet' Spies on Governments & Dalai Lama," *Hot Hardware* (March 29, 2009). http://hothardware.com/News/GhostNet-Spies-on-Governments—Dalai-Lama/

147   *Computer hackers in China*   Shane Harris, "China's Cyber-Militia: Chinese hackers pose a clear and present danger to U.S. government and private-sector networks and may be responsible for two major U.S. power blackouts," *National Journal* (May 31, 2008). www.nationaljournal.com/magazine/china-s-cyber-militia-20080531

148   *Even the main character from the book Where's Waldo?*   http://micro.magnet.fsu.edu/creatures/index.html. See our website for links to view some very cool examples.

You don't check for the infinite possible things   Sally Adee, "The Hunt for the Kill Switch," *ieee Spectrum* (May 2008). http://spectrum.ieee.org/semiconductors/design/the-hunt-for-the-kill-switch

149   *contrived computer chips*   Gus W. Weiss, "Duping the Soviets: The Farewell Dossier," www.cia.gov/library/center-for-the-study-of-intelligence/kent-csi/vol39no5/pdf/v39i5a14p.pdf

the largest blackout in North American history   Shane Harris, ibid.

150 *the Chinese have attempted to map our infrastructure* Siobhan Gorman, "Electricity Grid in U.S. Penetrated by Spies," *Wall Street Journal* (April 8, 2009). http://online.wsj.com/article/SB123914805204099085.html

could, in fact, be in the magnitude Shane Harris, ibid.

151 *We are devoted to the peaceful use of space* Howard W. French, "On Live Television, 2 Chinese Astronauts Begin 5 Days in Low Orbit of Earth," *New York Times* (October 12, 2005). http://query.nytimes.com/gst/fullpage.html?res=9803E7D6163FF931A25753C1A9639C8B63

If anyone wanted to know what the Japanese were planning Christopher Stone, "Chinese intentions and American preparedness," *Space Review* (August 13, 2007). www.thespacereview.com/article/930/1

152 *Moreover, by leveraging its manufacturing prowess* Craig Covault, "China Readies Military Space Station for 2010 Launch," *Space.com* (March 9, 2009). www.space.com/6391-china-readies-military-space-station-2010-launch.html

153 *In the 2,900 cubic kilometers* David Whitehouse, "Gold rush in space?" *BBC News* (July 22, 1999). http://news.bbc.co.uk/2/hi/sci/tech/401227.stm

154 *Scientists writing in the journal Nature have predicted* P. Michel, P. Farinella, and Ch. Froeschlé, "The orbital evolution of the asteroid Eros and implications for collision with the Earth," *Nature*. www.nature.com/nature/journal/v380/n6576/abs/380689a0.html

155 *Attach rockets to the asteroid* Based on Mr. Autry's personal conversations with Mr. Benson before his death.

Each year, three space shuttle missions "Ouyang Ziyuan's Moon Dream Coming True," *China Daily* (July 26, 2006).

156 *Chinese visionaries like Ouyang also see the moon* "Why does China want to probe moon?" *People's Daily* (February 7, 2007). http://english.people.com.cn/200702/07/eng20070207_348107.html

By the time the Chinese began to systematically do this Based on Mr. Autry's personal interview with Mr. Bigelow, October 21, 2010 in Las Cruces, New Mexico.

[T]he goal isn't just scientific exploration Michael Griffin, "NASA's Griffin: 'Humans Will Colonize the Solar System,'" *Washington Post* (September 25, 2005), p. B07.

Our only chance of long-term survival Richard Alleyne, "Stephen Hawking: mankind must move to outer space within a century," *Telegraph* (August 2010). www.telegraph.co.uk/science/space/7935505/Stephen-Hawking-mankind-must-move-to-outer-space-within-a-century.html

157 *Outer space is going to be weaponized* Shirley Kan, "China's Anti-Satellite Weapon Test," CRS Report for Congress (April 23, 2007). www.fas.org/sgp/crs/row/RS22652.pdf

plasma attacks against low-orbit satellites Michael P. Pillsbury, "An Assessment of China's Anti-Satellite and Space Warfare Programs, Policies, and Doctrines," p. 29 (January 19, 2007). www.uscc.gov/researchpapers/2007/FINAL_REPORT_1-19-2007_REVISED_BY_MPP.pdf

158 *Destroy or temporarily incapacitate all enemy satellites* Li Daguang, *Space Warfare*, National Defense University (NDU) Press (2001).

159 *While 150 Americans died in combat during the first Gulf War* Jack Kelly, "Estimates of deaths in first war still in dispute," *U.S. News* (February 16, 2003). www.post-gazette.com/nation/20030216casualty0216p5.asp

   As long as China's space program is in the hands of its generals Richard Fisher, Jr., "Closer Look: Shenzhou-7's Close Pass by the International Space Station," *International Assessment and Strategy Center* (October 9, 2008). www.strategycenter.net/research/pubID.191/pub_detail.asp

160 *In January 2010, Chinese space gunners* "Demarche Following China's January 2010 Intercept Flight-Test," *Telegraph* (January 12, 2010). www.telegraph.co.uk/news/wikileaks-files/china-wikileaks/8299323/DEMARCHE-FOLLOWING-CHINAS-JANUARY-2010-INTERCEPT-FLIGHT-TEST.html

161 *They let us see their lasers* "The militarization of space: Disharmony in the spheres," *Economist* (January 17, 2008). www.economist.com/node/10533205

   sudden decline in effectiveness "U.S. claims that China has used lasers to attack satellites," *Janes Defense Weekly* (October 16, 2006).

   At the same time, telescopes at the Reagan Test Site Ibid.

   The Chinese routinely turn powerful lasers skywards "The militarization of space," ibid.

162 *China looks set to pull ahead in the Asian space race* Jonathon Adams, "China is on path to 'militarization of space,'" *Christian Science Monitor* (October 28, 2010). www.csmonitor.com/World/Asia-South-Central/2010/1028/China-is-on-path-to-militarization-of-space

163 *These include a growing fleet of huge space tracking ships* http://scitech.people.com.cn/GB/7117881.html

   In January 2001, a space security commission "Report of the Commission to Assess United States National Security Space Management and Organization" (January 11, 2001). www.dod.gov/pubs/spaceabout.html

164 *[The] goal of a space shock and awe strike* "Military Power of the People's Republic of China," Annual Report to Congress (2009). www.defense.gov/pubs/pdfs/China_Military_Power_Report_2009.pdf, p. 14.

165 *On September 27th, a Chinese Shenzhou space capsule* James Dunnigan, "Chinese Space Walkers Stalk the Space Station," *Strategy Page* (November 27, 2008). www.strategypage.com/dls/articles/20081127232927.asp

   Each time China launches one of its manned www.astronautix.com/craft/shenzhou.htm

166 *In the process, China violated the so-called "conjunction box" range* Brian Weeden, "China's BX-1 microsatellite: a litmus test for space weaponization," *Space Review* (October 20, 2008). www.thespacereview.com/article/1235/1

   To understand the consternation this caused at NASA Ibid.

   had started drifting away from its intended trajectory Richard Fisher, ibid.

167   *A strong enemy with absolute superiority*   Robert L. Pfaltzgraff, Jr., Presenter,
      "China–U.S. Strategic Stability," Carnegie Endowment for International Peace
      (April 6–7, 2009). www.carnegieendowment.org/files/
      2009npc_prepared_pfaltzgraff.pdf

168   *An ordinary inexpensive weather-monitoring object*   Michael P. Pillsbury, ibid.

      Our future space weapons program should be low profile   Ibid, p. 11.

      We are on notice—but we have not noticed   Commission to Assess United States
      National Security Space Management and Organization, "Executive Summary,"
      Pursuant to Public Law 106-65 (January 11, 2001).
      http://space.au.af.mil/space_commission/executive_summary.pdf

171   *China's environmental problems are mounting*   Elizabeth C. Economy, "The
      Great Leap Backwards?" *Foreign Affairs* (September/October 2007). www.
      foreignaffairs.com/articles/62827/elizabeth-c-economy/the-great-leap-backward

      This soot-blackened city of Linfen   Bryan Walsh, "The World's Most Polluted
      Places: Linfen, China," *Time.* www.time.com/time/specials/2007/article/
      0,28804,1661031_1661028_1661016,00.html

174   *such pollution kills a staggering 700,000 Chinese souls annually*   World Bank,
      "Cost of Pollution in China: Economic Estimates of Physical Damages" (February
      2007). http://siteresources.worldbank.org/INTEAPREGTOPENVIRONMENT/
      Resources/China_Cost_of_Pollution.pdf

176   *America's three great rivers*   Jeffrey Hayes, "Water Pollution in China," *Facts and
      Details* (April 2010). http://factsanddetails.com/china.php?itemid=391&catid=
      10&subcatid=66#

      Waters that used to teem with fish   Ibid.

177   *Fuan's factory was shut down for illegally dumping*   Ariana Eunjung Cha,
      "China's Environmental Retreat: In Tough Economic Times, Promises Fall by
      Wayside," *Washington Post* (November 19, 2008). www.washingtonpost.com/
      wp-dyn/content/article/2008/11/18/AR2008111803625.html

178   *China's arable land, which feeds 22% of the world's population*   Worldwatch
      Institute, "Soil Quality Deteriorating in China, Threatening Public Health and
      Ecosystems," www.worldwatch.org/node/4419

179   *invisible pollution*   XuQi, "Facing up to 'invisible pollution,'" *China Environ-
      mental Times* (January 29, 2007). www.chinadialogue.net/article/show/single/en/724

      a copper sulfate compound used in insecticides and germicides   Worldwatch
      Institute, ibid.

180   *expert Fusuo Zhang of the China Agricultural University*   Natasha Gilbert, "Acid
      Soil Threatens Chinese Farms," *Nature* (February 11, 2010).
      www.nature.com/news/2010/100211/full/news.2010.67.html

      Up to 50-million tons of e-waste is generated worldwide   "Elevated Concen-
      trations of Toxic Metals in China's E-Waste Recycling Workshops," *ScienceDaily*
      (April 1, 2008). www.sciencedaily.com/releases/2008/03/080331092500.htm

181 *the price tag comes in the form of over 10 million tons* Central News Agency, "China Estimates About 11 Million Tons in Grain Reserves are Lost Annually," *Epoch Times* (November 22, 2007). http://en.epochtimes.com/news/7-11-22/ 62202.html

The world has never faced such a predictably massive threat Ray Hammond, "Climate change, food, poverty and the price of failure to the UK," *Friends of the Earth* (October 2009). www.foe.co.uk/resource/reports/climate_change_price_ failure.pdf

183 *[W]ithin 80 years, 30 million people* Dominic Casciani, "Asia-Pacific China's floods: Is deforestation to blame?" *BBC News* (August 6, 1999). http://news.bbc.co. uk/2/hi/asia-pacific/413717.stm

An industrial city—though China doesn't really have any other kind Bryan Walsh, "The World's Most Polluted Places: Tianying, China," *Time* (September 3, 2007). www.time.com/time/specials/2007/article/0,28804,1661031_1661028_ 1661017,00.html

189 *In fact, the latest Press Freedom Index published* "Europe falls from its pedestal, no respite in the dictatorships," Reporters Without Borders. http://en.rsf.org/press-freedom-index-2010,1034.html

and we've personally seen this happen Dissidents that Autry attempted to meet in Shenzhen on December 22, 2010 were removed from the airport by police based on meeting times that could only have been acquired from intercepting private emails. When a second meeting was scheduled via email for the following day, the participants received a phone call within an hour telling them "not to meet the American writer."

Do it repeatedly, and you are likely to get a personal visit Autry had somebody come to his hotel room to ask if he was "having trouble with the Internet and needed guidance."

or get busted by someone from a network of amateur enforcers Thomas Lum, "Internet Development and Information Control in the People's Republic of China," *CRS Report for Congress* (February 10, 2006). www.fas.org/sgp/crs/row/RL33167.pdf, CRS-7

[We must] further strengthen and improve controls David Bandurski, "Hu calls for stronger web controls," *China Media Project (CMP)* (February 21, 2011). http://cmp.hku.hk/2011/02/21/10152/

190 *If Facebook grew corn or built cards* Brendan Greeley and Mark Drajem, "China's Facebook syndrome," *Bloomberg Businessweek* (March 10, 2011). www.businessweek.com/print/magazine/content/11_12/b4220029428856.htm

and tens of thousands of these citizens have been locked up Malcolm Moore, "China ponders closing 'outdated' re-education labour camps," *Telegraph* (July 13, 2010). www.telegraph.co.uk/news/worldnews/asia/china/7887359/China-ponders-closing-outdated-re-education-labour-camps.html; "China: Twenty-One Pastors Sent to Labour Camps," *Release International* (March 4, 2008). www.releaseinternational.org/pages/posts/china-twenty-one-pastors-sent-to-labour-camps349.php

191   *A huge [Chinese] fleet left port in 1414*   Samuel M. Wilson, *The Emperor's Giraffe*. Originally printed in *Natural History* (December 1992), from the American Museum of Natural History. http://classjump.com/arduengoworld/documents/3394165161.pdf9

192   *Despite its isolationism, in the early 1800s*   "Economic Decline and External Humiliation, 1820–1949." www.ggdc.net/MADDISON/China_book/Chapter_2.pdf

      versus America's meager 3%   Catherine, "Share of GDP: China, India, Japan, Latin America, Western Europe, United States," *Visualizing Economics* (January 20, 2008). www.visualizingeconomics.com/2008/01/20/share-of-world-gdp/

193   *That makes Mao the worst mass murderer of all time*   Piero Scaruffi, "1900–2000: a century of genocides," (2009). www.scaruffi.com/politics/dictat.html

197   *Immersion in sewage, ripping out fingernails*   Jonathon Watts, "Torture still widespread in China, says UN investigator," *Guardian.co.uk* (December 3, 2005). www.guardian.co.uk/world/2005/dec/03/china.jonathanwatts

      It is a serious offense to drown or abandon female infants   The author has a photo of this sign.

198   *China alone stands to have as many unmarried young men*   "Gendercide," *Economist* (March 4, 2010). www.economist.com/node/15606229

      Indeed, even as other developing nations   Simon Elegant, "Why Forced Abortions Persist in China," *Time* (April 30, 2007). www.time.com/time/world/article/0,8599,1615936,00.html

      The cornerstone of China's no-choice policy   The law in Guangdong, for instance, stipulates that somebody who earned the average 200,000 yuan would pay 480,000 in fines: www.china.org.cn/english/government/224913.htm

      The not unsurprising result is that China has more abortions   "China concerned about abortions," *BBC News* (July 30, 2009). http://news.bbc.co.uk/2/hi/8175864.stm#graph; William Robert Johnston, "Summary of Registered Abortions Worldwide, through April 2010," (May 9, 2010). www.johnstonsarchive.net/policy/abortion/wrjp3310.html

      close to 13 million a year, and that's a conservative government estimate   The *China Daily* report has been censored after it embarrassed the government but is credibly referenced by the BBC here: http://news.bbc.co.uk/2/hi/8175864.stm

      61 pregnant women were hauled into hospitals in Guangxi   Simon Elegant, ibid.

199   *forced to have an abortion eight months into her pregnancy*   "Forced abortions for Chinese women," *Aljazeera* (October 20, 2010). http://english.aljazeera.net/news/asia-pacific/2010/10/201010208145793266.html

      Christian Pastor Liang Yage and his wife, Wei Linrong   Louisa Lim, "Cases of Forced Abortions Surface in China," *NPR* (April 23, 2007). www.npr.org/templates/story/story.php?storyId=9766870

      In fact, almost all of China's abandoned babies are female   "Case Study: Female Infanticide," Gendercide Watch. www.gendercide.org/case_infanticide.html

      many abortions are sex selective   Ibid.

and female infanticide is still common enough to require public campaigns   As noted by the sign in the quote on page 197.

Given that Chinese law bars Chinese couples under 35   "Adoption Law of the People's Republic of China," Consulate-General of the People's Republic of China in Vancouver. vancouver.china-consulate.org/eng/visa/t29786.htm

the biggest single holocaust in human history   Joseph Farah, "Cover-up of China's gender-cide," *Western Journalism Center/FreeRepublic* (September 29, 1997).

These "bare branches," as they are referred to in China   Even assuming China's 1.3 billion population stabilizes, with 19 out of every 219 becoming unmatched men, that's 112 million extra males. The total population of Japan is 127 million, and South Korea's population is 65 million. Assuming roughly equitable gender distribution, that's 96 million men.

The inevitable result has been a dramatic rise in prostitution   "Case Study: Female Infanticide," ibid.

200   *many as 100,00 North Korean women have been imported*   Carol Anne Douglas, "China: Korean women forced into sex slavery," *Washington Post* (March 3, 2004).

We have been cheated, murdered, raped   Kekenus Sidik, "Saving Kashghar," *Uyghur News* (June 2, 2009). www.uyghurnews.com/american/Read. asp?UighurNews=saving-kashghar&ItemID=DO-812009874210283431252

With the help of Stalin, Mao also managed to engineer a plane crash   "Communist China's Control over East Turkestan," *East Turkestan.* www.eastturkestan.net/china04.html

201   *According to the Inner Mongolia People's Party*   "Inner Mongolia FAQ," www.innermongolia.org/english/faq.htm#imfaq

forced abortions, forced sterilizations   "An Evaluation of 30 Years of the One-Child Policy in China," Tom Lantos Human Rights Commission (November 10, 2009). http://tlhrc.house.gov/hearing_notice.asp?id=1201

They told everybody to get out of the houses   "China: Detainees 'Disappeared' After Xinjiang Protests," *Human Rights Watch* (October 21, 2009). www.hrw.org/en/news/2009/10/20/china-detainees-disappeared-after-xinjiang-protests

202   *In today's Tibet, Han Chinese now own most of the shops*   "Han Chinese Migrants Killing Tibet's Way of Life," *Tibet Post* (July 26, 2010). www.thetibetpost.com/en/news/tibet/1021-han-chinese-migrants-killing-tibets-way-of-life

They have no jobs and they have no land   Claudia Joseph, "Torture, hunger, mobile sterilisation units   ...the brutal reality of Tibet 2008," *Daily Mail Online* (March 2008). www.dailymail.co.uk/news/article-549310/Torture-hunger-mobile-sterilisation-units—-brutal-reality-Tibet-2008.html

Of course, Chinese bankers have been executing the rental agreements   Edward Wong, "China's Money and Migrants Pour into Tibet," *New York Times* (July 24, 2010). www.nytimes.com/2010/07/25/world/asia/25tibet.html

I haven't met anyone who had been arrested who wasn't tortured   Claudia Joseph, ibid.

203 *I was forcibly taken away against my will*   Ibid.

We are part of a Chinese nation contributing to a great future   Edward Wong, ibid.

This world's youngest political prisoner has not been seen since 1996   "Gedhun Choekyi Nyima, the XIth Panchen Lama turns 20," Tibetan Centre for Human Rights and Democracy (April 24, 2009). www.tchrd.org/press/2009/pr20090424. html

By barring any Buddhist monk living outside China   "China Bans Reincarnation Without Government Permission," (August 22, 2007). www.huffingtonpost.com/ 2007/08/22/china-bans-reincarnation-_n_61444.html

204 *Chinese entrepreneurs have five-star factories*   Vivek Kaul, "Of China, five-star factories and sweatshops," *Daily News & Analysis* (July 28, 2008). www.dnaindia. com/money/review_of-china-five-star-factories-and-sweatshops_1180185

It is only when the foreign clients show up   Peter Foster, "Microsoft accused of using teenage 'slave labour' to build Xboxes in China," *Telegraph* (April 16, 2010). www.telegraph.co.uk/technology/microsoft/7597344/Microsoft-accused-of-using-teenage-slave-labour-to-build-Xboxes-in-China.html

205 *Now here's what life is like for workers at the Yuwei facilities*   "Dirty Parts/ Where Lost Fingers Come Cheap: Ford in China," National Labor Committee (March 1, 2011). www.nlcnet.org/reports?id=0629#Executive Summary

Twenty-one year old Worker "A" had three fingers   Ibid.

If there is an accident, even a death, there is no investigation   Based on a personal discussion with an American factory representative in Shanghai, April 2007.

206 *Among the 10- to 14-year-old children*   Dory Mineo, "Child Slave Labor in China," ihscslnews.org (November 2010). http://ihscslnews.org/view_article. php?id=326

They took advantage of my brother because he has a mental disability   Barbara Demick, "China's disabled exploited as slaves," *Los Angeles Times* (February 26, 2011). http://articles.latimes.com/2011/feb/26/world/la-fg-china-brick-factory-20110226

hands as red as freshly boiled lobster from handling hot bricks   Ibid.

207 *These nets were put in place to halt a rash of worker suicides*   Based on Autry's tour of the facility and interview with the chief legal consul and social responsibility officer on December 22, 2010.

208 *The police beat us indiscriminately*   "Labor unrest in China reflects more awareness of rights," *China Post* (June 10, 2010). www.chinapost.com.tw/business/asia/ b-china/2010/06/10/260097/Labor-unrest.htm

For example, Li Guohong, an oil worker in Henan   "Going It Alone: The Workers' Movement in China, 2007–2008," *China Labour Bulletin* (July 2009). www.china-labour.org.hk/en/files/share/File/research_reports/workers_movement_07-08_print_final.pdf, p. 41.

A case in point is that of a series of strikes and public protests   Keith Bradshier, "Strike Forces Honda to Shut Plants in China," *New York Times* (March 27, 2010). www.nytimes.com/2010/05/28/business/global/28honda.html

The lack of the usual police strikebreaking   Keith Bradshier, "A Labor Movement Stirs in China," *New York Times* (June 10, 2010). www.nytimes.com/2010/06/11/business/global/11strike.html

209   *The persistent desire to control the most intimate area of citizens' lives*   "Communique Concerning Chinese Catholic Assembly," *Catholic News* (December 17, 2010). www.catholicnews.sg/index.php?option=com_content&view=article&id=5367&Itemid=127

Communism is a secular faith that can brook no dissent   Karl Marx, "The abolition of religion as the illusory happiness of the people is required for their real happiness." Critique of Hegel's Philosophy of Right. www.marxists.org/archive/marx/works/1843/critique-hpr/intro.htm

Just consider the case of Yang Xuan   Malcolm Moore, "China jails five underground church leaders," *Telegraph* (November 2009). www.telegraph.co.uk/news/worldnews/asia/china/6667317/China-jails-five-underground-church-leaders.html; China Aid Association, "2009 Annual Report: Top Ten Cases of Christian Persecution in China" (January 19, 2010). www.purdue.edu/crcs/itemResources/NGO/Chinaaidreports/chinaaidreportC2009.pdf

In the early morning hours of Sunday, September 13   "The Persecution of Linfen Church," www.helplinfen.com/stories.html

210   *Moreover, unapproved printings and distribution of Bibles*   "Underground in China," Christian Aid Mission. www.christianaid.org/Missionaries/ByRegion/China/UndergroundInChina_print.aspx

When 10,000 adherents gathered in silent protest   CIST, "The Persecution of Falun Gong Is Jiang Zemin's Personal Vendetta Against the Will of the Chinese People and Government," Committee for an International Special Tribunal on the Persecution of Falun Gong. www.specialtribunal.org/articles/0004/

Of course, the Communist Party's harsh response has produced some serious blowback   *Epoch Times* newspaper and New Tang Dynasty TV.

211   *Falun Gong comprises between 15 to 20% of the Laogai system*   Ethan Gutmann, "China's Policies Toward Spiritual Movements," Congressional-Executive Commission on China (CECC) roundtable discussion (June 18, 2010). www.cecc.gov/pages/roundtables/2010/20100618/gutmannTestimony.pdf

Mr. Wang Jiangping is handicapped and can't knit as fast as the others   For more information, go to www.faluninfo.net

215   *China's growth has obvious and amazing benefits for the world*   Fareed Zakaria, "Does the Future Belong to China?" *Newsweek* (February 9, 2006). www.cis.gsu.edu/~dtruex/courses/IB8710/Articles/China/DoestheFutureBelong2China.pdf

216   *President Clinton will close years of political and economic debate*   "Clinton to sign China trade bill Tuesday," *CNN Politics* (October 10, 2000). http://articles.cnn.com/2000-10-10/politics/clinton.pntr_1_wto-membership-china-global-trade-regime?_s=PM:ALLPOLITICS

217 *In the West, liberal Democrats often expect* Ming Xia, "The Governance Crisis and Democratization in China," *New York Times*. www.nytimes.com/ref/college/coll-china-politics-006.html

218 *The essence of Western civilization is the Magna Carta, not the Magna Mac* Joseph Eaton, "What if China Doesn't Change?" *Taiwan Review* (January 1, 2008). http://taiwanreview.nat.gov.tw/ct.asp?xItem=25058&CtNode=1366

As if the world economy wasn't fragile enough "The Yuan Scapegoat: The U.S. establishment flirts with a currency and trade war with China," *Wall Street Journal* (March 18, 2010). http://online.wsj.com/article/SB10001424052748704743404575127511778280940.html

221 *The combined resources of Goldman Sachs, GSGH, and Gao Hua* www2.goldmansachs.com/worldwide/china/index.html

222 *the renminbi is very close to the price that it should be* Jim O'Neill, "Tough talk on China ignores economic reality," *Financial Times* (March 31, 2010). www.ft.com/cms/s/0/dc113472-3cfd-11df-bbcf-00144feabdc0.html#axzz1JGiq9vv8

Morgan Stanley Asia chairman Stephen Roach said Friday "Morgan Stanley: Yuan not to blame for US woes," *China Daily* (March 19, 2010). www.chinadaily.com.cn/china/2010-03/19/content_9616372.htm

223 *Last year the U.S. ran trade deficits with 90 countries* Kopin Tan, "A Better U.S. Fix for China Trade," *Barron's* (October 2, 2010). http://online.barrons.com/article/SB50001424052970204839304575520022191183034.html

I believe it is peace in our time Neville Chamberlain, *The Rise and Fall of the Third Reich*, Modern History Sourcebook: Neville Chamberlain: Peace in Our Time (1938). www.fordham.edu/halsall/mod/1938PEACE.html

I absolutely believe that China's peaceful rise is good for the world "National Defense, China, and the Constitution," *The 1789 Project* (January 20, 2011). www.the1789project.com/2011/01/national-defense-china-and-the-constitution/

225 *So far, America's economic relationship with China has been successful and beneficial* James Fallows, "China Makes, The World Takes," (August 26, 2008). http://delong.typepad.com/egregious_moderation/2008/08/james-fallows-c.html

227 *On Sept. 29, the House of Representatives passed a bill* Fareed Zakaria, "The Real Challenge from China: Its People, Not Its Currency," *Time* (October 7, 2010). www.time.com/time/world/article/0,8599,2024090,00.html

228 *hospitality to business, compliant unions* Ibid.

229 *help other low-wage economies like Vietnam, India, and Bangladesh* Ibid.

230 *Those who would build a Great Wall of America* Albert Keidel, "China's Growing Pains Shouldn't Hurt Us," *Washington Post* (July 24, 2005). www.washingtonpost.com/wp-dyn/content/article/2005/07/22/AR2005072202217.html

236 *If you put it in your body* "New Multivitamins Target Concern Over China's Quality Problems," *PRWeb* (February 22, 2010). www.prweb.com/releases/2010/02/prweb3633644.htm

238 *This nominally "Swedish" auto firm is now wholly owned* Norihiko Shirouzu, "Volvo Mulls China-Made Cars for U.S.," *Wall Street Journal* (January 13, 2011). http://online.wsj.com/article/SB10001424052748704803604576078002874055280. html?mg=com-wsj

Don't laugh; this happens Pacific Bicycle, parent of Schwinn brand, asserted its Chinese manufacturer performed all the QA tests, but it wasn't able to identify the manufacturer for a specific bike involved in an injury crash.

243 *help U.S. companies resist attempts by Chinese authorities* "Comprehensive List of the Commission's Recommendations" (2010). www.uscc.gov/annual_report/ 2010/ComprehensiveListoftheCommissionsRecommendations(page%20271).pdf

251 *strengthen its interaction with allies in the Western Pacific* Ibid.

258 *reliable, routine, access to low Earth orbit* Amy Klamper and Debra Werner, "NASA's New Direction Drawing Fire from House and Senate Lawmakers," *Space News* (February 26, 2010). www.spacenews.com/policy/100226-nasa-new-direction-drawing-fire-lawmakers.html

263 *Of course, the German government first chipped away at Ford's control* Simon Reich, "The Ford Motor Company and the Third Reich," *Dimensions: A Journal of Holocaust Studies.* www.adl.org/braun/dim_13_2_ford.asp

I've seen the future, and it works From the title page of Ella Winter, *Red Virtue* (London: Victor Gollancz, 1933).

Caught up in the excitement, Henry Ford ran to build a new auto plant Charles E. Sorensen, with Samuel T. Williamson, *My Forty Years with Ford* (New York: Norton, 1956).

264 *Zhou: Perhaps it is the national character of the Americans* Henry Kissinger, *Years of Upheaval* (New York: Little, Brown and Company, 1982).

INDEX